LETHAL GAMES

Ramona Fransson

English translation

Judith Bourque

FÖRLAG AB anomaR

Ramona Fransson: Lethal Games
© Ramona Fransson 2016
www.anomar–forlag.se
Translation: Judith Bourque
Cover and Layout: Mia Raunegger, design4u2.se
ISBN: 978-91-87779-32-9

For Thommy, my beloved husband and best friend

Police Coroner and Forensic Detectives

Greger Thulin   Chief Inspector
Address   Fiskaregränd 75, Skärhamn, Tjörn
Workplace   Serious Crime Division Gothenburg

Katarina Linde   Inspector
Address   Nordenskiöldsgatan 30, Gothenburg
Workplace   Serious Crime Division Gothenburg

Charlotte Engman   Forensic Detective
Address   Munkebäcksgatan, Gothenburg
Workplace   Forensics Division Gothenburg

Stefan Kronfeld   Chief Super Intendent
Address   Änggården, Gothenburg
Workplace   Serious Crime Division Gothenburg

Sara Kronfeld   Chief Coroner
Address   Änggården, Gothenburg
Workplace   Forensics Medicine Division Gothenburg

Annika Thorsson   Detective Sergeant
Address   Linnégatan 57, Gothenburg
Workplace   Serious Crime Division Gothenburg

Leif Griffén   Detective Sergeant
Address   Sommarvädersgatan 88, Gothenburg
Workplace   Serious Crime Division Gothenburg

Matthias Brodd   Special Inspector
Adress   Kungsladugårdsgatan, Gothenburg
Workplace   Special Investigations Department Gothenburg

Personal Gallery

The Caling family:

Knut and Astrid Caling have a daughter, Andrea, and
a son, Björn.

Andrea, a lawyer, is married to Arne Hildeng. They have
two sons, Kjell and Verne.

Andrea's brother, Björn Caling, is an artist and is unmarried.

The Hildeng family:

Olav and Elsebeth have two sons, Arne and Jon.

Arne Hildeng is a co-owner of the Pharmacy chain.
He is married to Andrea Caling and they have two sons,
Kjell and Verne.

Arne's younger brother, Jon Hildeng, is also co-owner of
the Pharmacy chain. He is married to Mette and they have
no children.

Much of this story takes place on the island of Tjörn, located about 60 kilometers from the second largest city in Sweden, Gothenburg. Tjörn is a very popular vacation spot for most of the Swedish population. What follows is a list of the many streets and favorite spots there, translated to English:

Kopparmärra	Copper Mare
Kungsportsplatsen	King's Gateway Place
Fredsgatan	Peace Street
Kyrkogatan	Church Street
NK Nordiska kompaniet	The Norden Company
	(a large department Store)
Gamle Port	The Old Gate
Järntorget	The Iron Square
Folkets hus	The Community House
Gunne(by)	A small village
Norra Hamngatan	North Harbour Street
Packhuskajen	Customs House Quay
Stora Höga	Big Hill
Adenmarks	A departement store
Biskopsgården	The Bishops Yard
Lillekärr	Small Marsh
Utby	Out village
Gårdstensbergen	Farm Stones Mountain
Klädesholmen Östra	East Clothes Islet
Skärhamn	Pink Harbour
Strandgatan	Beach Street
Bojens	Buoy

*"Gambling is the child of avarice,
the brother of iniquity,
and the father of mischief."*
                    French proverb

"Finally! A whole day off!" thought Chief Inspector Greger Thulin as he stretched his arms up toward the sky, took a deep breath, and felt the taste of salt and seaweed on his tongue. He walked slowly down Ankarvägen in Skärhamn and looked out over the sea that lay there in front of him without the slightest ripple on its surface. He had an unexplainable feeling that the ocean was that quiet in anticipation of his arrival. Greger squinted as he looked at the sun and felt its sharp rays sting his clear blue eyes. As his walk continued down Hamngatan, he noticed a man sitting on a wooden bench just to the left of the entrance to Atenes Warehouse. Greger watched him with curiosity. "I'm not the only one who's up early," he thought and kept walking. "I wonder if the mackerel are running today?" he mumbled to himself.

The bells in the church tower had just rung six chimes and the early sun's warm rays spread out over the county of Tjörn. The sunlight crept down in every nook and cranny between the fishing captains' houses and formed rectangular shaped shadows on the building walls. Two thin slices of clouds sailed alongside each other in the sky, and the ocean waited for the first morning wind. In the fishing boat harbor seagulls screamed loudly about their fresh breakfast.

Greger strolled slowly past the dock and gave a friend-ly wave to two fishermen who sat cleaning mackerel in the stern of their boat. He continued in the direction of his own boat, carrying the cushion for the driver's seat under his arm. After every boat ride, he was in the habit of taking the cushion back home with him. Carrying it back and forth like that guaranteed him a soft, dry place to sit the next time he went out. These days it wasn't a question of jumping down into the boat on flexible legs; now getting into the boat he looked more like the way a seal moves on land. But Greger was happy as long as he could manage to climb down into his vessel. He stood in the stern and looked out over the har-bor. It was June, and there were still plenty of places to dock a boat, except perhaps on the weekends. But in one month, boat owners from all over Europe would be fighting over the few spaces that Skärhamn's guest harbor could offer.

Greger lifted the seat cover, pulled out the heavy, clanking anchor and laid it down on the floorboards. "It's a good idea to check on the anchor now and then," he thought.

A scream suddenly arose from somewhere out over the ocean. Greger raised his head and looked around the har-bor. The fishermen on the dock stopped cleaning mackerel and looked toward the warehouse. Another human scream spread out through the harbor, went to a higher pitch, and was followed by a cry for help. Greger let go of the rope and stood up. His eyes scoured the surroundings, but he couldn't see anyone in distress. Laboriously puffing and panting, he climbed up and out of the boat and started walking along the wharf toward the southern part of the harbor.

When he got to the boat houses next to the guest harbor, twenty meters from the old customs building, he saw someone waving their arms in the air. Greger waved back and started moving faster. The person ran toward him, wildly gesticulating. The fellow had short, sun bleached hair with a long face, blunt nose, and a wide mouth. "He looks like he's about thirty years old," thought Greger. With his mixed Gothenburg and Bohus dialect, he asked what had happened.

"Can you help? Right beside my boat there's a woman who's sitting on the deck of her boat and she looks like she's in shock or something! I can't get a word out of her! I went below deck on her boat and found some guy lying completely still on one of the double beds." He kept waving his arms in the air as he spoke.

"Is he alive? Has anyone called an ambulance?"

"No, I didn't want to touch him. What if he's been murdered! I've seen enough detective stories to know you shouldn't mess things up for the police. But I *have* called the ambulance," he said, and suddenly stopped waving his arms. "Who are you by the way? You sound like a policeman. Are you the police?" Before Greger answered, he squinted at the sun and then looked into this man's dark gray eyes. "Strange," he thought. "His eyelashes are completely white."

"Maybe I am. Who are you and what is your connection to that boat?" asked Greger as he started to walk toward the boat in question.

"My name is Roland. They call me Rulle. And no, we don't know anyone on that boat. We arrived at the harbor late last night and just happened to find a spot beside them."

When Greger was about ten meters close to the boat, he realized it was a yacht. Could it be a Storebro? Once he was on board, the boat's luxurious details shouted out that this was indeed a Storebro, the Rolls Royce of yachts. Sitting on the well- cared-for teak deck was a woman looking straight ahead with an empty gaze. Greger stood right in front of her. He waved his hands and tried to make eye contact. But her arms just remained hanging motionless by her sides so he concluded that she must be in a state of shock. Greger walked over toward the salon and bent down to see more of the yacht's interior. He saw mahogany furnishing and two sofas upholstered in natural leather. "This is a boat I could only dream of owning," Greger thought to himself with a sigh. From this vantage point, he didn't see anyone in distress or a body, so he took a few more steps forward. He stepped down onto the floor of the salon and moved carefully ahead toward the bow of the boat. As he approached the sleeping area, he saw a man lying on the bed with large, hairy, well-tanned legs that were folded in a natural position. A dark blue blanket lay behind his back and covered his face. Greger placed two fingers on the man's legs and felt that they were cold, just as he had anticipated. He lifted the blanket to examine his face. "This guy looks like he's just asleep, but he's dead alright," thought Greger.

He heard sirens suddenly, and they were coming closer. He turned around, sighed out loud, and made his way back up the stairs with heavy steps. On deck, the sharp sun rays stung his eyes, and he squeezed them shut. The unidentified woman still sat motionless in the same stiff position. Greger went over to her and laid his hand on her shoulder, giving it a little squeeze. No response.

The ambulance pulled up and parked by the gathering crowd. The passenger door opened and a young woman with short, tousled hair jumped out of the ambulance. Greger yelled and waved to get her attention. The young woman walked quickly toward him, carrying a medicine bag in her left hand.

"Is he lying forward in the boat?" she asked. Greger nodded and watched enviously as she jumped on board with gazelle-like agility. A half a minute later she was back up on the deck.

"I'm sorry, but this is nothing for us. The man down there has been dead for several hours. You need to call the coroner instead."

"Excuse me … I haven't introduced myself. My name is Greger Thulin, and I'm Chief Inspector for Homicide," he said, stretching out his hand.

"Maja Park, Emergency Physician," she said, grabbing his hand and shaking it. "What I can do is write a certificate of death. By the way, what's homicide doing here?"

"I live at Fiskaregränd here in Skärhamn and was in my boat when I heard a scream. If I've understood the situation correctly, the woman who is sitting frozen stiff on the deck, is the wife of the dead man in the bow. Could you please have a look at her? She seems to be in a state of shock."

"Of course, no problem," said Maja and walked over to the woman. Greger went along since he wanted to speak with her and get some information as to what had happened; that is if it was at all possible to carry on a normal conversation with her.

Just as he was looking out over the wharf, a police car drove up and parked beside the ambulance. The ambulance driver, who had stayed behind in the vehicle now got out and spoke with one of the policemen. Greger had to squint again as he looked through the bright sunlight to see if he knew anyone in uniform. One of them came toward him with a smile on his face as he climbed on board.

"Don't you recognize me?" he asked. "I was on duty when

a body was found at Lyckebacken here in Skärhamn … last year, wasn't it? Or was it two years ago?"

"Could be, you look familiar. But I'm terrible at remembering people's names," sighed Greger.

"That's ok. I'm no good at that either. My name is Sune Koltman."

Greger introduced himself for the second time and realized that his day off was no longer a day off. He turned around to see what Maja was up to and saw that she was giving the woman in shock an injection. A few seconds later, she started to move around. With wide open blue eyes, she stared at Maja and then looked around slowly at everyone who was on board the boat. Her eyes froze again, and she shook her head. Tears ran down her cheeks, but she didn't utter a sound. Maja looked at the woman, shrugged her shoulders, and turned to Greger.

"I don't think we can do a lot more here. Maybe you can talk with her," said Maja and closed her bag. Greger sat down beside the woman and put his arm around her shoulders. He suddenly wished that it had been his colleague, Katarina Linde, sitting there instead of him. She was much more proficient at dealing with emotionally charged situations. Greger cleared his throat.

"Are you able to tell me what happened? Is that your husband lying on the bed down there?" She nodded and took hold of Greger's hand.

"Can you go get my brother?"

"Who is your brother and what's your name?"

"His name is Björn Caling. He's an artist and has an exhibition now at the Watercolor Museum," she said, with tears flowing heavily down her cheeks. "And my name is Andrea Hildeng."

"But your brother can't be at the museum this early…it's

only 6.30 in the morning!"

"He's staying at one of the guest studios behind the museum," she said, wiping away her tears with her hand.

"Hildeng," said Greger. "Is that a Norwegian name?"

"Yes, it is. My husband's parents are from Norway," she said, looking at Greger with pleading eyes. "Please help me! I can't take anymore!" Greger looked for Sune Koltman, who was still on board the boat. When they made eye contact, Greger waved him over.

"Do me a favor! Drive over to the studios that are behind the museum and see if you can find someone by the name of Björn Caling. If you find him, bring him back here with you," said Greger.

"I can't believe that Arne is gone! Just yesterday he was so full of life! We had dinner at a restaurant and then we returned to our boat," said Andrea and started to cry again.

"Which restaurant was it?" asked Greger.

"The one that looks like a boat. Right now I can't remember the name of it," she answered, wiping away more tears.

"Was it The Haddock?" asked Greger.

"Yes, that's it! That's where we were yesterday," said Andrea with a shiver. "But the four of us all ordered the same meal, so it couldn't have been something in the food!"

"All four? Who else was there besides you and your husband?"

"My brother Björn and one of his friends," she said, hanging her head. "Oh my God, how can I explain this to Kjell and Verne?"

"Who are they?" asked Greger scratching his head while he continued to think about the name Hildeng. He'd heard that name before … he was sure of that. The question was, where and why?

"They are our children," said Andrea, watching the police

car as it drove off.

"How old was Arne?"

"He was only fifty-six," she mumbled.

Greger felt that the best thing to do right now was to call his boss, Chief Superintendent Stefan Kronfeld. They might as well send the body to Forensics in Gothenburg for autopsy, he thought. Stefan would then in turn call his wife, Sara. She was one of Sweden's best forensic pathologists, and if there were something in that body that shouldn't have been there, she would be the person to find it. "If it turns out that Arne Hildeng died of natural causes, then I can have a few more days off," thought Greger. He stepped out onto the wharf, walked over to the ambulance and asked if he could borrow Maja's cell phone.

"Hi, Stefan. I just happened to have a body on hand and …"

"What? Where are you? I thought you were at home taking some time off!" interrupted Stefan.

"Well, yes, actually, but then I heard a scream and felt obligated to assist," said Greger.

"Who's been murdered?"

"I don't know if it *is* murder yet."

Stefan listened as Greger laid out the details, at the same time looking absent-mindedly at his nicely manicured fingernails. When he got out his calendar, he noticed that his wife's birthday was tomorrow. "Better not forget that," he thought to himself. On last year's birthday, she really lit into him for coming home without flowers.

"I think the best thing would be to call Charlotte and get her involved, even though we don't know at this point whether Arne Hildeng has been murdered or not," said Greger.

"Isn't Engman at your place?" asked Stefan. He caught his reflection in the window and combed his hand through his dark, gray speckled hair, correcting the placement of a few hairs.

"No, she decided to drive out to her aunt's cottage in Lerum to go swimming and relax for a few days. The cottage is out by Aspen Lake," said Greger, remembering yesterday evening.

He and Charlotte had been living together for six months and during the first months everything had gone smoothly between the two. Charlotte was a forensic detective, and since her working hours were the same as his, for the most part, there hadn't been much conflict. They had taken turns cleaning, doing laundry, buying groceries and cooking. But two days ago Charlotte happened to find part of a moldy sandwich, about as big as a dice, in the hamper and blew up. The dam really broke! Greger just stood there like a fool listening to all the accusations and didn't get a word in edgewise. When she finally stopped for a few seconds, he thought the whole thing was over. But then she added that it might be a good idea if they took a break from each other for a few days. She needed to see something else and someone else she said.

"Communication problems?" asked Stefan.

"Not at all," lied Greger. "She wanted to spend time with her nephew, that's all!"

"Do whatever you think is best. I'll call Sara and let her know. We'll send a vehicle to pick up the body," said Stefan. He didn't bother to wait for any additional comments and hung up.

Greger thanked Maja for the use of her cell phone and while they stood talking the police car returned. Sune Koltman sat up front and gave Greger a thumbs up. The car was still rolling when the passenger door opened, and a man jumped out of the car. He ran past everyone standing on the wharf without so much as a glance and jumped on board the boat. Andrea Hildeng threw herself into his arms. Greger understood that this must be her brother, Björn Caling. He gave them some minutes to be alone before he went on board again. A moment later it seemed as though Andrea had started to breathe normally again. She sat on one of the leather sofas on the aft deck, wiping her tears and blowing her nose in a paper napkin.

Greger took the opportunity to observe Björn Caling as he climbed back on board the boat. Judging from this man's effeminate appearance and body language, Greger came to the conclusion that Björn was probably homosexual.

"Oh my God," said Björn Caling to Greger as he stretched out a boney, claw-like hand toward Greger. "This is terrible! I can't understand what's happened!" he said as he waved his arms out in a heroic gesture. "I talked to him as recently as last night and he was just full of life …" When he spoke, he let his head drop, and dark brown curls of long hair hid his face as he began to cry. Greger saw his gray hair roots and realized that Björn dyed his hair. Andrea got up to hold onto her brother again. Greger had the feeling that everyone around him could see that he was uncomfortable. During the fifties, when he grew up, anyone who openly declared or was discovered as homosexual would have been fired immediately. Later, during his career he had met many homosexuals, and two of them worked for the narcotics division. But the ones he had met hadn't acted effeminate, neither in the way they dressed nor behaved, especially in comparison with Björn Caling. He was a woman, dressed in man's clothes, thought Greger.

"Were you with Arne Hildeng yesterday evening?" asked Greger, looking straight into Björn's light brown, eyelash framed teary eyes.

16

"Yes, of course, I was! It was a wonderful evening. We sat having dinner together in a gorgeous sunset with colors an artist's palette could never duplicate," answered Björn, gesticulating eagerly with his claw-like hands. Greger said, "Uh huh, uh huh," and nodded, but inwardly he was experiencing storm winds of uncertainty. What would be the correct way to behave in discussing emotions with a homosexual concerning other men? Once again he wished that Katarina was there with him. He missed the excellent analytical abilities she displayed without any noticeable lack of confidence.

"What do you think can have happened to Arne? Did he die of natural causes? Was he suffering from some illness?" asked Greger and immediately regretted his choice of words.

"What do you mean? Do you mean that he could have been murdered?" asked Björn as his dark brown, perfectly groomed eyebrows raised and then fell. He ended up staring at Greger with deep wrinkles in his forehead. Without blinking, Greger stared back. "That's preposterous! My brother-in-law hasn't been murdered. Who would want to murder him? He didn't have any enemies!" said Björn Caling, looking at his sister with wide open eyes.

"Murdered?" repeated Andrea, staring at Greger. "Why would Arne be murdered and by whom? It's just us here!"

All of a sudden, Greger felt like an elephant walking into a glass boutique. The questions that just passed through his lips could single out Arne's wife as a potential murderer. Statistically, it is most often someone close to the victim who is the killer if this was, in fact, a murder.

"Well, since your husband was not ill, since he didn't have a problem with his heart, and since he was only fifty-six years old and, in addition, seemed to be in great shape, wouldn't it be good to try and discover what it was that caused his sudden demise? Was he depressed?" asked Greger.

"Not in the least! Arne loved life, loved good food, enjoyed running and playing golf," said Björn, patting Andrea on the arm. "He did have problems with his stomach, however."

"That's not usually something you die of," said Greger, looking down.

The car that Chief Kronfeld had sent drove up to the wharf beside the police car. A young man dressed in a short sleeved light blue shirt jumped out of the car and walked in the direction of the boat. He said hello to Greger and held out a paper to be signed. Greger read through it and asked Andrea for a pen. He explained to her that this was just a document that would allow a forensic autopsy of the body. Andrea signed it and gave it back to Greger. She broke down again when the young man got back on board with a stretcher. Brother and sister held each other and cried. At the moment, Greger couldn't do anything more than give Andrea a pat on her shoulder and thank Björn. He gave them his business card and asked them to call him if there was anything at all they wanted to talk to him about. They thanked him for his help and assisted him off the boat. Sune Koltman was waiting stand by, leaning up against the police car.

"Do you need a ride anywhere?" he asked.

"No, thanks. I'm off duty today and intend to enjoy whatever is left of it," replied Greger. Sune grinned, hopped into the car and drove off. When Greger walked past the men in the fishing boat, he noted a curious expression on their faces. But he didn't have the energy to explain so he just smiled at them and walked off in the direction of his boat. He worked his way into it, laid out the cushion and sat down.

Then he bent over and picked up his fishing reel. He felt its weight and moved it back and forth between his hands. Suddenly his desire to go fishing just disappeared. The only thing he wanted to do right now was to call Charlotte and hear the sound of her voice. Greger was not the type to be angry for long, nor was Charlotte as far as he had noticed. Ten minutes later, out of breath, he stepped over the threshold of his home. Normally he would have taken off his shoes and put away the seat cushion, but now he just dropped everything he was carrying right down on the hall floor. He walked out to the kitchen, grabbed the telephone and dialed Charlotte's cell phone number. Slowly, very slowly, he heard her phone ring at least four times, and then started to lose hope.

Charlotte had walked back into the cottage when she saw the familiar number on the cell phone display. She was standing in front of the mirror in the bedroom. Her grayish blonde hair was cut short and stuck out in all directions. She noticed that her blouse that had been clean in the morning was now decorated with a coffee spot right in front. She felt dirty, but then she'd been weeding in the strawberry patch for three hours, and was feeling the results in her spine.

"Hi Greger, how are you?"

"Oh, Hi Charlotte. I miss you!" he said as he sat down at the kitchen table and breathed a heavy sigh.

"Ah ha, is that so ... well, to be honest, I miss you too," she said.

"I promise never to drop any more sandwiches in the hamper if you just come home!"

"Maybe it wasn't just the moldy sandwich in the hamper that made me angry. There are a lot of other things to talk about besides you being sloppy," said Charlotte. "I'm on my way home in any case. We can talk later."

"When will you be home?" asked Greger, looking at the clock.

"I'll be back at your house at twelve noon at the latest. You can make lunch for us."

Charlotte had already hung up when Greger noticed that he stood there nodding. What could he make for lunch? He could get on his bike and ride over to Hamnéns Fish. If nothing else it would be good exercise, he thought. They had a great take-away pain riche filled with mixed seafood that he knew Charlotte was particularly fond of.

Family Talk

Björn Caling and Andrea Hildeng walked together into the salon on the boat. They sat down at the table and Andrea's fingers tightly clutched the used napkin that lay like a ball in her hands.

"Have you called Mom and Dad?" asked Björn.

"No ... I haven't spoken to anyone else except you. I don't know if I can handle telling them over the phone." Tears ran down her cheeks and dropped down onto the flower printed tablecloth.

"Weren't Jon and Mette supposed to meet you here in Skärhamn today?" asked Björn taking hold of her hand. Andrea pulled back her hand and covered her mouth. Wide eyed, she stared at Björn.

"I've completely forgotten about that! Please, Björn ... can you stay with me today? Do you have to be at the Watercolor Museum? "How will I be able to tell Jon that his brother is ... gone?"

"Do you know what time they were supposed to arrive?"

"She shook her head, got up, and went to the toilet. Björn

overheard that she had vomited. He looked around the boat. Where did Arne keep the alcohol? He could use a drink right now. Others might have a look at the clock before having something to drink, but Björn didn't look at his calendar or his watch. He went by the feeling he had in his stomach. Andrea came out of the bathroom and went straight out to the kitchen. The sound of clinking ice helped him to relax. She had understood without him having to say anything. Andrea put down a glass with gin and tonic in front of Björn and took a large gulp of her own drink. Björn followed suit and they sat there in silence with their glasses in front of them.

"I can call Kjell and Verne if you'd like me to," said Björn after a few minutes.

"Kjell is working in the U.S. Verne is visiting Mom and Dad. Call Kjell first. I'll give you his cell phone number," said Andrea as she got up and took their empty glasses to the kitchen to refill their drinks. A minute later she was back and put a tray down in front of Björn with more drinks and her cell phone laying on it. Björn went for the drinks first and then picked up her phone. He stretched out his hand with the cell phone as far away from his body as he could to see the small numbers on the display. His reading glasses lay forgotten on the side table in his bedroom since he had left in such a hurry. A strange feeling came over him as he stared at the telephone. Here he was, in this boat, but Arne would never sit across from him anymore he realized and felt a shiver run through his body. He shook his head and pushed the ring icon by Kjell's name with clumsy fingers.

During the whole time, Björn spoke with Kjell, Andrea just sat still, listening to Björn's light, gentle voice. She could see Kjell in front of her, their first born, and he looked just like his father. Close-set, light blue eyes, with a nose as

22

straight as a ruler in an oblong face, thin black eyebrows and dark curly hair. His mouth was always closed when he listened, but he had a habit of grabbing a lock of his hair and twirling it around his pointing finger. After some minutes had passed, she knew that Björn would soon be handing her the phone. She felt more and more afraid with each passing second. How could she handle talking to her son? Andrea took a deep breath before she lifted the cell phone to her ear. Björn took her other hand and held it tightly.

"Hi, Kjell … No, I haven't spoken with Verne yet. I want you to come home as soon as possible!" she said.

Björn let go of her hand and looked down into his half full glass. It looked like he was listening, but his thoughts were elsewhere. He was thinking about yesterday evening with memories passing through his mind like scenes from a movie. He remembered Arne sitting in the sunlight at the restaurant, surrounded by what looked like a firework display of sparkling reflections on the blue and red glasses. Björn had been overwhelmed by an intense longing to have an easel in front of him with a brush in one hand and palette in the other. Yesterday he had, for a few quivering moments, so wanted to paint a portrait of Arne amidst all the intense color, and today Arne was dead. It was unreal. "When Mother finds out about this she'll have an attack," he thought, leaning back in the sofa and closing his eyes. "Dad, on the other hand, will go to the library and have a large brandy." The bottle would, of course, be hidden behind one of the countless rows of books that lined the walls from floor to ceiling. He would pour the brandy into a crystal brandy glass, and then sink into the well-worn green leather armchair and lift his feet up onto the leather footstool. In spite of the hateful situation, Björn couldn't help smiling as he thought about his father.

Dad had always taken refuge in the library. It was his way of dealing with anything unpleasant. There had been countless times during the years that his mother had tried to confront him, but now she had given up. It was pointless since he never responded. She would instead vent her irritation on the gardener or on anyone else who happened to be nearby. And after she'd done that, she would make her escape to the piano.

The black Steinway and Sons grand piano was placed in front of one of the paned panorama windows with a view of the fountain. She would sit down at the piano, take out Microcosmos by Bela Bartok, and let her fingers fly back and forth over the keys until she finished with a crescendo, completely exhausted. As a child, Björn had always hated those moments. He hated all of Bela Bartok's compositions. It all sounded disharmonic, and that was probably why his mother loved them. She identified with that kind of music, he thought, as he opened his eyes and drank up the last drops in the glass.

Andrea came back, sat down beside Björn and nodded in the direction of his glass.

"Sure, why not? This is a good day to get very drunk and blame it all on everything that has happened" said Björn, patting her on the chin. "Do you want me to call Jon? Now that I've had a few drinks, I could even handle talking to Mom for five minutes," he said, patting himself on the chest.

Andrea smiled a crooked smile for an answer. She started to feel the effect of the alcohol and for once it felt good to be a little drunk. Soon enough, she would be forced to deal with all the problems, and she would have to do it in a completely sober state of mind.

"I think I can handle it myself. Jon is always calm and sensible," said Andrea, dialling the number. "Hello Jon ... how is everything with you and Mette?" she asked holding her breath.

"Thanks, fine. But you don't sound Okay," said Jon as he turned around and looked at his wife. They were sitting on the flybridge, and Mette was behind him, lying on a britz in the sun. She changed positions, caught his eye, winked and smiled. He winked back.

"It's Arne," said Andrea, pressing her nails into her hands and hoping the pain would prevent her from crying.

"What about Arne? Problems with his stomach?" asked Jon slowing the boat down. Mette sat up and looked at her husband. She took off her sunglasses and tried to catch his eye again, but he avoided her by looking in another direction. The motor shut off and the boat lay still, bobbing up and down in the waves. Mette could see by Jon's body language that this was something serious. His eyebrows moved first up and then down. The sunburned hand that had just recently guided the boat forward was now being nervously run back and forth through his light gray hair. Mette put her bra back on and took two wobbly steps over the deck toward her husband. His voice was shaking, and his eyes filled with tears. In spite of having a sunburned back, she felt a cold shiver through her body.

"We'll be with you in about two hours," he said, finishing the conversation.

"Has something happened?" asked Mette, laying her hand on his arm.

"Arne is dead!" he said, shaking off her hand. Mette's eyes flew wide open, and she took a step backward. She was close to losing her balance and would have fallen into the water if Jon hadn't grabbed her at the last minute. Her thoughts were spinning. What had happened? How had he died? Was it an accident? She studied Jon's reactions without interfering. He obviously didn't want to talk about it since he'd turned his back to her. His whole body spoke the unspoken "Leave me alone!" In other words, everything was as usual in their relationship. Oddly enough, she didn't feel any emotion about knowing that Arne was dead. Was this what they called being in shock? She didn't feel as though she was shocked. She didn't feel anything! Suddenly she came to think of Andrea and that she must be devastated. She and Arne had loved each other. "Or at least their behavior toward each other had always been affectionate, in contrast to ours," she thought. And my God! Their children! Had anyone told Kjell and Verne? And how have they handled it? Her parents-in-law, had anyone told them?

The motor started up again, and the boat raced ahead full throttle. Mette climbed down into the salon and walked forward to the sleeping area. Her clothes were spread out on the double bed. She put her shirt on, but stood and hesitated with her jeans in her hand. She ought to take the chance to call her mother-in-law, Elsebeth, and tell her about Arne. It was a nasty thought, but in a way she thought it would be satisfying to hear Elsebeth take a deep breath and scream out her grief.

"Sweet revenge," she mumbled to herself and pulled on her jeans. She hadn't forgotten all the countless times Elsebeth had showered her with little sarcasms, and the reason was always the same. Mette had not succeeded in producing any grandchildren. Her mother-in-law was a master at camouflaging her poison arrows. They were aimed at Mette, and when they hit their mark, it hurt. When Mette and Jon had been married a year, and no bulge appeared on her stomach, Elsebeth's remarks had begun to hail at a more and more intensive speed. The first months it had been in the form of small sticks of a needle.

26

"Mette dear, have you gained weight? Could you possibly be ... no, you've probably just been eating too much chocolate!"

But then as time went by, her comments became more aggressive.

"I read an article today. It was about a woman who committed suicide after she found out that she couldn't have children. Isn't that terrible? I mean, it's not that important to be able to have children, or what do you think Mette?"

Even now, after 25 years of marriage, Mette still hadn't been able to get used to Elsebeth's nasty comments. There were times when she wished that her mother-in-law would drop dead.

Her feelings toward her father-in-law, Olav Hildeng, were different. Mette had discovered something about one of Olav's secret interests. For a long time, Olav was convinced that no one knew about his late night habit of surfing pornographic sites on the web. One late night in February, the two of them happened to be left alone in the Hildeng family's mammoth stone house. The place was three stories high, had two wings, and was landscaped with an English style garden complete with rose bushes and fountains. Elsebeth and Olav lived in one of the wings, leaving the use of the other wing for their children. Arne and Andrea moved out once they had become a couple, but Jon felt it was both more comfortable and cheaper to share the house with his parents. No one had bothered to ask how Mette felt about living there, she thought bitterly.

This particular evening Mette had decided to confront Olav with his little hobby. After midnight, she sneaked unnoticed over to her parents-in-law's wing of the house and into Olav's office. She hid in the dark behind the door and watched him for a long time. He was sitting hunched up by the computer. Suddenly he noticed that someone was there and just stared at her at first. She nodded toward the computer and he pretended not to know what she was alluding to. Mette then stepped forward, pushed two keys on the keyboard, and the screen immediately revealed what she had meant. Olav took a deep breath, leaned back into his chair, and starting looking at Mette's figure, up and down. After a few seconds, she got the uncomfortable feeling that he was going to make a pass at her. Confused about his behavior, she looked right into his blue-gray eyes and showed him with her stiff body that she was not interested in his games. At the time, Mette was forty-five years old and was what many would call a natural beauty with her billowing blond hair and slim body. Her best feature was her emerald green, feline eyes with long, thick, black eyelashes that waved up and down like a fan. But for sure, she didn't want to get any closer to Olav than she was right now. When Olav understood that, he had backed down, and then adopted an attitude of not being able to do enough for her. She had been satisfied for the time being but thought that there could come a day when she might need his loyalty. Until then his addiction to pornography could remain a well-protected secret between the two of them. Mette smiled as she remembered that incident. She got her cell phone out of her handbag and dialed the familiar number.

Her mother-in-law's shriek into the telephone filled Mette with satisfaction, but it also frightened her. She hung up, put her phone into her handbag, snuck into the toilet and locked the door. It took only a minute for the motor on the boat to shut down. She heard Jon running over the deck and realized he was on his way to the salon. He yelled out her name. Mette sat cringing on the toilet seat behind the locked door and felt her heart starting to beat faster.

"Why in hell did you call Mom?" screamed Jon, kicking on the locked door. "Couldn't you have waited until I talked to her?" Mette jumped at every kick. She knew that Jon could become very aggressive. Up to now he had never hit her, but he'd come close to it many times. The question was whether or not the phone call to Elsebeth would push him over the edge. Mette was holding her breath when suddenly everything got quiet outside the door. What was he doing? She could feel drops of sweat running down the back of her neck. A familiar melody came from Jon's cell phone, and she heard him talking to someone. His voice grew more distant, and when she heard his footsteps on the deck again she knew she was out of danger for the time being.

Greger Apologizes

Greger stood waiting in the door opening to his house. Charlotte's younger brother sat behind the wheel and gave him a little wave of recognition. Greger held back the feeling of wanting to throw himself all over her. Right now, it was better that brother and sister had time to say goodbye to each other in peace and quiet.

Charlotte walked toward him with her red purse and a green bag hanging over her shoulder. She smiled at him.

"Hi there honey … can you help me?" she asked and handed over the large green bag. He took it in one hand and put his other around her shoulders. A happy feeling spread through his whole body. He drew her near him when she stepped over the threshold and breathed in her smell. He was just getting in the mood to head for the bedroom when Charlotte stopped him in his tracks.

"I hope lunch is on the table! My stomach is growling!" she said, pulling herself away from his arms.

The kitchen table was covered with a yellow and white striped tablecloth that matched the curtains in the window.

Two candles in red candlestick holders were lit, and on the yellow porcelain plates lay the fresh pain riche with seafood mix. Greger had added some onion rings, slices of tomato and leaves of lettuce for the sake of appearance. Charlotte clapped her hands in delight.

"How sweet of you to remember! I love seafood mix!" she said sitting down at the table. After taking a big bite and rinsing it down with some water, she turned to him and asked, "Tell me now! What's happened while I was gone?"

"Well, I started out thinking I would take the boat out and go mackerel fishing," said Greger leaning back in his chair. Five minutes later Charlotte had stopped chewing and was all wrapped up in what Greger was talking about. When he had finished telling her about it all, she put the half-eaten sandwich down on her plate and wiped her mouth.

"I'll call Sara and see if she's found anything suspicious in the body. If Arne Hildeng has been murdered, you have to block off the boat immediately since that makes it a crime scene. I can't understand why you didn't do that right away!"

Greger rose from the table, gathered up the plates, glasses, and cutlery to fill up the dishwasher. Charlotte was watching him and suddenly got a bad conscience. Her outburst after finding the moldy piece of sandwich in the laundry basket had been unnecessary. It wasn't as though she had not been aware of Greger's sloppy side when she decided to move in with him. They had after all known each other for many years before they took the step to live together. Greger had even proposed, and she had said yes. True, they still had not gotten around to organizing the wedding ceremony, but that was not the most important. The important thing was that she was very fond of Greger but found it difficult to accept his nonchalant attitude about their agreed upon way of organizing things. He would often just walk through the door with dirty shoes on without wiping them off first on the doormat. And then he would drop his dirty socks on the floor by the bed, leaving them there for several days. He forgot to buy snacks and milk for their coffee break. In actuality one could see all these things as trifles, but when they were all lumped together it resulted in one thing…chaos.

She suddenly felt Greger's hand on her shoulder. Charlotte looked up and saw his clear blue eyes. His dark, bushy eyebrows were bow shaped and made his native American-like face look questioning. She stretched her face upward, felt his warm lips on hers and met his kiss.

"Do you think you could let Sara wait an hour?" asked Greger, running his hands through his hair as he looked at Charlotte. She got up and put her arms around him, pinching his bulges of fat on the side and kissing him on the neck.

"I don't think anything will be seriously affected if Sara will have to wait an hour," she said and smiled.

The telephone's shrill ring signal hurt Greger's ears. He groped on the bedside table with his hand, found the phone and pressed it to his ear.

"Hey, yes, it's Greger!" But the phone continued to ring. He looked with raised eyebrows at the strange thing he had in his hand. It was the alarm clock!

"Aren't you going to answer?" mumbled Charlotte with her face buried in her pillow. Greger grabbed onto the edge of the bed and pulled himself up. Now he could see that the cell phone was lying behind the base of the lamp. It was vibrating and moving around from all the ringing and just about to fall on the floor. He grabbed it at the last minute.

"Hi! It's Sara. Am I calling at a bad time?"

"No, no. Not at all," replied Greger, signaling with his hand to get Charlotte's attention. She pulled the covers up over her head. He tried to pull them down again, and Charlotte pulled back. Greger finally won. "I have a preliminary report on the blood tests we took, and it says here that he had unusually high doses of morphine in his body," said Sara. But of course, we'll send the samples to the Forensic Chemistry Lab in Linköping for further analysis, which takes a week or more."

"Are we talking about Arne Hildeng?"

"Yes, who else?" Greger's shoulders sank, and he sighed out loud. "Is there something wrong?" wonder Sara.

"Yes, there is in fact. According to Andrea Hildeng, the victim's wife, her husband was not depressed or seriously ill, but judging from what you've found, he could have been murdered. And, unfortunately, I never blocked off the boat as a possible crime scene. Your dear husband will not be pleased … so that you know," said Greger.

Sara laughed out loud at what Greger just said. He could see her in front of him with his mind's eye, this unbelievably positive, professional woman with big dimples and lively brown eyes. Right now, she was probably rocking on her heels and running her hand through her curly, thick, graying hair, just like she usually did when something amused her.

"Stefan can say what he likes, but you can hardly block off a boat before you know what has happened, can you? Was there anyone on board the boat that aroused your suspicions that a crime had been committed?" asked Sara.

"Well, to be honest, I did, in fact, feel a little suspicious, but that could also come from working on the police force too long. On the other hand, this was my first day off in a very long time, and I didn't want to have to focus on a new murder case. It was my intention, in fact, to go out with my boat, feel the smell of seaweed, and catch a few mackerel," said Greger.

"And I sent a hair sample to the Forensic Toxicology Lab just to check if Arne Hildeng had any hidden addictions. Do you want me to call Stefan and tell him about the boat? That way you can call the crime scene technicians and start your investigation instead of having to deal with him," said Sara.

"Thanks so much Sara; I'd appreciate that. In that case I owe you one," he said and hung up. Greger turned toward Charlotte and smiled at her hair that stuck out all over. He pinched her thigh affectionately.

"So what did Sara say?" Charlotte got up out of bed and got her clothes together while Greger updated her on Sara's findings. She could see Greger in the mirror hanging on the closet door as she got dressed in front of it. He was sitting on the bed with a worried expression on his face. His stomach stuck out, and so did his lower lip. His bushy eyebrows remained immovable as he focused on something that was invisible. Charlotte walked over to him and put her arms around his neck.

"Maybe we'd better get moving," she said. "I'll call the team and let them know about the case and you can get ahold of Katarina." Greger held her close and kissed her lightly on her nose. He tried to hold her attention, but she wriggled out of his grip with a smile on her face. In spite of the fact that they had just made love with each other less than a half an hour ago, Greger sensed an uneasy feeling. "Women are difficult to understand," he reflected. "Or is it just me that has a problem?" Maybe he could talk to Katarina about this? If there was anyone he was close to, with the exception of Charlotte, it was Katarina, he thought and felt a small wave of hope.

Katarina Linde sat in the backseat together with three crime scene technicians and thought about what Greger had said over the phone. In the midst of her thoughts, the driver of the car yelled and pointed. He was driving over Tjörn Bridge when he caught sight of fifteen small sailing boats. The other two passengers in the car leaned excitedly over to the right of the car to see better. The boats were sailing in a circle. "They are probably youngsters learning how to sail," commented Katarina's colleague. She nodded in a distracted way since she was thinking about something else altogether.

Her thoughts were with Matthias. He was in the United States, in Washington D.C. with the FBI learning more about intercepting telecommunications and would be gone another month. She missed him but at the same time thought it was nice to have time alone. These doubts concerned her. They had both chosen the form of partnership which meant being together but living apart, but most of the time she was the one to go over to his place for the night. They met for the first time over two years ago and a year ago he had proposed. Excited and happily surprised, she had said yes right away and then had misgivings a few seconds later. Sara Kronfeld, Stefan's wife, had been genuinely happy about their new love, and if there was someone's judgment she felt she could trust, it was Sara's. That was one of the reasons why she had just ignored her doubts. Even Greger, a widower for so many years, had found a new life partner in Charlotte Engman at about the same time. The question was whether or not Charlotte would be able to handle Greger's constant sloppiness, thought Katarina. After many years of practice, she had finally managed to take command over her irritation regarding Greger's hopelessly careless behavior, things like forgotten notes.

Katarina thoughts wandered back in time to that special evening with Matthias and she started to smile. They were sitting beside each other on the sofa at his place. The only light in the room was from the streetlight and two lit candles on the table. She remembered the noise of the streetcars outside his window. It was seldom quiet on Kungsladugårdsgatan, but then it wasn't any more quiet on her street. She felt lucky that she hadn't been forced to choose between the two apartments since she was much happier with her place on Nordenskiöldsgatan in the Linné area. The view from her living room window was of nothing more than the building across the road, but being so close to the Slottsskogen Park with all that it included meant a lot to her. Mattias had stretched out his hand to get his glass of wine from the table and she had noticed in the light from the street that his hand was shaking. Katarina put her hand on his arm and he put down the glass. When he turned toward her, his eyes were filled with tears and without a word, she took him in her arms. And then they just sat there, with their arms around each other in complete silence. Suddenly someone rang the doorbell. Mattias jumped, got up from the sofa and went out to the hall. When he came back, he had his hands behind his back and a mysterious smile on his face.

"We're approaching the harbor," yelled the driver of the car. "Is this where we are supposed to turn right?" he asked, pointing.

Katarina was brought out of her daydreaming and looked around. They were on Hamngatan in the center of Skärhamn. She caught sight of the schooner Atene, which lay anchored to the left of the boat club's warehouse and told him to turn right at the next entrance. As the car approached the guest harbor, she noticed a gathering of people. She asked the

36

driver to drive over to the group and park. When she got out of the car and walked toward the boat, she was surprised to see two identical boats lying beside each other. Greger stood talking with Charlotte and didn't notice her arrival. She put her hand on his shoulder.

"What's this? These boats are identical! Which boat is it?" asked Katarina, nodding at the same time toward Charlotte. Greger turned toward her, shrugged his shoulders and pointed to the boat that was closest.

"The one called Andrea! The other one is called Elsebeth and they are both Storebro. Not everyone can afford a Storebro 40 Biscay I might add," said Greger.

"Do I sense a little envy?" asked Katarina, poking Greger playfully in his side.

"After you've been on board we'll have something to talk about," he said with a grin.

While they stood there talking, Charlotte and her team had changed to their protective overalls and were ready to go onboard. Yet another car with detectives arrived and blocked off the area with blue and white tape. A group of about ten people who stood there staring and had started asking questions were moved aside.

"Have you spoken with Andrea Hildeng?"

Greger squirmed and looked hastily at the boat before answering Katarina's question.

"I was hoping you could handle that part. She's with her brother, Björn Caling."

"Have you checked to see if there is anyone in the other boat who might have a connection with the victim?" asked Katarina.

"No ... I ... um ... we thought it would be better to wait until you came," said Greger and felt the usual uncontrollable twitches in his right eyelid. "Why is there always some revealing detail?" he thought with irritation.

Charlotte left them and climbed on board the boat with her team. They disappeared down into the salon, but she came back up on deck just a few seconds later. Charlotte walked to the stern of the boat and waved Greger over.

"There's not a soul on the boat! Where are the victim's wife and brother?" Suddenly a man came out of the boat that lay alongside and turned toward Charlotte.

"Who are you and why are you onboard my brother's boat?" he asked.

With her hands in the air and raised eyebrows, Charlotte looked at the person who was apparently addressing her. "Well, can I have an answer?" asked Jon.

"And who are you?" she asked, after having introduced herself.

"My name is Jon Hildeng and I am Arne's brother," he said stretching out his hand. Charlotte bent over the railing to meet his outstretched hand. His grip was warm and powerful. When he unexpectedly smiled at her, his whole appearance suddenly changed. Studying him, she discovered that this man was extremely charming. His smile deepened the furrows around his mouth, and straight, white teeth dominated his face. Charlotte realized that she was still standing and holding his hand all the while that she was studying him. She pulled her hand back and felt a red blush spread over her face. Greger, who had stood watching, made himself look away and caught sight of a woman with billowing blonde hair climbing onto the deck. Andrea Hildeng and Björn Caling came along with this woman.

"Oh God, I guess the whole family's here," thought Greger. He started watching the woman with the blond hair. "She's very attractive," he thought, and had to stop himself from whistling out loud. In the meantime he had completely forgotten that Katarina and Charlotte were standing only a meter away from him. He cleared his throat, resumed his composure, and went to meet up with Andrea and her brother Björn.

Charlotte stepped out of the boat and stood beside the others. Even she had noticed the delicate woman with the enormous hair. "And it even seems real," she thought, feeling poisonous envy spread throughout her body. Katarina had also noticed the woman and was wondering why she kept her head bent down and her hand up against her cheek. Katarina stood still while she was watching her and waited as the entire group made their way up on deck. "Greger has placed himself in the middle of the group and seems to have taken charge," thought Katarina. Now that Mette Hildeng was a mere half meter from Katarina, she could clearly see the swelling on the right side of Mette's face. The bruising must have taken place recently since it was still red. The sensitive blood vessels in the face can break from being hit. At first there is a pinkish red discoloration, which later turns to a bluish purple. "I wonder what has just happened here?" she thought with curiosity and took a step closer to the group.

"Had you planned to meet here?" asked Greger, addressing his question to both the Caling and Hildeng families.

"After we met in Strömstad last Thursday, we decided to all go to Björn's exhibition together," said Jon and nodded toward Andrea. Mette chimed in with a

"Yes, that's right!" Her eyes looked nervously around as she spoke.

"Have you had a fall on the boat?" interjected Katarina, looking at Mette. Jon gave her a quick look and turned to Katarina.

"When Andrea called and told us about the tragic news, I

cut the motor out too quickly and Mette lost her balance from the jerk and …"

"I just tripped and fell," answered Mette as she straightened up and looked Katarina right in the eyes.

"When can we bury Arne?" asked Björn, who was running his shaky hands through his hair.

"When forensics has taken all the tests we can send his body to the funeral home you have chosen," said Greger. "They are most likely finished already today, with taking the tests I mean," he added.

"We haven't chosen a funeral home yet," said Andrea, taking a deep breath. I'm sure that Arne's parents, Elsebeth and Olav, will also have something to say about it. I know that Elsebeth usually has an opinion about most things."

"You can say that again," mumbled Mette. Björn put his arm around Andrea's shoulders while Katarina noticed that a strange expression came over Jon's face. For a minute, she thought that Jon could be jealous of Björn. Or was it Mette's remark about his mother that had irritated him?

Greger excused himself from the group for a moment and asked Katarina to come with him.

"Do you have any idea what can have happened?" asked Greger.

"To be honest, I don't, but something's wrong here, I'm pretty sure of that."

"It's strange that no one has asked why I've come back and am asking questions," said Greger. "Hasn't it even occurred to them that I might suspect someone of murder? We'll go back now and drop the bomb. I want you to watch and see who reacts first!"

That turned out to be impossible since they all looked equally shocked at the same time when they heard what

Greger had to say. Everyone started talking at once. Andrea screamed and cried simultaneously. Björn's facial color turned gray, and he abruptly let go of Andrea. He took two steps in the direction of the boat but didn't make it in time before he had to throw up. Some of it splashed onto his pants when it landed right in front of his feet. Katarina noticed that Mette looked anxiously at Jon. He, on the other hand, didn't see her attempts to make eye contact.

Greger gave Katarina a questioning look and hoped that she would give him support. For the moment, he felt that the whole situation had become pretty chaotic, and he doubted that they would manage to get any sense out of anyone.

"Can I have a few words with you alone, Mette?" asked Katarina taking a step closer. When Jon overheard what she said he walked over immediately to Katarina and put himself in a protective position in front of his wife.

"Why do you want to talk to her? And about what? We weren't even here when Arne died," he said, glaring at Katarina.

"We want to talk to each one of you, but not at the same time," answered Greger. "I understand that it was frightening when I said Arne may not have died from natural causes."

"What do you mean 'may not have'? A minute ago you just told us you were convinced that Arne has been murdered," said Jon with an aggressive tone of voice.

At the same time, Charlotte walked over to Greger, whispered something in his ear and then went back to the team who was now in the process of taking off their protective clothes.

"We can talk about this here and now, or else you can all come with us to the station," said Greger, shrugging and throwing his arms in the air. Björn's facial color had returned to its normally pinkish hue, and he looked at Katarina with a careful smile.

"I'd prefer to stay here in Skärhamn if at all possible. The director of the museum wants to have a meeting with me in an hour, but up to then I'd be happy to answer any of your questions," he said. Katarina returned his smile and they walked off in the direction of the Watercolor Museum.

"Do you think it would be possible to get a cup of coffee at the Museum?" asked Katarina.

"Of course," said Björn, who took the chance to give Andrea an encouraging pat on the arm. She remained in the same position and gave Björn a nervous smile as an answer. Greger walked over to Charlotte and exchanged a few words with her. He wanted to know if the technicians had found anything useful.

"We took the contents of the medicine cabinet with us to hand over to Sara at Forensics and took fingerprints from anything that might be of interest," answered Charlotte. "We didn't find anything suspicious just from looking around."

"Are you going to go to Gothenburg with the team?" asked Greger. She nodded, got into the car, and waved to him through the window. His eyes followed the car until it was out of sight.

"Could you come along with me so we can talk?" asked Greger and nodded in Andrea's direction. Jon took a step forward, but this time Greger stopped him from standing in front of Andrea. In spite of the fact that Jon was over a decimeter taller than Greger, the air just went out of him. He backed up two steps and refrained from making a scene. He then grabbed Mette under the arm and pushed her in front of him in the direction of the boat.

"We are on the boat if there is anything you want," said

Jon to Andrea, without turning around.

"You need to realize that Jon is upset. Normally he is both very entertaining and friendly," said Andrea sighing deeply.

Now that she was standing close by, Greger noticed that her breath smelled of alcohol. He had smelled the same coming from Björn, but decided not to make any comments about it. "In view of the current situation, if they've had a few drinks one can hardly blame them," thought Greger. He looked around on the wharf and discovered that there were still quite a few people who were hanging around out of curiosity. Greger went over to one of the men who stood eagerly discussing with a woman dressed in a pair of white shorts and a clear red jersey. When they noticed that he was on his way over toward them, they stopped talking and turned toward him.

"Have you left your statements to any of the policemen? That is, if you've seen something," said Greger. They both shook their heads. "Has any one of you seen or heard anything unusual during the night?" asked Greger looking out over the five persons still remaining on the wharf. They all shook their heads in silence. "Thank you. I have no further questions!" said Greger. He turned around and walked back to Andrea. Together they started walking in the same direction that Katarina and Björn had gone five minutes earlier.

Greger walked into the Museum Café and saw Katarina sitting at a table across from Björn. He nodded toward her and directed Andrea toward one of the available tables.

"Would you like anything else besides a cup of coffee?" he asked.

"Thanks…a cup of black coffee will be fine," said Andrea looking down at the table. Greger watched her as she stirred her coffee with a spoon. The feeling he had was that Arne's death had been a terrible shock for her, even though she was trying to act with composure. He could see that her hands were shaking and that her jaws were clenched. When Greger lifted his cup up to his mouth, the smell of coffee spread into his nostrils, and he sipped slowly.

"How is your relationship with Arne's brother Jon?" asked Greger as he put his cup back down on the saucer. She looked confused about the question, and the cup she had just lifted up remained hanging in the air for several seconds before she answered.

"Sometimes he calls and asks legal questions about the pharmacy chain in Norway. I am a lawyer specializing in business law. Beyond that, we socialize the way most large families do I suppose; we are together over Christmas, Easter and Pentecost. Otherwise we don't get together very often," said Andrea, looking down at the table. Greger could see that his question had been provocative and sensed that she wasn't telling the whole truth.

Mette Broods Over Her Situation

In the boat, Mette was sitting by the table in the salon. Jon went over to the refrigerator and took out a bottle of sparkling water. He put it down in front of Mette and ran his hands through his short hair. Then he dropped the bottle opener on the floor and hit his head on the edge of the table when he was on his way back up. Swore and muttered. Mette sat still, waiting. Without thinking about it, she raised her hand to her cheek and stroked lightly over the swollen bruise. She discovered that it was still tender, but the pain inside of her was worse. That Jon had hit her wasn't something to be lightly forgotten, if she could ever forget. There was no excuse for his behavior! Elsebeth had hurt her so many times and Jon had never come to her defense, not once. He had always pretended to be *so* busy doing something else when Mette had approached him with tear-filled eyes to try and get him to intervene against his mother. That she had finally managed to shake up her mother-in-law definitely didn't render getting hit in the face. Jon got up quickly and walked over to the bar. She heard the ice maker machine start to rumble and then ice

45

clinking in a glass. He returned to the table with his drink, which judging by the smell was a gin and tonic. That was one of his favorites, and it had also been Arne's favorite drink. The situation was absurd. Here they were, sitting opposite each other, and Mette wondered whether or not Jon had even a single thought in his head about his dead brother. She knew that Jon had always been jealous of Arne. The greatest cause of his envy was that Andrea and Arne had two healthy sons. Jon had always avoided her pleas to let the doctors examine him as well for their shared problems. That had been difficult for her to forgive. But still the most painful part of it all was Elsebeth's verbal attacks. They were etched into her brain.

"I think it was very unwise of you to call my mother and tell her what had happened," said Jon and took a gulp from his glass. "Don't you agree?"

It took several seconds before the words sank into her consciousness. Anger reared up inside her. She felt like taking the bottle of sparkling water and hitting him in the head with it. Instead she took a deep breath, looked up and met his gaze.

"Maybe it wasn't the smartest thing I've ever done, but in view of the way your mother has treated me all these years, maybe it wasn't so strange," she said, looking down. Jon muttered something impossible to hear but didn't actually say anything. That surprised Mette since she had expected a cutting remark in return. Jon had an absent expression on his face and didn't seem to be following the conversation. She could see that his thoughts were elsewhere.

"How do you want to arrange Arne's funeral?" asked Mette in an attempt to get away from the subject of her mother-in-law. Without answering, Jon got up from the table. He took his drink and his cell phone and then left her alone in the salon. She heard his footsteps up on deck and assumed that he was talking with his mother on the phone. Mette was wondering what the next step would be. She thought Elsebeth would want to take care of the funeral. She would want to, no matter what Andrea or anyone else thought about it. Elsebeth was used to being in control, even over her husband.

"I've talked with Mom, and we're going home now," said Jon, putting down his glass with a bang. "I only want to wait for Björn and Andrea, so they know where we've gone." After he said those words, he went into the master bedroom and closed the door. "Home" thought Mette and sighed out loud just thinking the word. She'd never had a home, actually. Her parents had died when she was eleven years old, and after that an elderly woman related to her father had taken care of her. That woman had passed away when Mette was nineteen years old and had just begun her education as a pharmacist. That was how she had met Jon. During a trip with a classmate on their way to Strömstad she had been bitten by a wasp and her leg swelled up. She had gone to the pharmacy to ask for help, and it was Jon who had taken care of her. It turned out that he was also studying to become a pharmacist and had just begun practicing at the pharmacy. He ended up asking both Mette and her classmate to go out in the evening. Mette fell head over heels for Jon's charm, his smile, and his attention. She was in seventh heaven, in love, and so happy that she answered yes right away when he proposed three months later. It was after that that she met her future mother-in-law, Elsebeth.

The Police Station at Ernst Fontell Place

Greger sat in the assignment room together with Katarina and Charlotte. Stefan Kronfeld had just left the room and he had been whiny. He was upset with Greger for not blocking off the boat right after finding Arne Hildeng and immediately treating it as a crime scene. There was a notebook on the table with Sara's report. In it she had written that Arne Hildeng had died of an overdose. There was no indication that he had abused narcotics. The lab report on his hair samples showed no signs of drugs.

"Did you get a chance to talk to them?" asked Charlotte.

"If you mean Andrea and Björn Caling, I talked with Andrea and Katarina took care of Björn. But I can't see either of them as a potential murderer," said Greger.

"I agree with Greger. We never got the chance to talk with Jon or Mette, unfortunately. I'd like to know if it was Jon who gave Mette that bruise and if so, why. I didn't think his story about her falling in the boat was true. Even if she did back him up," said Katarina.

"I thought Jon seemed very nice," said Charlotte, smiling

48

at the memory of their meeting.

"I noticed that," retorted Greger, who couldn't help sounding touchy. Katarina looked at him with surprise and cleared her throat loudly.

"Don't tell me you got jealous?" asked Charlotte.

"No, no ... not at all," said Greger, retreating quickly.

"I can't believe Jon or Mette could be involved," said Charlotte. "They weren't even there!" She ignored Greger's facial expressions and gathered her papers as she started to get up out of her chair. "We'll wait for the report from the Forensic Medical Lab to see what those pill bottles from the boat contained. In the meantime we'll just have to wait and see," she said.

Greger turned toward Katarina and with a pleading look asked her to remain in the room. Charlotte said goodbye and went her way. Katarina leaned back in her chair and waited with curiosity to hear what Greger had to say.

"How are you these days?" asked Greger.

"How I am?" echoed Katarina. "Why are you asking me that? Do I seem to not feel well?"

"No, no ... that's not what I meant," said Greger, clearing his throat. "What I meant was, or rather, what I'm wondering about is whether or not you miss Matthias?"

Katarina went quiet, leaned forward in the chair and looked at Greger with her golden brown eyes. She brushed away one of the chestnut colored curls that was in the habit of falling in front of her eyes.

"Last year, when I had my fiftieth birthday, I thought I would never find a new life partner again. Fortunately, Matthias came into my life, and it was even more fortunate that he didn't want to have children. Right now, he is in the U.S. as you know and will be home in about a month. But if I'm going to be honest, which you know I always want to be with you, there are moments when I am happy we are still each living in our own homes," she said. Greger bent his head down and looked away. Katarina leaned over closer to him and took hold of his arm. "I'm so sorry! For a minute I completely forgot about your daughter Johanna," she said.

"I can understand that you aren't constantly reminded of her existence, but I am. Even though six years have passed since she died, as soon as I remember it, it feels like it just happened yesterday," said Greger, sighing loudly. "The question I think many parents who are in my situation ask themselves is 'What did I do wrong?'"

"But surely you don't still believe, after all these years, that you did something wrong?" said Katarina. "You couldn't help that your wife Elvy was depressed and didn't have the will to live any longer. And that Johanna ended up with the wrong crowd after her mother died is nothing you should take the blame for," she said firmly. "Does this discussion have anything to do with your relationship with Charlotte?" asked Katarina all of a sudden. Greger nodded. "Have you had a fight?"

"Yes and no," he answered. "It's just that something feels wrong."

"What is it that doesn't feel right? You're going to have to be more detailed if you want me to help you," she said. "Because this is what you want, isn't it?"

"I thought that since you are a woman and the same age as Charlotte … "

"I am actually four years younger," said Katarina, interrupting with a smile.

"Yes, yes, but you know what I mean," he said, running his hands through his hair. "The other day she found a tiny bit of moldy bread in the laundry hamper and that resulted in me getting a scolding. A very big one," he said and sighed heavily.

"But it couldn't have been that little piece of bread that made her angry. The anger that came out then has probably been building up inside her for a while," said Katarina. "It can't be a secret for anyone who is close to you that you are sloppy, right?"

Greger shook his head.

"Do you want me to talk to Charlotte? Ask some leading questions?"

"No, I don't want that. I just thought that you might have some good advice to give me. Should I buy some flowers or maybe some jewelry?"

"No, I think you should avoid that. A better idea would be if you tried to learn to pick up after yourself," said Katarina laughing.

"But it is so difficult to change one's behavior!" said Greger and groaned. "I've always been hopelessly sloppy. Even when I was a kid! When my mother sent me to the store to buy groceries I always forgot something just because I'd lost the list along the way!"

"Maybe it would be better if the two of you each lived in your own place?" said Katarina.

"But Charlotte loves Tjörn just as much as I do! And I was the one who proposed and asked her to move into my place. Now I can't ask her to move out!"

"I think you should talk with her anyway. If you aren't happy in the relationship, she's most likely not either," said Katarina, wrinkling her forehead. "Nothing is going to get better by not talking about it."

"You're right! I'm going to try to talk with her right away," said Greger and got up. "Now we should get back to figuring out the Caling and Hildeng families. There is an answer somewhere as to why Arne Hildeng is no longer amongst the living."

"You're sure as hell right about that," said Katarina, digging after her cigarettes in the pocket of her jacket that was hanging on the chair. "I have to go outside and have a cigarette."

"So you haven't managed to quit yet?"

"No, but who knows. One of these days I might actually try to stop," she said.

"Ha! That'll be the day!" said Greger laughing. He stopped laughing the minute he saw Stefan Kronfeld in the door opening.

"Oh, I see you are having a good time at work ..." said Stefan. "Well, then this job is too soft! I just came by to say that Sara called and has informed me that nothing of out of the ordinary was found in the medicines Charlotte and her team collected from the boat. The contents of the bottles were as marked," he said and then turned around and left.

"That man really has a strange way of delivering news," said Greger, making a face.

"But he has his better moments. Otherwise Sara would never have married him," said Katarina.

"I just can't see what that bouncy, smart, independent and absolutely charming woman sees in that buffalo!" said Greger.

"Maybe the same things that Charlotte sees in you," said Katarina. For a few seconds Greger looked at her with a surprised expression on his face and then laughed out loud.

"No wonder I like you so much," he said and gave her a hug.

"In view of what we just found out from Stefan, we have to start all over again. I was hoping that the morphine that was found in Arne's body would turn up in one of those bottles,"

52

said Katarina.

"Yeah, and Charlotte didn't find anything useful on the boat either," said Greger. "The question is, where should we start to look? Could he have had the morphine with him himself?"

"What are you saying? That he arranged his own death? That it was suicide? Why would he? According to the conversation I had with Björn Caling, Arne was feeling good. He was happy with everything and definitely not suffering from depression," said Katarina shaking her head.

"We'll have to start by mapping out the last week in his life. If we don't find anything there we'll have to go even further back in time. This means getting in touch with everyone who had contact with him during those days," said Greger.

"I can call Andrea and ask where they are going. And we need to book interviews with each of them at the same time," said Katarina.

The Hildeng Family in Strömstad

In Strömstad, Elsebeth stood waiting on the family's private wharf to meet them. Jon steered the boat in toward the dock and Mette sat beside him on the flying bridge. When she caught sight of her mother-in-law, the thin woman with the pointed chin and sharp tongue, she knew what would be waiting for her. But she braced herself and deliberately looked right past Elsebeth. As soon as the boat was docked, Elsebeth climbed on board. In spite of her age, she was surprisingly agile. With just a few steps, she was up on the flying bridge. She didn't give Mette any recognition, but instead threw her arms around her son's neck.

"Poor Mom," said Jon, stroking her hair. Mette could see that the thin body shook from crying and that even Jon's eyes filled with tears.

"Shall we go up to the house? Why don't you take your things with you? Your clothes will get damp otherwise," said Elsebeth, releasing herself from Jon's arms. Mette turned around and started to pick up the clothes that lay spread out here and there in the boat. In the meantime, Jon and Elsebeth went up toward the house. Mette looked out through one of the ventilation openings and could see that they were holding each other as they walked. They looked like they were a couple.

The clothes filled two large suitcases. She dragged them over to the aft doors. Jon would have to carry them up to the house from there.

"Mette, would you like a glass of wine?" asked Olav, when she walked through the glass doors on the terrace. She nodded and walked over to her father-in-law. His lips were trembling and his smile nervous when she took the glass from his hand. He was probably still worried about her knowing that he surfed pornographic sites at night. But for the time being her thoughts were elsewhere. She smiled back at Olav and went to sit in one of the lounge chairs placed out on the sunny terrace. Olav followed after and sat down in the chair beside her.

"Have you seen Andrea yet?" asked Olav, staring down into the wine glass he was holding in his hand. Mette nodded and looked out over the ocean. The view from this house was so magnificent. It was possible to look out over the ocean and the islets from all of the rooms that faced west. That was the only good thing about living here, she thought.

"Well, how did she take it? Is she unhappy?" he asked, looking straight at Mette.

Without thinking about it, she held her hand over her cheek. The bruise was probably hidden by her recently applied make up. And besides, she didn't need to worry with regard to Olav since his sight wasn't very good at a distance.

She turned toward her father-in-law and glared at him. What did he mean by that? Should Andrea have been happy? What kind of a weird question was that?

"What do you mean?" she asked. "Aren't you sad about your son being dead?"

Olav bent his head down again and rubbed his pointing finger around the edge of the glass to make a squealing noise.

"Sure, of course I am, but …" His sentence remained hanging in the air, and the reason was that Elsebeth had just come out on the terrace with Jon. Her ice blue eyes swept over Mette and then got stuck like glue onto Olav. Elsebeth took two steps and pulled the wine glass out of his hand. She placed it on the table and stood right in front of him.

"Haven't you got anything better to do than sit here and guzzle wine?" she asked. "You could, for example, go get Jon's baggage from the boat. Come on! Get up and make yourself useful!"

Olav slowly pulled himself up from out of the lounge chair and walked off without a word. An unpleasant feeling spread in Mette's stomach. The silence on the terrace after Olav left was oppressive, but at the same time, Mette didn't dare to break it. She knew from experience that if she should happen to utter something that didn't suit Elsebeth, she'd just get a humiliating remark back.

Mette decided to leave them alone. She got up and realized she'd have to walk past Jon to get into the house. She didn't want to have to look him in the eyes, so she concentrated on the fluttering curtains hanging to the side of the glass doors. Just as she passed Jon, he took a step in her direction. She jumped nervously and lost her balance for a moment, but then regained her equilibrium and hurried into the house. Mette happened to see Elsebeth start to smile a crooked smile. Tears filled her eyes, and she hurried toward the long corridor that connected their side of the house with her parents-in-law's. The sound of her weeping that even broke out into heartbreaking wails echoed back and forth between the

56

stone walls. She ran up the broad staircase into one of the three bedrooms on the upper floor and walked over to one of the windows. Her breathing was fast and hoarse as she wiped her eyes with a tissue. Through the veil of tears, she could see part of the terrace. Just as she leaned forward, Elsebeth looked up. Mette stepped quickly back into the bedroom.

Once again, the same uncomfortable feeling she'd had in the morning started to spread throughout her body. Why had she stayed in this horrible family all these years? She looked slowly around the room. Every time she put her foot in here she was reminded of her failure to have a child. Mette walked over and stared at the wallpaper that she and Jon had chosen over twenty years ago. It was a warm, vanilla-like color with hundreds of red, blue, green and purple floating balloons. She briefly touched the white curtains with yellow braided silk ties. Then she looked at the golden yellow rugs that were hand woven. Everything was prepared for the child that never arrived, so it could have lived in a gender neutral room. Suddenly she felt her eyes well up with tears again. "Maybe I should find the courage to ask for a divorce," she thought and trying to find some warmth she wrapped her arms tightly around herself.

Early Morning Bomb

It was 2.15 am when the sound of the telephone woke Katarina. She threw herself out of bed, walked two steps over to the bureau and answered. She had intentionally left her cell phone there since it was over by the wall in her bedroom, which made her wake up faster and start thinking clearly.

"We have a war going on in town," said Greger, coughing. "That means you're not off work anymore. How fast can you get here?"

"Where's here?"

"Forgot to tell you! Come to Vasaplatsen. We have one person dead and another on the way to Sahlgrenska Hospital. We also have a bomb threat under a car on Vasagatan," said Greger.

"I'm on my way," said Katarina and hung up.

She arrived fifteen minutes later to a scene at Vasaplatsen that really did look like it was in the midst of a war. A car parked at the beginning of the street was still burning in spite of the foam two firefighters had sprayed on it. Two fire engines, four police cars, the picket force and a lot of other personnel ran back and forth to their vehicles. Behind the blockades, a curious crowd had assembled as well as journalists waiting in line to speak with someone who handled meeting the press. Katarina managed to find Greger, who was talking on his phone.

"Do we know anything about who's behind this?" asked Katarina after Greger had finished.

"No, not yet, but we think HD is involved. Heaven's Devils were active as recently as last week and according to surveillance of their phones it has to do with the Bandits.

We've also had them under surveillance," said Greger.

"What's happening with the car bomb? Do we know who owns the car?"

"I haven't received that information yet," said Greger. Just as they were talking, Charlotte came over to them with a paper bag containing a driver's license.

"This was found by the firemen after they managed to put out the fire in the car. It lay just outside," she said. Greger looked closer at the license, but it wasn't possible to read the name. Parts of the identification number were still intact however. From the photo he could see that it was a man, but it was difficult to ascertain his age.

"Could the license belong to the person who is being transported to the hospital right now? asked Katarina. "Or do we already know who this is?"

"No idea, but we're working on it as you can see," said Charlotte and returned to her colleagues with the piece of evidence. Suddenly a police in uniform showed up by Greger's side. He patted him on the arm.

"Are you Greger Thulin? We just found out that the person we sent in an ambulance to Sahlgrenska Hospital is Verne Hildeng. The family lives in Hovås, but we haven't been able to reach them."

Katarina and Greger both stood there with gaping mouths, staring at their colleague.

"Did I say something wrong?" he wondered. Greger was the first to regain his voice.

"Not at all! Thank you very much for this information. *Very interesting* I must say," mumbled Greger.

"What's this supposed to mean? Is this guy related to Arne Hildeng?" asked Katarina. Greger nodded.

"When I first tried to speak with Andrea Hildeng, right after I arrived at the boat, she mentioned her children's names. One was Kjell and the other was Verne. But what this means, I have no idea," said Greger, scratching his beard stubble. Maybe Verne Hildeng just happened to be in the wrong place at the wrong time. It's happened before! Let's get to the hospital and see how he is."

There was complete confusion in the emergency room at Sahlgrenska. The nurses were trying with varying degrees of success to calm four persons down who were yelling at any personnel that came their way. Greger pushed through all the hysterics and managed to reach the plexiglass. A woman with a tightly closed mouth and glassy stare sat behind the reception window. She jumped when Greger knocked on the glass and then stared at him with an open mouth. He smiled a friendly smile and pushed his police badge up against the window. It opened with a squeeking sound.

"Good God! What took you so long?!" yelled the receptionist. "We've been waiting for you for over a half an hour!"

"For us?" asked Greger, turning around to see where Katarina had gone.

"Yes, we called the police to get help with the fighting here that's gotten out of control," she said sounding somewhat more calm. She even gave him a smile.

"I'm sorry, but we're not here for that reason," said Greger. "We're looking for a patient who arrived here with the ambulance about an hour ago."

"I see … who is that?"

"His name is Verne Hildeng," he said.

The receptionist hammered away on the keys of the computer a few seconds and got out a pad to write on. She gave Greger the written note.

"Could you call some of your colleagues so we can get some help with our problem?" she asked.

"Perhaps we can …" mumbled Greger, looking desperately around for Katarina. He finally saw her. She stood talking with one of the nurses a few meters away. He breathed a sigh of relief.

"I'll get back to you," he said to the receptionist and made his way through the crowded room towards Katarina.

They took the elevator up to the section and a nurse helped them find the right room. She advised them to take it easy with Verne Hildeng. Verne was not seriously injured from the bomb detonating, but he was in shock. He never got as far as getting into the car, but it went off when he was standing close by.

"Have you been in touch with his family?" asked Greger. She shook her head.

"We've spoken with Verne, and he says it's not necessary," said the nurse and left them alone.

Katarina opened the door and walked into the room. She walked over to the foot end of the bed and looked at Verne's face. It was obvious that the pressure from the bomb had thrown him down onto the street since his face was full of scratches. They introduced themselves and showed him their badges.

61

"Why were you standing beside the car?" asked Katarina.

"It wasn't my car! It belongs to my friend Janne. He was going to drive me home," said Verne. "Is he OK?"

"We don't actually know how he is yet," answered Greger.

They knew that one person was dead, but since they didn't have the name of that person yet, it didn't necessarily have to be Janne. That was why he didn't think there was any point in saying who the dead person *might* be.

"Do you have any idea why your friend's car has been rigged up with a bomb?" asked Katarina.

Verne looked around nervously and then looked at the glass of water that was on the bed table. He lifted the glass of water to his lips and drank. After that he looked at Katarina and shook his head.

"What does your friend work with?" asked Greger.

"He works at a restaurant," answered Verne.

"And what about you? What do you work with?" asked Katarina.

"I'm studying law," he said.

"Are your parents Arne and Andrea Hildeng?" asked Greger.

"Yes, why? I've said that I don't want anyone to get in touch with them. Have you done that anyway?" asked Verne, pursing his lips together. Greger gave Katarina a quick look. She nodded. Verne was watching their facial expressions.

"No, we haven't contacted them, but we have some bad news for you regarding your father," said Katarina. "He is dead unfortunately."

Verne's mouth gaped wide open and he stared at them for several seconds before he was able to speak again.

"What happened? How did he die? Is he ... wasn't he together with Mom?"

Katarina described briefly what had happened, all the

while observing Verne's body language. But she couldn't see anything to indicate that he had been involved with his father's death.

"Where is Mom now?" asked Verne.

"We left her alone with her brother Björn, and now they are both with your uncle Jon and his wife Mette," answered Greger.

"So Kjelle is still in the U.S. then?" mumbled Verne.

"You mean your brother Kjell?" asked Katarina.

He nodded, and at the same time his eyes filled with tears.

"If you can excuse me, I'd like to be alone for a while," said Verne, turning his head away. Katarina laid her hand on his arm and gave him a light squeeze.

"We understand. I'm leaving our business cards on the table. Should you happen to think of something related to the accident with the car, if you saw anyone hanging around there or if there was anything that seemed strange, we'd appreciate it if you get in touch," she said.

After they had left the hospital and sat in the car on the way to the police station, Katarina took the chance to smoke. She rolled the window down and let the early, warm summer wind blow in her hair. Greger drove slowly through the almost empty streets. Katarina caught sight of a magpie picking eagerly through an abandoned McDonald's box hoping to find the remains of a hamburger. Everyone does what they need to do to survive, she thought gloomily. The city of Gothenburg was waking up and in just a few hours the traffic would be standing still from all the car owners who were looking desperately for a parking place. The cars would be spitting out their exhaust fumes as usual, and the trees on the avenue would get their daily dose.

"Want to go have breakfast at Hannes on Odinsgatan? I'm

hungry, and there's no point in going home. What do you say?" asked Greger. Katarina nodded.

After breakfast, they drove back to the police station and both were on their way to the assignment room when they met a nervous Charlotte having a conversation with Stefan.

"So what have you two accomplished?" asked Stefan pausing to talk with them.

"Quite a lot, as usual," answered Greger, sticking out his lower lip. Charlotte recognized that facial expression. It was the way Greger looked when he was unhappy.

"Okay, write a report and put it on my desk so I don't have to go get it from my mailbox," said Stefan and walked on.

"He is such a character," said Greger making a face.

"I heard you!" called Stefan out, waving with his hand without turning around.

"I hoped that you would!" yelled Greger back, but this time smiling from ear to ear.

"I might have something that would interest you," said Charlotte walking toward the assignment room. Greger took the chance to put his arm around Charlotte's shoulders and was happy to discover that she didn't shake it off. "I've written a report and put a copy in everyone's mailbox, but since you're here, you might as well find out about it already now," said Charlotte sitting down at the rectangular table. She took a paper out from the notebook and put it down in front of Greger. He read and hummed, then gave it to Katarina who repeated the same procedure and returned it to Charlotte.

"So what was new about that? We already know that the contents of the medicine bottles didn't contain anything out of the ordinary," said Greger.

"That wasn't the part you were supposed to read," said Charlotte with irritation. "The interesting part is that the

64

bottles didn't have a single fingerprint! They had been wiped off!"

Her sentence echoed through the room. Greger stretched out his hand toward Charlotte and asked to read the document one more time.

"Maybe someone cleaned the boat and wiped everything down, including the medicine bottles," said Greger with a sigh.

"It's obvious that you aren't used to cleaning," answered Charlotte with some irony. "Why would someone only clean some bottles that are in the medicine chest? Nothing else was wiped off. We found Andrea's, Björn's and Arne's fingerprints all over, but there was nothing on those bottles! I do think that is strange."

"The mistake we made was not barricading off the boat after you had found him," said Katarina. "But then, we didn't know what we know now! Maybe we should take a drive out to Strömstad. When I spoke with Andrea, she said they were going to spend time with her parents-in-law. They live in Strömstad. Andrea was quite sure that Elsebeth Hildeng wanted Arne to be buried there."

"I have a feeling that that Elsebeth is a real bitch," said Greger.

"Seems so, judging from the way Mette acted when Andrea just mentioned her name," said Katarina. "What do you say? Shall we drive out to Strömstad?"

Talking in the Middle of the Night?

Mette was awakened by the sound of angry voices. She sat up in bed and looked at the clock. It was 2.07 am. She tried to hear where they were coming from and who it was that was fighting. She sneaked out of bed and put her ear up against the bedroom door. The voices didn't come from the corridor. Could there be people out on the terrace in the middle of the night? She walked over to the window and pulled away the curtain. In the moonlight, she could make out two persons, but couldn't see who they were. Since she and Jon had separate bedrooms, he could be one of the people on the terrace talking with, or rather fighting with, someone. To find out if it was Jon or not, she would have to walk over to his bedroom. The thought of stepping out into the long corridor, sneaking over the creaking wood floor and risk getting caught by him wasn't the least bit tempting. Mette returned to the window, but now the terrace was empty. The only shadows she saw were from the furniture that was lit up by the cold moonlight. She walked over to the bedroom door and held her breath. Not a sound to be heard. Finally she gave up, went back to bed, got under the sheets and tried to fall asleep again.

At breakfast the next morning, Mette watched to see if Jon or anyone else in the family was behaving differently. But everything was as usual. Elsebeth sat in her place as usual, by the short end of the table, in a cloud of expensive perfume. Jon sat by her side on the right, and across from Elsebeth, five meters further away, sat Olav rustling the morning paper. Mette's place was always across from Jon's, but today she made a point of sitting to the left of Olav.

"Andrea and her family are coming here with their boat in the afternoon," said Elsebeth, raising her eyebrows and looking at Mette.

"Are the boys coming too?" asked Olav from behind the newspaper.

"As far as I can remember Kjell and Verne are still part of the family," answered Elsebeth in a sarcastic tone. "And see to it that you put the newspaper down when you talk to me!" Olav put his paper down enough so that half of his face was visible.

"Did you say something my dear?" he asked. Elsebeth's answer to Olav was a snort. She turned to Jon and her facial expression changed. The deep wrinkles in her forehead smoothed out, and her small, narrow lips had a softer line. She put her hand on top of his.

"How are you, Jon? Could you sleep last night? If you want me to I can call Dr. Olsén and ask him to come over," said Elsebeth, with a voice like a summer breeze.

"Thanks Mom, but that won't be necessary. I've slept very well. It's nice of you to ask," said Jon, stroking her hand.

Mette had seen Elsebeth completely twist and turn in order to be able to wrap herself around Jon before, but this time it made her feel sick. Arne had only been dead for three days and Elsebeth was acting as if there had never been anyone else except her one son Jon. Suddenly she couldn't handle sitting at the table and watching this macabre theatre. Mette got up and hurried out of the room. She walked out on the terrace, felt the smells of the sea, heard the waves rolling in on the rocks, felt the wind caress her hair, and could finally breathe out. A quick look behind her assured her that no one else had followed her there. She was looking forward to being with Andrea, but not Verne. He reminded her too much of Elsebeth in the way he behaved, she thought.

"Oh my dear, look at you!" said Elsebeth clapping her hands together when she got sight of Verne. He dragged himself out of the boat with the help of Kjell, who more or less lifted Verne up onto the dock.

"What happened to him?" asked Jon as he helped Andrea carry their bags ashore.

"A car exploded, but fortunately Verne hadn't gotten into it when that happened. His friend wasn't as lucky. He died," said Andrea in a low voice and bent her head down. Mette stiffened up as she listened to Andrea. She wondered if Elsebeth had heard what had just been said. But a quick glance at her mother-in-law reassured her that Elsebeth was as hard of hearing as usual. She never listened to anyone. Elsebeth talked on hysterically and threw her arms around Andrea. For a moment, Mette thought that Björn hadn't come along, but then she caught sight of his lanky body climbing up onto the dock. His dyed brown, curly hair blew in his face, and he kept trying pull it away with his sinewy, claw-like hand. When Björn caught sight of Mette, he gave her a big smile. That smile felt like a caress. "It's wonderful to have at least one friend I can trust," she thought with consolation.

At about six in the evening, Mette walked out on the terrace again. Olav lay in one of the lounge chairs and looked like he was asleep. She took a few steps closer. When she saw the blue tone of his lips in contrast to his loose, white, wrinkled skin, she got worried and panicked. She raised her hand in the direction of his throat. Just as she was about to feel if there was a pulse, Olav opened his eyes and stared at her in surprise.

"What's the matter? Has something happened?"

Mette backed away. His breath was terrible. The smell was like something completely rotten.

"No no, nothing has happened," answered Mette, who by this time had created some distance to the horrible odor.

"Why were you leaning over my face then?" he asked and pulled himself up into a sitting position.

"I thought you looked a little pale," she said with a flat tone and walked over to the railing. He got up out of the chair and followed her. Positioning himself beside her, he looked out over the ocean that happened to be calm for the moment.

"What do you think happened to Verne? He looks like he's been dragged through the streets. I wonder if someone beat him up."

"Why do you think someone beat him up?"

"Because the people he associates with are not what I would call very proper," said Olav.

"I heard Andrea say that a car had exploded and that Verne had been knocked to the ground from the shock wave," said Mette.

"Aren't you at all curious as to why he was near a car that exploded?" asked Olav and went back to the table to fill his glass with wine. She stood still and watched Olav. "He certainly becomes a new man as soon as Elsebeth is out of earshot and out of sight," thought Mette.

"Don't you think he was just at the wrong place at the wrong time?" she asked when Olav returned with his glass filled to the brim. He smiled, raised his glass as if to make a toast, took a gulp and put it down on the edge of the railing.

"No, actually, I don't think so," he answered and looked at her with a smile.

"Are you saying that this has something to do with the way Arne died?" asked Mette holding her breath. Olav stopped smiling and stared at her with wide open eyes.

"What in god's name are you talking about?"

"Well, because Arne was murdered …"

"Murdered?" he yelled. "What are you saying? Was Arne murdered? Who says so?"

He staggered and Mette grabbed hold of him. Suddenly she didn't know what was going on. Didn't Elsebeth and Olav know that their son had been murdered? Hadn't Jon told his parents what had happened? Her mind was spinning and she couldn't think of a single thing to say to Olav. Then Jon came out on the terrace. Without even looking at Mette, he rushed over to his father, took him by the arm and dragged him over to a chair.

"Could you please leave us alone?" asked Jon, glaring at her. Without a word, Mette turned around and walked into the house. On her way to their part of the house, she bumped into Elsebeth who was carrying a filled tray. The sound of the glasses, the bottles and the tray as they hit the stone floor was deafening. Mette stood as if her feet were glued to the floor, looking at the catastrophe.

"Well don't just stand there staring!" hissed Elsebeth. "Get out to the kitchen and get a floor brush! And bring a pail and some paper towel! My God woman, you are clumsy!" Mette took a step in the direction of the kitchen, but then she changed her mind.

70

"Are you still here? Go on, get going!" said Elsebeth and bent down to pick up some glass.

"I'm not going to the kitchen to fetch a goddam thing! Do it yourself!" snapped Mette and hurried away. She didn't bother to wait for a reaction, but she did feel satisfied. For the first time in twenty years, she had dared to talk back to her mother-in-law! "Why have I waited so long to do that?" she wondered. When she got up to the second floor, she knocked on one of the doors. A few seconds later Björn Caling opened the door and let her in. She went straight in and sat down in one of the armchairs by the window.

"I am so goddamn tired of the Hildeng family," she said and bent her head down.

"What's going on? Is Elsebeth on your case again?"

"Not just her; even Jon," sighed Mette. "I don't think I can stand this anymore!" As soon as she said that she started to cry. Björn rushed over and put his arms around her. He rocked her as he held her and said comforting things. Andrea happened to come into the room, and she looked at what was going on with interest. Not saying anything, she stepped quietly into the room. After a while, she cleared her throat. Björn turned around and nodded. He gradually let go of Mette's shoulders, and when she caught sight of Andrea, she blushed.

"I'm sorry … I didn't mean to rush into Björn's room … but I just didn't have anywhere else to go," she said sniffing.

"What's made you so upset?" asked Andrea, stroking Mette's hair.

After Mette told them what had happened on the terrace, Andrea and Björn were quiet for a long while. Andrea finally got up from one of the armchairs. She walked over to the door, stood still there for a moment, then suddenly grabbed the handle and opened the door quickly. Mette watched what she was doing with curious interest.

"One can never be sure who might be standing behind the door listening when you are at the Hildeng family home," said Andrea. "What you just told me comes as a surprise," she said. "I can't understand why Jon has kept it a secret from his parents that Arne didn't die a natural death."

Mette could tell by Andrea's body language that she was upset. She walked to and fro over the rug, sometimes running her hands through her dark blond hair and sometimes wringing them nervously back and forth.

Someone knocked on the door suddenly. Two loud knocks. Andrea stopped and stared. She put her finger up to her lips, pointed to Mette and then to the bathroom door. When Mette had disappeared into the bathroom, Andrea went to open the door.

"Hi, Jon. Are we having dinner soon?"

"Yes, but that's not why I'm here," said Jon stepping past her into the room. "I'm looking for Mette. Have you seen her?" They both shook their heads. "You mean neither of you has seen her since you got here?" They both shook their heads again. Jon walked over to one of the windows and looked out.

"Are you expecting visitors?" he asked and turned toward Andrea. She didn't answer but walked over to Jon to see what had caught his interest. A car was on its way toward the house. There was no doubt about where it was headed since the road didn't lead anywhere else.

"I'm not expecting anyone. What about you?" asked Andrea looking at Björn. He shook his head and looked surprised when he went over to look out the window. Björn could see that the car drove up to the front entrance, but after that he couldn't see anything else. When Andrea turned around to speak to Jon, he was already on his way out of the room. He didn't even bother to close the door. Andrea closed it, went over to the bathroom and told Mette that the coast was clear.

"Thank you for not revealing me," she said and gave Andrea a quick hug. "I think I'd better get out of the house without anyone seeing me. That way you won't get accused of keeping me hidden," she said and smiled with trembling lips.

"Well, it seems as though Jon has got something else to think about right now," said Björn. "Someone is making an unexpected call … a car just drove up to the front entrance."

Jon was on his way down the broad staircase that led to the square shaped hall when he saw Verne come through the front entrance door. Verne seemed a bit startled when he caught sight of Jon, but a second later greeted him cheerfully.

"The visitors were for me," he called and came limping towards Jon.

"Is your foot still bothering you?" asked Jon sounding concerned. "I can call a doctor if you want me to."

"Yes it still hurts, but I think I'll be fine in a few days," answered Verne and rubbed his ankle.

"How *are* you?" asked Jon, looking deeply into Verne's eyes. Verne avoided his glance and gave a mumbled reply along the lines of everything being ok. "I understand that you miss your father. And I miss my brother," said Jon, his eyes filling with tears that he wiped away quickly. He put his hand on Verne's shoulder. "I want you to know that you can always come to me if there is anything you need."

"Hey Jon! What are you two talking about?" asked Kjell, who seemed to have come out of nowhere. "Who was it that just came for a visit? Or had they come to the wrong place?"

"Oh, it was just one of my friends from school. He wanted to know how I am doing," answered Verne.

"Did he come all the way from Gothenburg to see how you are? Doesn't he have a phone?" Kjell stood on the last step of the staircase with his arms crossed, waiting for his little brother to answer. Verne's light eyebrows lifted and then fell, but then he seemed to relax. He smiled toward Kjell and ran his hand through his dark blond, short cut hair.

"His parents have a summer cottage here in Strömstad. That's why he stopped by personally instead of calling."

"What do you say, boys … shall we go out on the terrace and see what kind of delicious food your grandmother has arranged for dinner?" asked Jon, interrupting the conversation between the two brothers.

Kjell shrugged his shoulders and turned around to walk up the staircase. Jon waited for Verne so he could put his arm around his shoulder and they walked in the same direction as Kjell.

Mette stood behind the curtains by the terrace doors and peeked out. She saw Jon's back where he stood at the grill, and beside him stood Verne. Björn had a glass of wine in his hand and was leaning on the railing to enjoy the view out over the ocean. Olav sat slumped in his chair by the table and stared down at his empty plate. Beside him sat Elsebeth with a handkerchief in her hand. She lifted the tissue up to her eyes with trembling hands and wiped away tears that were non-existant. Andrea had squatted down beside her and was stroking her hand continually. Kjell sat two chairs further away and seemed to be absorbed in reading a newspaper.

Mette had the feeling she was going to walk straight into an inferno. She would have preferred to turn on her heels and walk away. But where would she go? She had nowhere to escape. During all the years they had been living under the same roof as her parents-in-law, there had never been

74

any talk of her finding an occupation. Jon saw to that already the year they celebrated their first anniversary. She had been rather carried away, carefree and thoughtless. The idea was that she would become a mother, take care of their home, the children, and her beloved husband. The years passed, her womb remained empty and then her heart as well. For every year that passed, Jon's expressions of affection became less in number. In the beginning, there were passionate kisses and long nights of making love. Now they were living in separate bedrooms. It felt as though it all had been for nothing. What was it, actually, that she had been waiting for? Mette tried to shake off all the nasty feelings. And now, idiotically enough, she was hiding behind a curtain and waiting. No matter what was going to happen, she was convinced that it wouldn't be anything that could benefit her. Unawarely she shrugged her shoulders and stepped out on the terrace.

"Well, it's about time! So nice of you to come and keep us company," said Verne, smiling at her. She saw through that smile. It was only on Verne's lips and didn't reach all the way up to his eyes. She nodded toward him and started to walk in the direction of her chair by the table.

"Hey, what's your rush? Shouldn't you ask me if I need any help before you sit down?" asked Jon staring at her. Mette stopped in her tracks, and her smile froze. Out of the corner of her eye, she saw that Andrea was getting up out of her chair.

"Let me," said Andrea. "What do you need help with?"

"Mette lives here! You're the guest, Andrea," said Elsebeth, glaring at Mette. She felt her face flushing and tried not to look at her mother-in-law.

"Of course I'll help," said Mette and started walking over to the table.

"Okay, but then we'll do it together," said Andrea, grabbing

Mette's arm and nearly dragged her away from the terrace, out toward the kitchen.

"Hey, what's going on here?" asked Andrea, looking over her shoulder. She didn't want anyone else to hear her question.

"To be honest, I probably know less about that than you do," said Mette and let herself be led through the corridor. Once they were in the huge, restaurant-sized kitchen, Andrea stood in front of one of the four refrigerators. Mette ran her hand over the dining table of polished oak. It felt soft and smooth on her palm.

"Did Jon get a hold of you after you left Björn's room?"

"No, I sneaked outside and took a walk. I didn't want to have to see him," answered Mette. Andrea gathered her courage and asked the question she had wanted to ask for quite a while.

"Was it Jon who hit you on the boat? You didn't fall like you said, did you?" asked Andrea. Mette nodded and started shaking.

"Are you frightened of him?" Mette nodded again. Andrea leaned back up against the door to the refrigerator room. She still had one more question but wasn't sure she would get an answer.

"Do you have any explanation as to why Jon didn't tell the others about how Arne … that Arne was …?"

Mette understood that Andrea was having a hard time talking about how Arne had died and helped her fill in the hateful word. Andrea sighed, and complete silence spontaneously arose between them. Mette hardly dared to breathe and just let the air pass very slowly through her nostrils. When one of the kitchen windows suddenly closed with a bang, Mette's heart jumped enough to make her scream. She looked at Andrea with wide open eyes and she looked

76

at Mette. Then they both looked at the window and started to laugh. The laughter brought tears to Mette's eyes, but this time they were tears of relief. Andrea sat down on the kitchen floor, and Mette did the same.

"The Hildeng family is hardly a cheerful story," said Andrea chuckling. That made Mette laugh even more. Andrea took her hand and squeezed it hard.

"I think I'm really starting to understand what it's been like for you all these years," said Andrea. Mette leaned back toward the wall and looked up at the ceiling. She felt safe and relaxed when she was with Andrea.

"Yes, it has not been all that easy. The first years when we were newly married were good, but then when you got pregnant and had your second son, things got worse each year. Jon was so envious then and took it out on me," said Mette, sighing out loud. I had to listen to him saying that I wasn't a real woman."

Andrea let go of Mette's hand suddenly and got up.

"That must have been tough for you! What do you say? Should we go get some bottles of the house's best wine and keep the others company?" she asked, brushing her clothes off and offering a hand to Mette. She looked up and took Andrea's hand so she could be pulled up off the floor. Then they walked together into one of the wine refrigerators filled with vintage wines being kept at just the right temperature.

Greger and Katarina at the Hildeng Residence

"Are you sure this is the right way?" asked Greger, staring at the GPS receiver. Ever since it had been set up in the car, Greger thought it was more difficult to drive the car in peace and quiet. Without being able to control it, he looked at the GPS screen all the time instead of keeping his eyes on the road. He had a clear memory of Stefan's face when they had stood by the car, and the technician had assembled the GPS.

"You'll get used to it," had Stefan said sarcastically and laughed at him.

"We've been on route 176 and then Ringvägen, so now we are on Backestrandsvägen. A private road will show up soon and a sign that says The Hildeng Park," answered Katarina. "Right now we are on the right road anyway! We just have to make sure we don't miss that private sign."

Greger cast a glance into the rear mirror and was surprised to see an ambulance approaching at a high speed with its blue light on. He drove off to the side and let it by. Katarina looked at him and raised her eyebrows in surprise.

"It's a sunny Sunday morning, the time is eight thirty, and

we are practically alone on the road. Why am I getting the strange feeling that ambulance is on its way to the same address as we are," said Katarina.

"You're not alone with that thought," said Greger while he stepped on the clutch, put the car in gear and stepped on the gas pedal.

After five minutes, they arrived at the house and the first thing they saw was the ambulance parked by the front entrance. Greger noticed that Andrea Hildeng was on her way into the house together with the emergency medical technicians who were carrying a stretcher.

"This time I'm blocking off everything right away," mumbled Greger as he jumped out of the car. Katarina was right after him.

"Hello there! What's happened?" called Katarina, waving at Andrea who had stopped by the entrance when she caught sight of them.

Greger could see already from a distance that Andrea was upset. Her hair was uncombed, and the look that came from her blue eyes was confused.

"Has someone called for you?" asked Andrea, staring at Greger with wide open eyes. "There's been an accident! It's horrible ... and such a short time after Arne! I don't understand how this could have happened!"

"What has happened?" asked Katarina putting a hand on Andrea's shoulder.

"Elsebeth, my mother-in-law, is lying motionless at the bottom of the stairs. Jon found her this morning. I don't know much more than that. I want to go in and hear what the EMTs have to say," said Andrea pulling her hair and walking into the house.

"Yes, let's go in together," said Greger, moving quickly.

After having been out in the strong sunlight, it was difficult to see clearly in the dark hall. Katarina could make out the contours of someone dressed in an orange vest standing over something that looked just like a pile of clothes from her perspective. She went closer, followed by Andrea and Greger. She could see the wide stairway and on the last step sat Jon. He was holding his mother's hand tightly in his. Tears ran down his face. Greger walked over to the man who stood closest to the body and held up his police identification. He then tried to establish contact with Jon, but he showed no signs of being willing to let go of his mother's hand. Greger took his arm and asked him with a loud voice to let go of her hand. That turned out to be more difficult than he thought it would be. He was forced to pry Jon from his mother's body. Katarina saw the struggle between the two men and went over to Jon to take hold of his hands.

"Please, Jon! Look at me! Focus on me! We have to let the EMTs do their job," said Katarina shaking his hands. Finally, it seemed that Jon heard her voice and he started to calm down. Katarina let go of his hands.

"How is she?" asked Andrea, leaning toward the man standing closest to the stairs. "Is she alive? She's alive isn't she? Please, someone, answer me!" The man took hold of Andrea's shoulders and turned her away from the body.

"I'm the Emergency Physician and am afraid to say that she has passed away," said the doctor and turned toward Greger.

"What was the cause of death?" he asked.

When Andrea heard those words, she screamed out. Jon got up from the stairs and took her straight into his arms. Loud, heavy steps were approaching from the left, and Katarina caught sight of Björn. He came running out from a long corridor. Further away in the corridor she could see an older man who was hobbling along with two younger men at his sides.

"I want this whole area blocked off and treated as a crime scene," said Greger.

"Why?" asked Jon. He put the question to Greger, but his eyes were fixed on the motionless body lying on the floor.

Greger didn't bother to answer. Instead he punched in the number for the police in Strömstad since it was time to connect with the local police force. If he didn't, things could turn sour later on; he knew that from experience. Katarina stood at some distance from the staircase and waited for the other members of the family. She might as well inform them about the situation as soon as possible.

No one noticed Mette, who was standing still up at the top of the staircase. A crippling feeling of anxiety started to spread throughout her body. She understood that something serious had happened to Elsebeth. When she heard Andrea's scream, she suspected that Elsebeth was either dead or badly hurt. Mette had also recognized Greger Thulin right away, but couldn't understand why the police from Gothenburg were there. Had someone called them and if they had, why? Mette realized that she had to walk down to all the others, but wished with all her heart that she could just be invisible and walk past them all, out through the door.

Katarina suddenly noticed Mette and could tell from her posture that something was stopping her from coming down. The fact that Jon adored his mother was a fact that Katarina had understood from her very first meeting with him. She remembered that Jon didn't like what Mette had mumbled about her mother-in-law in Skärhamn. And that the mother-in-law wasn't the most popular person in Mette's life wasn't so hard to understand. But how would she react to the news that she was dead? Katarina took a few steps up the stairs in order to get the chance to talk alone with Mette, before Jon got his claws into her. Mette felt herself stiffen when she saw Katarina coming up the stairs, but decided to be cooperative.

"Hi, Mette! How are you doing?"

"Not very well, but mostly I'm worried about what's happened to Elsebeth," she said and took a harder grip on the handrail by the stairs.

"I'm sorry to have to tell you that she is dead," said Katarina.

Mette had tried to prepare herself for bad news. But now she realized that it didn't matter whether you were prepared or not. When the truth washes over you like a downpour of rain, chances are you won't have an umbrella. Mette stood still and sat down on one of the steps with a thud. Katarina sat down beside her.

"How did she die?" asked Mette, staring straight ahead.

"We don't know yet, but we have blocked off the stairs and part of the hall," answered Katarina.

"Why? Do you think that …? "

Mette turned toward Katarina and looked into her golden brown eyes. Katarina nodded and took hold of her hand at the same time.

"But, to be honest, one of the reasons we are blocking off the area this time is because we should have done it when Arne was found dead on board the boat. Better to be safe than sorry, if you understand what I mean," said Katarina, surprising herself by being so open. Mette got up, turned toward Katarina and stretched out her hand.

"I wish I had thought of that," said Mette and pulled Katarina up from her sitting position.

"What do you mean?"

"That I should have played it safe," answered Mette,

rushing down the stairs. Katarina watched her go and wondered what she had meant by that. But she couldn't come up with a single guess.

Outside the house Greger stood waiting for the local police from Strömstad to show up. In the meantime he stood scraping his shoes in the gravel with some irritation. He had agreed with Katarina that Charlotte and her team of technicians would come as soon as possible. "They'll probably get here before the locals do," muttered Greger. He looked down toward the road and caught sight of a car that that was driving up at way too high a speed, creating a cloud of sand. The police car abruptly stopped one meter from Greger, leaving him standing in a large cloud of gravel. He coughed, rubbed his eyes, and walked over to the car. A man and a woman dressed in police uniforms jumped out of the car. And from the passenger side of the car a man came out dressed in Scottish plaid shorts and a white t-shirt. He looked around, and his eyes landed on Greger.

"What in hell is this guy wearing?" thought Greger, staring at the person in front of him. But then he saw the shoes. They were golf shoes! Unawarely, Greger's lips formed a smile. "Uh huh, his game of golf just went up in smoke!" thought Greger.

"Hi, my name is Jörgen Hult. They call me Hultman," said the man in the golf clothes. "You must be Greger Thulin? Quite a mansion they've got here!"

"Yes, it's a real manor and that's correct, I am Greger Thulin. By the way, has Sven Ähling stopped working on the force?" asked Greger, shaking hands with Hultman. He remembered Sven as a reliable and knowledgeable inspector who was about forty. It seemed a bit too early if he had already retired.

"He was unfortunately forced to quit," said Hultman, ordering the other police to go into the house. Greger remained in the same position and waited for more.

"He was threatened," said Hultman, whispering.

"But it must have been more than that! We are more or less threatened every day. It's a part of the job," said Greger, shaking his head.

"Well, he just couldn't take anymore when he received email with pictures of his family and a detailed schedule of what they all had been doing during the day," said Hultman.

"What are you saying? Couldn't you see where the email was coming from?"

"Sure, but it turned out to be a computer café in Gothenburg without any camera surveillance, so that's where the tracks stopped," answered Hultman.

"But my impression of Sven when I last met him was that he was really a tough guy," said Greger.

"Yes, he was! But having your children aimed at can be very threatening. All of a sudden your job is not worth that much, even if you enjoy it," said Hultman.

"Did you have any suspects?" asked Greger.

"Sure, but there's a difference between suspicion and evidence produced in court," said Hultman. We've had and had even then Heaven's Devils under surveillance. They have rented a big place within our area, but unfortunately we haven't been able to get them for anything criminal," said Hultman, sighing out loud as he walked toward the house. Greger lumbered after him, and started to think about his dead daughter for a moment. If he had ended up in Sven's situation and Johanna had been alive, he would have stopped working for the police for sure. "I wonder how many policemen have quit because their family's lives have been threatened. It would be interesting to see some statistics on

84

that," Greger thought. In the door opening he met up with Hultman who was discussing something together with the police in uniform.

"On the phone you said that you were bringing in a team of crime scene technicians. When will they get here?" asked Hultman.

"I expect them to be here any minute," answered Greger.

"Shall we gather the families and tell them what has happened," asked Hultman. "Or did you have something else you wanted to do?"

"I forgot to tell you something that could influence the investigation," said Greger and took Hultman aside. "That means we might have two murders in the same family. Doesn't that sound strange? The advantage is that it is ninety-seven percent certain that the murderer is here within the walls of this house, according to statistics," said Hultman and smiled toward Greger.

"Yea and we know how well statistics coincide with reality," he mumbled.

Suddenly the front entrance door opened, and Charlotte and her technicians came in together. She nodded toward Hultman and walked over to Greger. He gave her the necessary information and she assigned the tasks to her team.

"I'm going to have a talk with Katarina," said Greger. "We need to talk about what has happened right away. It's better now that everyone is here."

Most of the family was already sitting in the salon that was located off the hall. Olav sat together with Andrea in one of the rust-red corduroy sofas. That sofa was placed under a window, and in contrast to the sunlight they looked like dark silhouettes. Mette was sitting in one of the armchairs, and Björn sat on the arm of the chair with his arm around her shoulders. Greger noticed that Mette had her hands tightly folded and pushed down in between her thighs. In spite of her attempts to regain composure, her legs were shaking uncontrollably. Katarina stood by one of the doors to the salon and was talking with the Emergency Physician. Kjell and Verne were way down at the other end of the room by the fireplace. Neither of them said a word.

"Have you told any of them anything?" asked Greger, leaning over closer to Katarina. She shook her head.

"I'm just saying ... have you had anything to do with ...?" yelled Jon as he ran into the salon. His dark, noisy voice became quiet when he was met by staring glances and gaping mouths. Greger and Katarina only saw Jon's back but that it had stiffened on the spot. Greger cleared his throat, and Jon turned around.

"Can we assist in some way?" said Greger, looking at him.

"What would that be? I haven't seen much happening from your direction," snorted Jon. He turned around and sat down on one of the empty sofas. He looked up at Verne and Kjell, who were still standing by the fireplace and nodded to them.

"It's good that everyone is here. We'd like to tell you what we think happened," said Greger looking out over the group that was sitting there with resolute expressions on their faces. Katarina collected herself, felt more relaxed, and took a few steps into the salon. She had already picked out one of the armchairs to sit in, the one that was a half meter from the fireplace. Its position made it possible to look out over all the family members at the same time. At the very same moment she sat down on the soft cushions, voices could be heard from the hall and they were increasing in strength. A woman's voice could suddenly be heard over the others. Björn and Andrea's eyes met, and Andrea shook her head slowly.

Greger took a few quick strides into the hall to see what

86

was going on. The first thing he saw was an older woman who stood yelling right in the face of one of the uniformed police. Hultman stood beside her, as well as an older gentleman who was staring down at the floor.

"Hello there! Who are you?" asked Greger walking over to the woman.

"I want to see my family!" said the woman in a loud voice to Greger. "My children and grandchildren are here and you won't let me in! That's very rude!"

"If you could tone it down a little perhaps that would make things easier," said Greger taking a deep breath.

"My name is Astrid Caling and I am the mother of Andrea and Björn," she said with a considerably lower tone of voice. This is my husband Knut."

"I wonder how many more family members are going come dragging in," thought Greger with a sigh.

"I would appreciate it if you could wait here a moment, and I will get your children," said Greger and returned to the salon. He nodded to Björn and Andrea and they got up to walk over to him.

"That's our mother out in the hall, isn't it?" whispered Andrea.

"How much do you parents know about what has happened?" asked Greger.

"Nothing as a matter of fact!" said Björn. "Neither Andrea nor I managed to call them. Mamma has probably read about it in the newspaper, or else some neighbor has told her that Arne's been murdered. There is always an abundance of 'thoughtful' neighbors," said Björn shrugging his shoulders as he walked out into the hall. He could see that Elsebeth's body had already been removed and that the blue and white tape blocking off parts of the area and the stairs could hardly be seen in the shadows. "Hopefully Mom hasn't noticed that," thought Björn and walked toward his parents with outstretched arms.

"I can't understand why you haven't called and told us!" said Astrid Caling, scolding her son at the same time as she was being hugged.

"But Mother dear, I needed to take care of Andrea first and foremost," said Björn, patting his father on the arms.

"How is Andrea?" asked Knut Caling.

"She's just taking it one day at a time, but of course it was a great shock for her," said Björn.

As they stood talking, Greger was thinking about what he should do. Should he get Katarina and ask her to inform the Calings about Elsebeth's death? Or maybe wait and see if Björn would say something and then Greger would remain to do some questioning. Hultman caught his eye and nodded as if he understood the dilemma.

"How has poor Elsebeth handled Arne's death?" asked Astrid. Björn looked at Greger for just a few seconds, but that was enough. Astrid turned immediately toward Greger. "And what does that look mean? Is there more bad news that you are keeping from us? Can someone please have the decency to answer me!"

Astrid Caling took a step away from her son and stood right in front of Greger. The black pupils in her gray-blue eyes were focused steadily on Greger's eyes. Her posture was reminiscent of a rhino ready to attack.

"Excuse me for being blunt, but perhaps we should have a seat and talk about this in peace and quiet," said Greger and gave Astrid a smile. But she didn't smile back. Her mouth puckered up and looked something like a wrinkled chanterelle. Astrid gave her husband a poke as if to demonstrate that she expected a response.

"Yes, um, perhaps we should go sit down in the salon,"

said Knut, looking confused as he looked around.

"No, I'm sorry. It's better if we go to the kitchen. We can talk alone there," said Björn and took his mother under the arm. She pulled her arm out of his grip, stuck her nose in the air, and walked with determined steps in the direction of the kitchen. Björn looked at Andrea, who joined up. She gave him a quick nod and a smile before she started to keep her mother company. Knut Caling lumbered along behind them.

"Is there anything you can tell me about Elsebeth's death before you leave?" asked Greger. "Was she in the habit of getting up in the middle of the night to walk around the house?"

"I'm not the right person to express an opinion actually. I didn't know Elsebeth very well. But she treated me rather decently," said Björn.

"In what respect?"

"I mean concerning my homosexuality. Otherwise, Elsebeth was very demanding of those around her. I got off easy most of the time," answered Björn.

Greger scratched his head and looked at Björn. Suddenly he felt uncomfortable and didn't really know how to form his next question.

"But Elsebeth was always kind to Andrea. With Mette it was just the opposite," said Björn, immediately regretting what he'd just said.

"Could you elaborate on that?" asked Greger.

Hultman cleared his throat audibly and gave Greger a pleading look.

"I don't know, but it feels like I'm not contributing much here," he said. "If you don't need me, maybe I can get back to my golfing friends? You can always call me tomorrow."

"Sure, go ahead! We can talk tomorrow," answered a relieved Greger.

While Hultman and Greger were saying good-bye, Björn

was thinking through how he was going to avoid Greger's question. It didn't feel right to be talking about how Mette experienced Elsebeth's attacks.

"It would be better if you asked your question directly to Mette," said Björn.

"Yes, you could be right about that," answered Greger and returned to the salon.

Chief Coroner Sara Kronfeld

At Forensics on Monday morning, Greger, Katarina and Chief Coroner Sara Kronfeld leaned together over Elsebeth's dead body.

"Have you found anything to indicate that she was pushed down the stairs?" asked Katarina.

"No, the only thing I can see is that the wounds show she has fallen. Her neck is broken, and she has five broken ribs, as well as leg and arm fractures," said Sara, lifting up one Elsebeth's lifeless arms.

"Had she been drinking alcohol?" asked Greger.

"Not in any large amounts. She was probably a little drunk since the blood alcohol content was 0.8. I'll probably get the rest of the lab test results this afternoon. Just to be thorough I asked for a quick toxin analysis," said Sara.

"What we know from Charlotte's fingerprint inspection of the stairwell is that Elsebeth was holding on to the railing as far as step three. After that, she hasn't touched it. The rest of the fingerprints belonged only to the other family members," said Greger, sighing out loud.

"Has Stefan been at you?" asked Sara looking at Greger with her gentle brown eyes. He nodded. "Don't bother about him!" she said, laughing out loud. You're just doing your job. If there is no evidence of a crime, then there isn't one, right? Maybe Elsebeth just lost her footing and fell. It wouldn't be the first time some elderly person fell down the stairs and killed themselves. Probably not the last either," said Sara and took off her mask.

"We're going to have a meeting with Stefan in a half an hour. What we have to show him is that we have two dead persons within the same family, but no evidence to reveal what actually happened," said Greger. "I hope Stefan has an appointment with his dentist soon, because after our visit he'll be grinding his teeth for sure!" They went out into the corridor and could hear Sara's laughter echoing behind them all the way out to the exit.

Stefan Kronfeld stood mirroring himself in the window glass. He was fussing with his recently trimmed and still lightly moist gray hair. He made a face and ran his hand over his freshly shaved chin. One hour earlier he had been in the workout room and run on the treadmill. He was meticulous about his outer and inner, the direct opposite of his wife who was a chain smoker and hated all types of sports. In spite of their differences, he loved his wife and had great respect for her professional expertise. Smiling, he looked at the clock. The knocks on the door were punctual.

"Greger is at least smart enough to come on time," he thought, sitting down in his chair. "Come in!" he shouted.

Katarina and Greger walked into the room and immediately sensed a faint smell of the exclusive after-shave Van Gils. Greger made a face when he realized Stefan had yet another new, custom-made suit and looked like he was straight out of a men's fashion magazine. Every time Greger was with Stefan, he was reminded of his far too high calorie meals, and that sitting in an armchair in front of the television wasn't the best place to exercise. The only exercise he got was lifting his glass of beer to his mouth. "On the other hand, Stefan doesn't have to get out of bed at two a.m. in the morning to stare at a charcoal burned body," thought Greger with irritation.

"Have a seat! Well, what have you got?" asked Stefan, leaning back in his armchair with his hands clasped behind his neck.

"We might as well just say it like it is. We have nothing to go on," said Greger looking at Stefan as he sat down in the chair in front of him.

"I see. And what are you going to do about that?" asked Stefan. "You must at least have an idea about how you're going to solve it?"

Silence broke out in the room. It got heavier. Katarina wanted to look at Greger, but didn't dare. Should she say something? After several more seconds of silence, she took a deep breath and opened her mouth.

But then Greger said, "Of course we have theories about how, when and why with regard to Arne Hildeng, but there's not enough to prosecute anyone." He gave Katarina a quick look. "When it comes to his mother Elsebeth Hildeng, it seems that it was just an unfortunate fall that led to her death."

"What were you about to say," asked Stefan turning to Katarina.

"Um, the same as Greger actually," she answered.

Stefan stood up, pressed his knuckles against the table and leaned forward.

"Alright, then I'll tell our Chief Prosecutor Marianne

Konttii that she can relax this week too," said Stefan and walked over to open the door. "Thank you very much. Oh, and one more thing before you go ..." They stopped walking through the open door and turned around. "I'm bringing Matthias Brodd home," said Stefan and looked at Katarina. "The reason is that we have strong indications a gang war will break out soon. We need to have him here. Just so you know," said Stefan and closed the door behind them.

"Well that's good news," said Greger, patting Katarina on the shoulder.

"Yes, it is," she mumbled and wondered why Matthias hadn't called and told her.

"Your phone is ringing," said Greger and gave her a friendly poke in the side. She got her cell phone up from her coat pocket and stopped to push the answer button.

"Hi! So it's you! Yes, I was just told. When will you arrive?"

Greger took a few steps away to let her have her conversation in peace and quiet. He knew that it was Matthias who had called. That reminded him of Charlotte and their problems. It was time to deal with them. The question was how he should behave? He didn't want her to move out but also realized that the fights about his sloppiness weren't going to end as long as he wouldn't change. He couldn't change! He was convinced that he had tried in every possible way. Suddenly an idea came to him. Greger waited eagerly for Katarina to finish her conversation. He would need her help.

"You look happy anyway," said Greger when Katarina walked toward him.

"Yes, I'm excited! We haven't seen each other for almost two months. Good thing I have a picture of him in my wallet," she said with a little giggle.

"While you were talking to Matthias, I got an idea ... but

94

I need your help. It's about how I can solve our problems so Charlotte will stay with me," said Greger smiling broadly. "Follow me to my room and I'll show you!"

He put Katarina in front of the computer and wrote down on a piece of paper what he wanted her to search for. She wrote the word in on the search engine and found several links. Greger wrote the telephone numbers down.

"Thanks for helping! Now don't say anything to Charlotte! This is going to be a surprise!" he said and walked through the door whistling. Katarina was laughing as she followed him out.

"Aren't we due now for a meeting in the assignment room?" she asked looking at the clock.

"Yes, you're right," said Greger. "Do you think you can run the meeting without me? Since Charlotte and her team will also be there, I'd rather get finished with this first," he said, waving the piece of paper.

"Sure … go ahead. I'll handle this," she said, smiling.

Katarina walked in the direction of the assignment room. Her thoughts traveled back to the last time she and Matthias were together before he left for the U.S. They had been at his place. She remembered the doorbell ringing, and that Matthias had returned with his hands behind his back. He had a secretive smile on his face. When he pulled out the small velvet box she realized that it must be jewelry. Smiling to herself, Katarina remembered how relieved she was when she realized that the box contained a necklace with a heart shaped charm and not a wedding ring. Matthias had put the necklace on her and kissed her neck. Unconsciously, she touched the gold heart that was hanging around her neck. Of course, she missed him! Mattias would be landing at Landvetter Airport tomorrow morning at nine o'clock. It was too bad that she couldn't be there to greet him, but they would meet at her place at five pm after work. If she were lucky maybe they could have lunch together.

Katarina walked into the assignment room and discovered that Charlotte was already there talking with Sara. There was a total of seven persons in the room. She greeted them, walked over to the whiteboard and put up the material they had on Arne and Elsebeth Hildeng.

"We informed the Caling and Hildeng families in Strömstad," began Katarina.

"Where's Greger?" asked Charlotte.

"He's late … he'll be here as soon as he can," said Katarina and knew she was lying, but hoped that she would be forgiven if it were discovered.

"In the folders in front of you is all the information we have at present," said Katarina turning to Sara. "Have you got anything to add?"

"No, unfortunately. Regarding Arne Hildeng's death all we know is that it was due to an overdose of morphine. Beyond that, there were no other injuries. As for his mother, Elsebeth, all of her injuries were due to falling from the stairs. The cause of death was a broken neck," said Sara.

"We dusted for fingerprints and collected fibers, but that didn't produce anything," said Charlotte shrugging her shoulders.

"Yes, we don't have much to go on. Certain statements from family members have been confusing. Verne Hildeng said that his grandmother was often up walking around during the night. When he said that, Olav Hildeng raised his eyebrows, but no one objected to what Verne said. The other statement came from Andrea Hildeng who claimed that Elsebeth didn't have any enemies since she was such a thoughtful woman. With the exception of these statements, nothing of interest came out of their mouths. At the same time, the content of Jon's outburst toward Mette points in her direction as being the one who could have pushed Elsebeth," said Katarina.

"The accident that Verne was involved with … what do we know about that?" asked Charlotte.

"We checked up on his friend Janne Kopec who died in the explosion and found out that he worked extra as a guard at the Kollgate Restaurant," said Katarina.

"Could there be any connection between that explosion and Arne Hildeng's death?" wondered Charlotte.

"So far we haven't found any connection, but never say never. We're in the process of mapping out what Kopec did during his last days of work and what he did during his free time. We're of course keeping Chief Prosecutor Marianne Konttii informed as we go along.

Just at that moment Greger came in through the door. His face was covered with a blinding smile.

"Hi! Sorry to be late, but there were some important errands to be taken care of," he said, hugging Charlotte's shoulder. She looked at him with surprise when he pulled out the chair with a scraping sound and sat down with a thud.

"You're just in time for the coffee break," said Katarina.

"Okay, let's have some coffee then," said Greger.

Kjell and Verne Hildeng in the Summer House on Tjörn

Kjell Hildeng was sitting in the yellow wooden house with burgundy trim, in a hammock overlooking meadows filled with daisies and two grazing horses. On the table in front of him was a glass of elderberry flower juice. He lifted the glass and put the edge up against his lips. He breathed in the smell of the elderberry, and that brought back a memory from his childhood. His grandmother had shown him one of the four large elderberry trees that were in the garden by the front entrance. She had picked a large basket of elderberry flowers, and now they were to be cleaned before boiling them to make juice.

"If we were to wait until the fall, until the flowers turn into berries, we could also make juice out of them, but the taste is not as mild as it is from the flowers," she had said, taking his hand and leading him into the kitchen.

"Want to go for a round of golf?" asked Verne and sat down in front of him.

"You don't think that would be a little too nonchalant so soon after our father's and our grandmother's deaths?" asked

98

Kjell, putting his glass down on the table. He looked at his little brother and wondered what it was that had made them so different. As far as appearances went, he looked just like his father, according to everyone who had seen them together. Verne, on the other hand, with his dark blond hair and almond shaped blue eyes, was more like their mother (except for his behavior and lack of empathy), thought Kjell. They were sitting on the veranda of the summer house in Gunneby on Tjörn. The house had belonged to the Caling family for generations. Thanks to the fact that their parents had kept up with the costly repairs, they could enjoy summers there with rounds of golf and great swimming. Now their father was dead, probably murdered, and the only thing Verne could think about was golf!

"How much do you think we'll inherit from Elsebeth?" asked Verne suddenly.

"Inherit? What makes you think we'll inherit anything at all?" said Kjell, looking with surprise at his brother's facial expression, which had begun to look greedy. His lips were pursed and his eyebrows wrinkled into a strange shape. "And, by the way, aren't you the one studying law? You ought to know that Grandfather would be the first to inherit, not us. And when he dies, it will be Jon who is next in line. Haven't you got to that chapter yet?" asked Kjell with a grin toward Verne.

"She could very well have written a will that would give us our inheritance now instead," said Verne looking glum. "Of course I've read the inheritance laws!"

"Do you need money? Is that why you're asking?"

"No, I don't need money," answered Verne and got up. "I can see that there won't be any golf today. Then I might as well drive into Gothenburg and find something fun to do."

With those words he turned around and started walking

toward the veranda door. He met Andrea and Björn in the doorway, who were on their way out to the veranda. Andrea was carrying a tray with a pitcher of elderberry juice, a plate of sandwiches, and six glasses.

"You aren't leaving now are you? Mom and Dad are also coming out on the veranda soon. We thought it would be nice with some sandwiches and Mom's homemade juice," said Andrea.

"Sorry, I've got to go. I've made plans," said Verne and disappeared.

Björn looked at Kjell and shrugged his shoulders.

"There's no point in getting upset. That's just the way he is, my little brother," said Kjell.

"But it was just a little more than two weeks ago that he was in the hospital after a car explosion and after everything else that has happened I would think he would be feeling a little more emotion," said Björn and sat down beside Kjell.

"Mom, there's something I've been meaning to tell you, but there just hasn't been any appropriate opportunity before now," said Kjell and took Andrea's hand in his.

When she looked at her son her eyes well up with tears. Looking at Kjell was like looking Arne in the eyes once again.

"While I've been working in the States, I've met a girl," he said. Andrea nodded and encouraged him to keep talking. "We've known each other almost a year and have been together for seven months. Her name is Isabell," said Kjell and closed his eyes, thinking of what she looked like.

"How did you meet? Is she American? How old is she? What does she work …? "

Kjell laughed, and wildly waved his hands in the air.

"Take it easy! I'll tell you! She's not American, she's Swedish. Isabell works at the same office I do and she's twenty-five years old."

"So are you going to migrate to the U.S.A now?" asked Björn and smiled. "Are you going to live in the U.S.A.?" yelled Andrea, horrified. "But what for?"

"Mom, please! We are not going to move there! Isabell is on her way home as we speak. She's on a plane that will land at Landvetter Airport tomorrow morning at nine o'clock. The idea was that we would travel together, but then you called, and it wasn't the right time to tell you," said Kjell with teary eyes.

Andrea hugged him and ran her hand through his hair. In some way, she felt comforted by the thought of meeting Isabell soon and realizing that she might become a grandmother one day. In spite of the darkness they were in now, the future had begun to look bright, she thought.

Verne at Casino Cosmopol

Verne parked the car by Packhusplatsen and glided into Casino Cosmopol. Even though it was early in the day, the casino was full of people. He walked over to one of the roulette tables. Verne watched as the ball spun round on the wheel, bounced and finally landed on number 17, black. A shiver of expectation flowed through his body. He pushed his way in between an elderly, gray-haired gentleman in a suit and an elderly woman with dyed purple hair, dressed in a glittering, floor length dress. Reaching into his pocket, he pulled out 4 five hundred crown bills and threw them over to the dealer. With the help of a rake, the dealer shoved boxes filled with blue markers over the table. Verne filled his hand with markers, and the feeling of having them in his hand gave him a familiar rush of adrenalin. He placed a ring of markers on the number 13 and ten markers on black. Eager hands filled with markers in different colors flew over the table and did what they could to cover the roulette mat. The dealer had to use his rake several times to correct mistaken bets and to stack markers on top of each other. When he announced "No more bets" with a loud voice, all the hands pulled back. Then, in endless silence, all eyes followed the magic ball that would make them richer or poorer. When the ball stopped in slot 25, red, a roaring murmur was heard from the public gathered around the table. Verne lost his bet, but hurried to repeat his earlier strategy. Number 13 would bring him luck; he was convinced of that.

"Excuse me, can I get through?" asked a light and melodious voice.

Verne turned around and looked into a pair of brown eyes. He was about to snap and say that everyone has to wait their turn, but when he saw that the brown eyes belonged to one of the most beautiful faces he had ever seen in his life, he broke out into a smile. Shoving the man standing next to him aside, he made a spot for the young woman.

"Please, you can stand here beside me," said Verne, gesturing with his hand that she was welcome.

She gave him a smile for an answer, took out 2 five hundred crown bills from her handbag and threw them nonchalantly onto the table. Verne studied her movements with fascination and let his eyes wander over her body. Her dress was long, dark green, skin tight and designed with a low cut, both in the front and the back. There was no sign of her wearing any panties. The thick dark brown hair was casually pinned up with three rhinestone hairpins. Verne could sense her perfume … a mixture of vanilla and lily of the valley. For a few seconds, he forgot all about marker number 13, but came to his senses and leaned over the roulette table.

The ball stopped on number 11, black. Disappointed, Verne realized he had forgotten to pick a color. That resulted in less of a win. He picked up the chips the dealer pushed forward and held them a moment before he placed them around the number thirteen. This time he also placed a chip on the color black.

"Could you possibly help me get the dealer's attention so that I can place a single chip on number 36?" asked the young woman, turning toward Verne.

"Of course," answered Verne and motioned to the dealer as he announced what he wanted with a loud voice.

"Thanks for the help," said the woman.

"You're welcome! We gamblers should always help each other," said Verne.

"Oh, so you call yourself a gambler … do you play that often?" she asked.

"Well, gamble and gamble … I enjoy it," said Verne. "It's a moment's relaxation."

"It's the same for me," she replied.

Verne could just barely take his eyes off the beautiful woman by his side. But at the same time he knew that if he wanted to invite her for a drink he would have to leave the roulette table. He asked himself if it was worth it. Twenty minutes later he had lost all his chips. Then he took the chance and asked her. To his surprise, she said yes.

"My name is Mahtab," she said and stretched out her hand.

"What a beautiful name! Where does it come from?" asked Verne after presenting himself.

"It's Persian and means moonlight," said Mahtab, looking down when she saw Verne's eyes examining her.

They walked into the bar, and Mahtab sat down in one of the armchairs with the grace of an angel. Verne couldn't stop staring at this beautiful creature.

"Are you here alone?" he asked.

"No, I'm here with my sister," she answered, lifting her glass delicately to her lips.

"Tell me, how is it that a girl like you comes into a casino dressed as though you are going to a ball? Is that something you often do?"

Mahtab lowered her head and giggled.

"This is actually the first time we've come here," she said, looking him in the eyes. "We had heard that the guests here were proper, and we like to gamble."

"Are you born in Sweden?" asked Verne. "Your name is different and you look oriental ... I hope you don't mind my asking?"

"Yes and no. I understand that you are curious, but I get that question very often and am a bit tired of it," answered Mahtab as she put her glass down on the table and leaned back. But I'll answer. I was born in Sweden, here in Gothenburg. But my parents come from Iran. So in other words, I am a second generation immigrant. I have two brothers and one sister.

"Are you Muslim?" asked Verne, feeling ridiculous as soon as he asked the question.

Mahtab signed out loud.

"No. If I had been a true Muslim I would not be sitting here having a drink with you," she answered, sighing one more time. "Now maybe I can ask you some questions?"

"Of course," said Verne, feeling at once relieved.

They had been talking for about a half an hour when sud
denly Mahtab's sister appeared and greeted Verne. They looked a lot like each other, but Verne thought Mahtab was prettier.

"I'm afraid I have to leave now," said Mahtab and started to get out of her chair.

"Could I ask for your phone number?" said Verne. Mahtab wrote her number down on a napkin and gave it to Verne.

"I hope you call soon," she said, leaving him with a smile.

Verne remained sitting and stared at the napkin. He would have preferred that she had stayed there with him a little longer. There was something about this woman that made him feel in a way he had never felt before. She seemed a little shy, and yet she radiated class. Tomorrow he would call her; he'd already decided that. He could wait one day, but not more, and put the napkin carefully away in his pocket.

Together with her sister, Mahtab jumped into the back seat of a black Mercedes that had been parked in front of the main entrance to the casino. A man was sitting in the driver's seat, drumming with irritation on the steering wheel.

"What a long time you took! Well, did you get him? Is he dangling on the hook now?" said the man, laughing.

She wanted to say, "Shut up Amir", but knew better. That could make things worse. She glanced at her sister who sat looking out the window. She had her iPod on and was listening to her favorite songs. It was good that she didn't see this as anything more than an adventure, thought Mahtab.

"I'm doing my part of the agreement and you do yours," answered Mahtab, slamming the door shut with a bang. "Drive!"

Verne returned to the roulette table and took out four more five hundred crown bills. He laid them out on the table and waited for the box of chips. Two hours later the money was gone, and Verne was just as frustrated as usual when that happened. He picked up his cell phone and dialed a number. A half an hour later he walked out of the casino to the parking lot and sat in his car to wait. A red car pulled up beside Verne's and a man sitting in the passenger's seat nodded to him in recognition. Verne got out of his car, opened the back door of the red car and sat down in the back seat.

"How much do you want to borrow this time?" asked the man sitting in the passenger's seat in front of him.

"I need ten thousand crowns," said Verne staring straight ahead.

"When will you pay it back?" asked the man, stroking his dark beard with his hand.

"As soon as possible," answered Verne.

"You already owe me eighty-five thousand crowns, and with this that'll be almost a hundred thousand. So 'as soon as possible' won't be good enough for the boss. I'm sure you can understand that," said the man with a quiet voice.

"He knows that I always pay him back," whined Verne. "Don't mess with me! I need the money!"

"You've paid back so far, but now your debt is a little too big, wouldn't you agree?" asked the man, lighting a cigarette.

Verne sighed and leaned back in the car seat. He'd been borrowing money from this Turk for several months now without any hassle. Why were they giving him a problem now, he wondered, feeling irritated.

"Maybe you could do us a favor? A favor that would bring down your debt considerably," said the man, flicking the ash off his cigarette outside the open window.

"What kind of a favor?" asked Verne, and felt uncomfortable about being in their grip.

"Doesn't your old man own a Pharmacy chain in Norway?"

Verne was shocked into silence, and his thoughts were racing. How had they found out about that? But at least they didn't know that his father was dead, he thought with some relief.

"And since he's dead, it must be you that owns it now," said the man, showing his gold tooth as he grinned. He threw his cigarette butt out the window.

Verne's heart was beating fast, and his mouth was dry. What could he say? What did they want from him?

"Well?" said the man, turning around in his seat to stare at Verne. "Do you want to do us a favor or not? For your own sake?" From the tone in this man's voice, Verne realized that a no was out of the question. He would say yes, and then when he got out of their car and was back in his own, he would forget this idiot.

"I know what you're thinking, but forget it! We know where you live," said the man, and turned around again to look out the front window.

In the meantime, the driver of the car hadn't said a single word. He sat listening to his iPod and drummed with his fingers on the steering wheel to the beat of the music. A shiver ran along the back of Verne's neck, and his hands felt sweaty. The man took out an envelope and threw it to him in the back seat.

"There's ten thousand in the envelope and I want you to call within an hour and give us your answer." He put his hand on the driver's arm and squeezed it. Instantly the driver took the iPod out of his ear, turned the key and started the car. Verne realized that the conversation was over and got out. With the gas pedal floored, the red car was gone in a flash. He stood staring in the car's direction and wished he could disappear. How was he going to solve this? He couldn't talk with Kjell; he knew that already. The last time they had talked about gambling, he had said that gambling could perk up the routine of everyday life, but Kjell vehemently disagreed. Kjell thought that all forms of gambling, especially casinos, were evil. They just create a gaming addiction, Kjell had said. Verne had then protested and said that he didn't have an addiction. He only played to pass the time, nothing else. And besides, he won quite often. Kjell had left the conversation shrugging his shoulders and said: Do what you want, but don't come to me to borrow money. That last sentence was forever etched in Verne's memory. That's why he knew it was pointless to go to Kjell.

Greger Prepares a Surprise for Charlotte

Greger stood by the window waiting for the cleaning firm to arrive. Out of all the companies Katarina had found on the web, this was the one he chose. Finally, the car showed up. He walked out of the house and gave the woman who had come to clean a warm welcome. The car that she had parked out in front guaranteed that she came from the Bohuslän Cleaning Service.

"How do you want to set this up?" asked Greger.

"If possible we'll come every Thursday between one and three p.m.," answered Laila Stenberg, looking out of the dirty windows.

"That's sound great! Can you wash the windows once a month? Do you do laundry also?"

"Here is a list where you can check off what you want done. When you've filled that in I'll take it with me. If there's anything you want to change, just call this number," said Laila and handed him a business card.

Greger sat down at the kitchen table, checked the boxes saying what he wanted done and then wrote his signature.

Laila took the paper and stretched out her hand.

"Thank you and we can start already this Thursday. I hope you have some extra keys we can use?"

"Of course," said Greger and gave her a key ring. Laila gave him a receipt for the keys in return.

On the way back to the Police Station at Ernst Fontell's Place, Greger sat whistling behind the wheel. Finally, he and Charlotte would be able to spend time with each other instead of fighting about who was going to clean up after whom. This was a solution that she would undoubtedly be pleased with, he thought. On his way to the Department, Katarina was the first person he met, and she looked anything but happy.

"Has something happened?" asked Greger.

"I'll say," she answered, shaking her head. Stefan Kronfeld is in a terrible mood and wants a meeting in the assignment room. But he hasn't said what it's about. I'm on my way there now."

"I might as well come along," said Greger, scratching his head.

They stepped into the room and saw that Charlotte was sitting at the rectangular table with her team of forensic technicians. Beside her sat Sara and Stefan Kronfeld. Matthias Brodd was sitting at one of the short ends of the table and to his right four persons from the Special Investigations Department. Katarina halted in the doorway when she caught sight of Matthias. A wave of warmth washed over her when she saw the familiar face. She was one second from throwing herself past the table and covering him with kisses. One glance from Stefan was enough to stop her. Matthias smiled at her and tried to signal to her with his fingers that they could meet after the meeting. She nodded.

"Good, everyone is here," said Stefan. He got up and

walked over to the whiteboard. "Everyone here has met Matthias, Head of the Special Investigations Department and his personnel," said Stefan and everyone nodded. "Good. We've been monitoring Heaven's Devils and found out that Hazim, their leader, is going to meet with Amir, the leader of Xantinos. We expect a fight," said Stefan, pointing to photographs of Amir and Hazim that were up on the whiteboard.

"Do we know where they'll meet?" asked Greger.

"No, not yet, but we have a man undercover who we hope can tell us soon," said Matthias. "At present we just have surveillance only at certain points. We're trying to identify people they meet and talk with. We followed one person from HD's gang yesterday and managed to get a good photo of someone we haven't seen before. We're doing all we can within our budget restrictions," he said and avoided looking at Stefan after he spoke. Matthias got up and put the photograph on the whiteboard beside the other photos.

"We also have the possible murder of Arne Hildeng that no one seems to be able to explain in any common sense way," said Stefan, growling. "He died from an overdose of morphine, and no one knows how it was administered, and his mother, Elsebeth Hildeng, has fallen down a flight of stairs and broken her neck. Could there be others within the same family who might die soon without any explanation?" asked Stefan and stared at Greger.

"We certainly hope not!" broke out Katarina. "Actually, one of the sons was close to being killed from a car bomb on Vasagatan, but he survived."

"What? Which one of the sons was involved in that?"

"Verne Hildeng! We went to Sahlgrenska and spoke with him. That's when we found out that he was the son of Arne and Andrea Hildeng. It seemed as though he was just at the wrong place and the wrong time," said Katarina.

"Why hasn't anyone told me about this?" hissed Stefan with his eyes riveted on Greger. Katarina looked first at Stefan and after that raised her eyebrows as she looked at Greger.

"Yes, well, um, I don't know … but I believed …" began Greger.

"Believe! That you can do in church! Here we don't believe! Here we know!" grunted Stefan and turned his back toward the group. Greger turned toward Sara and tried to smile, but his mouth didn't want to. She shook her head, put a finger up to her lips and looked at the same time in the direction of Stefan.

"Maybe we should look more into what Verne is up to," said Matthias in an attempt to get the subject up on the table again.

"It's best that you in Special Investigations take care of this. Otherwise I won't find out about anything," answered Stefan and walked out of the room with determination.

"I thought that you had written a report about what had happened," said Katarina.

"And I thought that you had!" said Greger and shrugged his shoulders. "Well, now we know!"

"I can get out the report from the technical investigation that was done on the car," said Charlotte turning toward Matthias.

"And you can have the autopsy report from me. The name of the person who died from the car bomb was Jan Kopec," said Sara.

"Good. We might as well get onto this right away," said Matthias. Everyone got up out of their chairs and started to leave the room one by one. The only two left were Katarina and Matthias. She threw her arms around him and kissed him. He kissed her back and held her tight in his arms.

112

"I've missed you more than you can know," he said, looking into her golden brown eyes.

Her answer to that was to kiss him again. Afterward, she pulled herself slowly out of his arms and took a step backward to have a good look at him.

"You are even better looking than I remember," said Katarina and laughed. "In spite of looking at your photo every night before I go to sleep! Speaking of photos, what did you just put up on the whiteboard? I'd better go and have a look."

Katarina walked over to the whiteboard, studied the pictures and whistled out loud when she recognized someone.

"That guy, the one who's getting out of the red car, his name is Verne Hildeng," said Katarina.

"Oh yeah? The one who almost got blown to bits … that's interesting. Wonder what kind of business he has with Hazim's boys?"

"How much do you know about Heaven's Devils?"

"They're interested in anything that generates money, just like Xantinos. Anywhere where there is money on the black market they are involved. Prostitution, drugs, casinos, smuggling alcohol and cigarettes … you can buy whatever you want twenty-four hours a day as long as you pay cash. They don't take credit cards!"

"Maybe not yet, but in a few years they'll probably have their own banks!" said Katarina grinning.

"Aren't you the pessimist! Don't you believe in my job? I'm never going to give up hunting these gangs down, just so you know. Let's tell Greger about the photo of Verne Hildeng. He could use a little encouragement," said Matthias, taking Katarina by the shoulders and leading her out through the door.

"How was your flight, by the way?" asked Katarina on the

way out.

"Alright, relatively speaking. Sitting on a plane isn't all that fun, but I was lucky enough to have some nice company," said Matthias.

"Oh yeah? Anyone I know?" wondered Katarina.

"No, I don't think so. It was a young woman with nice legs by the name of Isabell," said Matthias.

"Nice legs! Is that the reason why the flight went well?" said Katarina and pinched him in the side.

"Ouch! Are you jealous or what?" asked Matthias and laughed out loud.

"Not in the least!" answered Katarina and laughed along with him.

At The House in Strömstad

Mette sat under the roof of the veranda and leafed through a magazine. The weather had changed from sunny, warm and dry to dark clouds rolling in over the ocean, giving it a gray color. The air was stuffy, and soon it would begin to rain, she thought. In a way, it was relaxing to be left alone out here. It was seldom that the other members of the family wanted to sit on the veranda when a thunder storm was on its way. Jon had hardly spoken to her during the last few days. He'd been talking on the phone a lot. That was a relief. Right after Elsebeth's death, he'd accused her of shoving his mother down the stairs. What a horrible accusation! She had become very upset and reacted by screaming and crying. It wasn't until the police had called and said that they had classified Elsebeth's death as an accident that he had stopped staring at her with hate in his eyes. She should actually thank Verne for having said what he did at the time. With a convincing tone of voice, he had stated that it was common for Elsebeth to be up walking around during the night. But Mette had always disliked Verne and his slippery behavior. Suddenly she heard Jon's voice and

115

the content was about the funeral. She realized he was talking to the funeral home. The plans had been changed since now they had to arrange for two funerals, not just one. A shiver ran through her body. Lightning broke through the sky and was followed by low thundering.

"So you're sitting out here all by yourself? May I join you?"

Mette looked up in confusion and saw Olav, who was standing right beside her chair. He pulled a chair over and sat down.

"Do you like to watch when lightning strikes? So do I," said Olav. "If I could only figure out a way to store the energy that comes from lightning, I'd become a millionaire in a flash!"

Mette stared at her father-in-law. It was as though some stranger had sat down beside her. She hardly recognized the man whom she had gotten used to calling father-in-law.

"How are you?" she finally managed to get out.

"I feel very good as a matter of fact," said Olav and patted his knees. "Better than I've felt in many years. Now I can surf the web as much as I want without feeling ashamed or guilty. Isn't that a wonderful feeling?" She nodded in surprise.

"Of course I'm grieving for Arne; he was our first born son, but since he and Andrea live in Gothenburg, and he traveled so much for his job, we only saw each other a couple of times a year, at Christmas and Midsummer. You know what I mean! Jon is away all the time too. Even my vacations were dedicated to running the business before I left it all to the boys four years ago. And besides, Elsebeth had control over the contact with our children and grandchildren. That was how she wanted it," said Olav and made a face. "Who in hell would dare rebel against that?!"

Mette couldn't help but smile when she heard Olav. He

was actually quite right in what he was saying. Elsebeth had always controlled everything and everyone. Even Mette felt relief over Elsebeth having vanished for good from her life, but that was not something she said out loud. Mette heard footsteps approaching, and she knew it was Jon.

"Now everything is ready for the funerals," he said with a hoarse voice. He turned around for a brief moment and cleared his throat.

"I appreciate you taking care of that my boy," said Olav. "Could you be good enough to tell Andrea and the rest of the family?" Jon nodded and walked off again.

Olav got up slowly from his chair, put his head to the side, and looked at Mette.

"You won't need to worry about what I'm doing during the night anymore," bragged Olav and walked slowly back into the house.

Mette shook her head, smiling. The Hildeng family was really quite similar to the Adams family of the 1960 TV series fame. That family had, in addition, a deep-voiced Butler that was two meters tall, but beyond that the craziness was a perfect match. For a few seconds, she thought about the funerals that lay ahead. They would be torturous, she knew that. But afterward she would try to decide how she wanted to spend the rest of her life.

Surprise for Charlotte

Greger and Charlotte sat together on the veranda in the house on Fiskargränd and had dinner. Charlotte had prepared butter fried Plaice fillets with new potatoes. Beside the cold white wine, Greger had poured some ice cold snaps into hand painted frosted glasses. The sun was on its way down, sinking like a giant orange down into the ocean and coloring the horizon in purple. Slices of clouds lay high up in the sky and formed fantasy shapes. Charlotte put down her silverware, leaned back in her chair and enjoyed the moment.

"It is just so wonderful to sit here and watch the sunset," she said and sighed. "At times like this I feel incredibly privileged."

Greger smiled and felt happy. It didn't matter that the snaps had helped with their good mood. Just to be able to sit and watch the last rays of sun caress Charlotte's face, to see her eyes glitter, gave him a rush. The feeling was priceless.

"When we come home from work tomorrow you're going to get a surprise," said Greger and lifted his glass in a toast.

"Really? What kind of surprise?"

"If I tell you about it, it won't be a surprise," said Greger.

"Well, if you've talked about A you have to tell me B. I don't want to have to sit here all evening and the whole day tomorrow and wonder what you've planned," said Charlotte and took ahold of her wine glass.

Greger looked down and pretended to be thinking. He enjoyed keeping Charlotte in suspense. He listened to her protests and understood that she was very curious about the coming surprise. He looked up, met her dark blue eyes, and smiled at her.

"You're right! I wouldn't have been able to keep it a secret anyway, so I might as well tell you! Tomorrow a cleaning firm will arrive to clean the whole house," said Greger and clinked his glass to Charlotte's. "Cheers!"

"Hey, that's smart! What an incredibly good idea," she said smiling broadly. "I haven't even thought of that possibility … hiring a cleaning firm, I mean. And nowadays we can even deduct some of the cost as 'household services'."

"That's a good idea," said Greger. "I've hired this company to clean every Thursday. That way we can spend our free time together instead of cleaning."

Charlotte got up out of her chair, walked over to Greger and hugged and kissed him.

"You're not only a good policeman; you're smart too," she said.

While the water dripped through the filter in the coffee pot, they sat quietly and relaxed in their chairs. The only sound that could be heard besides the twittering birds was the coffee maker brewing coffee.

"Do you think that Elsebeth Hildeng really fell down the stairs?" asked Greger all of a sudden.

"Well, since you obviously seem to doubt that she fell, maybe you should tell me your theory first," said Charlotte.

"What bothers me is that she didn't have any injuries on her knees or hands. If she tripped and lost her balance, shouldn't she have bent over and tried to protect herself from the fall with her knees and hands?" wondered Greger.

"There are a lot of different characteristics about falling accidents, and the only thing we can be certain of is that it is very difficult to determine if it is an accident or murder," said Charlotte. "But it's better to free someone who is guilty than condemn someone who is innocent, I believe."

"I agree with you on that. It's just that I can't let it go," said Greger. "And Arne Hildeng's unexplainable death bothers me too. He died of an overdose of morphine, and all of the bottles of medicine were wiped down, but only the medicine bottles. The only other person on board the boat besides Arne was his wife. Theoretically, she should be one of the suspects."

"Yes, but what's the motive? What motive could she have had to kill him? Money? Cheating? What do you think?" asked Charlotte.

They were interrupted by a telephone signal. Greger got out of his chair and rushed into the kitchen. He could hear the signal from his cell phone but couldn't find it.

"Well, answer it!" called Charlotte.

"As soon as I find the damned telephone I'll answer," mumbled Greger and finally managed to find it in the pocket of his coat hanging in the hall.

"Why did it take so long for you to answer?" asked Katarina. "Nevermind! We have a badly burned body behind a dumpster on Packhuskajen and a man with first-degree burns."

"Do we have any witnesses?" asked Greger.

"Several who have seen a car speed away and then shortly afterward there was a fire behind the dumpster. But we don't know how many were in the car, nor do we have any description."

"What does the man with first-degree burns have to say?" wondered Greger.

"He has epoxy glue in his mouth, so he's not saying much at all! Not even his name!" answered Katarina. "We'll take him to the station whether he wants to go or not."

"I can't get to Gothenburg. Not unless you send a car and get me. We've had wine and snaps with our dinner," said Greger.

"There's no rush. You can't do anything now anyway. Just wanted to let you know what's happening. I'll see you tomorrow," said Katarina. "Sleep well!"

Greger returned to Charlotte after the phone call and told her what Katarina had said.

"Do you think this could be the beginning of the gang war?" asked Charlotte.

"It wouldn't surprise me. This has been cooking quite a long while according to Matthias. The market for their criminal activities is probably not big enough for more than one actor. Right now we have two large gangs and God knows how many smaller ones. And they all seem to have easy access to weapons. Most of the weapons come from former Yugoslavia. They seem to have a never-ending supply and demand," said Greger.

"At least we can forget about the whole thing until tomorrow," said Charlotte and stroked his arm.

"You are absolutely right about that. Tonight we are just going to relax," said Greger and poured some brandy.

Katarina and Matthias Are Called Out

Katarina sat together with Matthias in his room. They had just had a short interrogation with the young man who had first-degree burns and the Chief District Prosecutor had decided to arrest him. After that he was sent to be locked up. Medically trained personnel had been summoned to care for his wounds.

"Should we interrogate him again today or should we wait until tomorrow?" asked Katarina.

"We'll wait until we know who he is. It will probably take a couple of hours before we know. Maybe we'd better let Greger join us," said Matthias and answered his cell phone.

"We'll be right there," he said and hung up.

"Now what?"

"We have a shooting on Blendas Gata on Hisingen. One person has been shot," said Matthias and was already on his way out the door.

There went their evening together out the window.

"Typical," thought Katarina, feeling irritated. She had already bought a kilo of shrimp and a freshly baked pain riche that she had stuffed into the personnel refrigerator. She might as well take it with her to the car. But then she stopped herself on her way to the personnel room and changed her mind. If they had time over to eat shrimp it would be very messy and if they were forgotten the stench would be unbearable. Katarina shrugged her shoulders, turned around and hurried to catch up with Matthias.

"How is your sister by the way?" asked Katarina after they had driven the car out of the garage.

"Agneta is fine. The last time I talked with her she sounded a little mysterious. My guess is that we'll soon be hearing the pitter-patter of small baby feet. I really hope that I'll be an uncle soon," said Matthias and smiled.

"How old is she?" wondered Katarina and felt, strangely enough, a stab in her heart when she realized Matthias could become an uncle.

When she met Matthias three years ago, and it turned out that he didn't want to have children, she had breathed a sigh of relief. She knew that her biological clock had struck twelve, and it was too late for her to have children. The realization that she would never experience the joy of having grandchildren she had come to terms with. But the thought that Matthias could become an uncle hadn't occurred to her. Katarina let out a silent sigh. At the same time, she couldn't help but hope that she would also get to spend time with this child. It could be a surrogate for the children she had never been able to experience.

"The fifteenth of August Agneta will be thirty-eight years old. So it's high time for her to get pregnant," said Matthias and laughed a little.

When they arrived at Blendas Gata, a police in uniform had blocked off the area, and the technicians were already at work. Matthias took charge and asked what had happened. Were there any witnesses?

"Are you kidding? We're in an area that's called little Gaza Strip! Do you think that people here are standing in line to be witnesses?" said the officer.

"I know what this area is called! I just want to know if there is anyone who is willing to talk with us. They can do it anonymously!" hissed Matthias. A feeling of powerlessness crept over him. He remembered what he had said to Katarina just a few hours ago … about never ending the chase for gang members. But at moments like this he wished he was back in the USA. Not because there was any less crime, but because the efficiency and methodology were on a higher level. "We have a lot to learn," he thought.

"Okay, but the way things are right now, we can't even get anyone to say anything anonymously," said the officer and groaned out loud. "Believe me, we've tried. They see us as the enemy, not the cavalry that's come to help! The Masoud Garakoei family that fled from Iran had a lunch restaurant not far from here. They are a living example of what happens if anyone reports a crime committed by a gang. How good were we at protecting that family?" asked the officer as he put a wad of snuff under his lip and then sent some black spit over his shoulder.

"The damn thing is that he is right," thought Katarina, chewing on her lower lip.

"What do we know about the man who was shot?" asked Matthias.

"It's a man of about fifty to sixty years of age and he has no identification with him. For the time being, we are calling it a robbery with murder," said the officer.

Right at that moment Matthias' cell phone rang. Katarina could see by his expression that it was serious. His hand went to his face and rubbed the beard growth on his chin.

"Another one! This time it's on Norra Hamngatan in Brunnsparken. What the hell is going on?" said Matthias and started to walk back to the car.

"It's still light out, the night is young, and we have two murders," said Katarina and got out a packet of cigarettes from her pocket. "You don't mind if I smoke do you, as long as I roll down the window?"

"No, go ahead and smoke. Even if cigarettes shorten your life it seems that there's a greater risk that you'll be shot to death on the street than dying of lung cancer," said Matthias. He put the blue light up on the top of the car and stepped on the gas.

When they got to the blocked off area at Norra Hamngatan, they showed their I.D.s to two men in uniform who were standing in front of the crime scene tape to keep the curious away. Several journalists who had already heard about the murder were there waving their press I.D.s and cameras.

"Don't let the press inside the tape!" yelled Matthias when he saw someone with a camera in their hands trying to get past the blockade.

Katarina walked over to the body that was surrounded by personnel from the police and saw that it was a man of upper middle age. His face was uninjured, but his white shirt was drenched in blood.

"Do we know who this is?" she asked a woman dressed in a white overall with a mask covering her mouth who stood close by.

"Yes, and we have notified his family. He is married and has one son," said the woman as she continued to collect evidence.

"And his age?"

"He's fifty-two," answered the woman.

Matthias stood beside Katarina and stared at the victim. He had checked and found out that there was no previous record of this man with the police. If this was the same scenario as the victim on Hisingen, suddenly they had two murders within the duration of an hour, he thought.

"Does the murder on Hisingen have any connection with this shooting?" called one of the journalists from behind the crime scene tape.

Matthias turned toward the journalist and stared at him. Then he looked back at the victim. Katarina touched his arm and looked up at him.

"You know how it is … they're just doing their job," she said.

"Sure, but they mess up mine at the same time," said Matthias with clenched teeth.

An hour later they sat together with Special Investigations along with five more detectives. Everyone was there with papers in their hands, talking a mile a minute. The atmosphere was electric. The man with the lighter burns had been identified. He was a member of Xantinos and was still unwilling to talk. The only two words that came out of his mouth were, "No comment." Tests taken from the burned corpse that was found behind the dumpster on Packhuskajen were on their way to the National Forensic Center in Linköping for identification. So far everything was under control. But they were having difficulty discovering a motive for the fatal shootings of the men who had been found on Blendas Gata and Norra Hamngatan. They searched, discussed, and argued, but couldn't agree on an acceptable motive to explain the brutality of the methods.

The clock was approaching two thirty a.m., and the smell

in the assignment room had become something like the stench from a stale cellar. There was a cup of cold coffee in front of Katarina as well as a box on the table with two pieces of cold pizza that hardly looked appetizing. She was tired and felt like her brain was in a jar of thick syrup.

"I must be getting old," she thought in dismay. Ten years ago she used to be alert even at this time of night in spite of having worked all day. Now the only thing she could think about was getting home to go to bed. That wouldn't mean that she'd get much sleep, but at least she'd be able to stretch her body out and rest her back.

For the moment, they couldn't do anything more than wait for the technical results, such as what caliber the bullets were. Was it the same weapon that was used for both shootings? It would take at least one week to get the answers if they were lucky, she thought. It could also take longer since it was all about priorities. Which crimes were the most important to investigate? This lay outside of her influence, which was sometimes very frustrating.

Opposite Katarina sat Matthias with documents containing identification information for the fellow in custody who was a true believer in "Silence is Gold". His name was Massoud, and he was born in Gothenburg. His parents had sought asylum from Iran in 1981 and been given permanent residency permits for Sweden two years later. Massoud was born in 1985. He had two sisters and one brother. None of his siblings had a police record. Which didn't necessarily mean that they hadn't committed any crimes; it just meant that they hadn't been caught at it, thought Matthias. Massoud had been brought into custody four times before he had reached the age of fourteen. For three of these instances, he had been placed in an open detention center but the fourth time he was placed in a secure detention center.

Matthias gave Katarina a crooked smile.

"I think I'm starting to get cynical because it's so late," he said, leaning back in the chair and stretching his long legs out under the table.

"What do you mean?"

"I'm reading about Massoud, the one whose lips are sealed shut. He has three siblings, none of whom has a police record. Instead of thinking that that's because they are law-abiding and well-behaved, I thought probably it's because they've been lucky enough never to get caught. That's cynical," said Matthias.

"I thought that was an occupational hazard," said Katarina. "I have the same symptoms as you. I see things in morose colors, like dark instead of light. How long can you hold Massoud?"

"One or two days more, at the most. After that, the Chief District Prosecutor will decide whether or not to put him under arrest. And it's going to take several days for the Forensics Lab to find out who the burned person is if they ever find out," said Matthias. "But I'm willing to bet a hundred crowns that Massoud wasn't there just by accident."

"No, but it's like Stefan says … believing we can do in church. Here we have to know," said Katarina. A prosecutor can never go to court and say 'We think this person has committed a crime, but we can't prove it.' Sometimes I actually wish it could be the other way around; that a person is guilty until proven innocent. But who in hell would dare to say that out loud?" she said and laughed. "That would create quite a commotion! Dear Massoud, please be kind enough to prove to the court that you are innocent!"

Matthias tilted his head as he looked at Katarina. He was longing to be with her, but now he was so tired that the only thing that mattered was sleep.

128

"Can I come sleep over at your place?" he asked. "I haven't had time to buy groceries and it might be good to have a little breakfast when we wake up in a few hours."

"Absolutely. I was hoping you'd say that," said Katarina.

Greger's Mood Changes

Greger walked into the Department at 9.00 am on the dot. He was in a good mood. The evening with Charlotte had been even better than he expected. It was such a relief that the cleaning problem was solved. Sure, it wasn't free of charge, but it was worth every cent, thought Greger humming to himself.

"You seem to be in a good mood," said Stefan giving Greger a thump on the back. "I hope the reason is that you are close to solving all the murders that are piling up on us." Greger pulled away from the back thumping with a jerk and stopped in his tracks. He turned toward Stefan with his bushy eyebrows raised.

"What do you mean by all the murders that are piling up on us? Yesterday Katarina called and told me about a burned body behind a dumpster on Packhuskajen, but I haven't heard about any more than that," said Greger.

"A man has been shot on Blendas Gata and one on Norra Hamngatan in Brunnsparken. Yesterday. We have no idea what's going on. There might be more shootings," said Stefan and walked in the direction of this office.

Greger's good mood disappeared, and the only thing he had in his head now was to get hold of Katarina. What was going on? Would they have to call in the National Police Force? He'd prefer to avoid that, but better to call them in early on then getting them involved when it was too late. He was after all the boss for the Special Investigations Department and responsible for who should be called in. If it turned out that even the recent murders were connected to the criminal gangs maybe they didn't have much time. Greger knocked on Katarina's door. No answer. He hurried on to the assignment room. Empty!

"Where is everyone?" he thought out loud. A door opened all the way down in the corridor. A familiar face showed itself. "Hi, Leif! Have you seen Katarina or Matthias?"

Leif walked toward him. He was an impressive sight, Criminal Inspector Leif Griffén. Almost two meters tall in his bare feet and muscular. Anyone who met him for the first time automatically took a step backward. And then when they heard his Gothenburg dialect, most couldn't help but start laughing.

"Nope, haven't seen 'em anywhere! Maybe they're grabbin' something to eat? I'm all wrapped up with yesterday's shootings ... you know about that, right?" asked Leif.

"I found out about it five minutes ago," said Greger.

If you didn't just happen to know that Stefan Kronfeld and Leif Griffén were childhood friends and had grown up on Hisingen together, you would never even think that it could be possible. They were complete opposites in every possible way. Leif's lightning quick responses and his love of soccer for example. He never missed his favorite team's hometown matches. For that he would exchange work passes with anyone so that he could watch his beloved team play. Stefan was on the other hand totally uninterested in soccer. Sure, he exercised every day, but to yell oneself hoarse amongst the public at a soccer match or some other team sport was unthinkable for Stefan. Greger shook his head.

"I know that Matthias is going to have a meeting in the assignment room. You can always come to that," said Leif.

"I will," said Greger and walked into his room. He sat down in front of his computer and stared at the screen, but couldn't manage to get anything done. He got up again, opened the door, and walked toward the assignment room. No one else was there yet, so he walked over to the whiteboard to study the photos that were mounted there. Suddenly he recognized Verne Hildeng. What was he doing there? Was he a member of the HD gang? And if so, why? The kid seems to be well-off, studying law and have parents who cared about him, even if one of them was dead now. He just didn't seem to be the type that would belong to a gang, thought Greger. Looking at the community as a whole, it was most often those who came from outside of Europe who had the most difficulties with finding work in Sweden. On the other hand, when it came to joining a gang, it didn't matter where you were from. The most important thing was what you could contribute. Oddly enough, the gangs were highly integrated with members coming both from Sweden and from a barrage of different nationalities. In those circles what mattered was whether or not you were talented enough to kill someone at the times deemed necessary by the gang leader, and that was that, thought Greger.

"Hi Greger, how was yesterday evening?" asked Matthias as he stepped into the room carrying a pile of folders. "I thought you might want to be present when we interrogate Massoud, the guy we are holding in connection with the burned body on Packhuskajen. We won't be able to keep him much longer if we can't get some evidence."

"Wasn't that the guy with his mouth full of glue?" said Greger chuckling.

"That's the one, but who knows? Maybe you can get him to loosen up," said Matthias.

"Hmm, well, it's happened before," said Greger and straightened up. "Will you also be there?"

"I thought you and Katarina could do the talking. We'll film it as usual, and I'll sit behind the window," said Matthias.

Greger stood waiting for Katarina outside of the interrogation room. He asked one of his co-workers to bring in an ashtray. The woman raised an eyebrow but did as she was asked without complaint. Greger knew very well that a ban on smoking had been imposed on all of the rooms at the station, but in certain cases he defied the rules and knew that he wasn't the only one.

"Then it's okay if I take the chance to smoke too?" said Katarina.

"Of course. Just don't forget to offer Massoud a cigarette. That's the whole idea," said Greger stepping into the room.

Five minutes later, the guard came in with Massoud. With his eyes half closed, he stopped in the middle of the room. It was first after he noticed the ashtray that he walked over to the table and sat down.

"Hi Massoud, would you like a cigarette?" asked Katarina, holding out the package. He shook out a cigarette from the pack and put it in between his lips. Then he stretched forward his bandaged arm to receive the lighter. Katarina kept holding the lighter a moment just for emphasis. Massoud lit his cigarette and returned the lighter.

"I want to inform you that we record everything that is said here," said Greger. "Could you tell us what happened last Wednesday evening on Packhuskajen? Did you know the person who died in the fire?"

"No comment," answered Massoud, taking a drag on his cigarette. He pulled the ashtray toward him and shook off the ashes with his finger.

"Does that mean that you don't want any legal assistance?" asked Katarina.

Massoud just grinned at Katarina for an answer and shook his head.

"Don't you think it's terrible that a human being has lost his life?" wondered Greger. He was feeling powerless in the face of Massoud's behavior. "You have a brother and two sisters. How would you feel if they ended up in the cemetery when they were still young?"

Katarina saw that his body got tense, his eyes narrowed and became darker. For a minute she thought Massoud would throw himself over the table, and she prepared herself. But instead he took a deep breath, reached out and crushed his cigarette to oblivion, and leaned back in the chair with his arms crossed over his chest. He didn't make a sound.

Greger looked at Katarina, and both of them got up at the same time.

"We're not getting anywhere, but should you change your mind and want to talk you can always call this number," said Greger, leaving his business card.

Massoud got up and slowly ripped the card into small pieces, sneering at them as he let the bits float down over the table.

Greger shrugged his shoulders and left the room together with Katarina. As they walked in behind the window to Matthias, Katarina cussed and swore.

"Where in hell have they learned to be so goddam cold?" she yelled. "Why don't they have any feelings?"

"Science says that no one is a born murderer, but when you

meet someone like Massoud, it sure makes you wonder," said Greger and sighed.

"I've had Verne Hildeng under observation, and I think we should bring him in for interrogation," said Matthias. "We don't have enough for prosecution. It's not enough to just have met with guys from Hazim's gang, but he might be able to tell us something. If nothing more, we might make him a little nervous."

Mahtab Broods Over her Situation

Mahtab stood in front of her locker. Her work pass was over for the day, and she had just taken off her coat when she heard a text signal from her cell phone. It was Verne. He wanted to meet her at the casino already this evening. Mahtab sat down on the wooden bench that was in front of the long row of lockers. When she read his text, she regretted having gotten involved. All of this was just for her little brother's sake. If he hadn't asked her and her sister for help, she would never have gone along with meeting Verne. Mahtab had only met Amir one time before he had picked them up outside Casino Cosmopol, and she hadn't liked what she had seen. But then Massoud said that if she didn't help him, something bad would happen to someone in the family. Mahtab shuddered at the thought of those words. Why had Massoud gotten involved with this gang? She had studied to become an assistant nurse and was very happy with her choice of profession, even if the pay was low. Her sister had just completed her education and would get a job right after graduating. Their older brother had already moved away from home and worked as a

136

chemist. Of four siblings, it was only Massoud who had not been able to adjust. He had always been something of a mischief maker. In school, his teachers would send notes home ... notes that Massoud would deliberately rip to pieces. Nor did any teacher dare to contact their parents. Perhaps that wasn't so strange since neither of them could speak Swedish very well. In spite of the resistance she felt, Mahtab called Amir to get instructions before she answered Verne. The conversation with Amir was short, and when she hung up, she felt a shiver run through her body. How could she get through this without getting hurt?

Kjell Comes Home to Tjörn

Andrea walked over to the set table for the fourth time and adjusted one of the white linen napkins that had fallen over. She looked at the clock and realized that it would be one more hour before Kjell and Isabell would arrive. Björn had promised to be there as well, and that felt reassuring. She sat down on one of the veranda chairs and looked out over the flowering meadows. Kjell had said that he wanted to show Isabell their summer cottage on Tjörn. Their winter home, the house in Hovås, was filled with too many reminders of Arne. And since Elsebeth had died at the house in Strömstad, he wanted them to meet Isabell in another environment, something warm and cozy. That left the house in Gunneby as the best and only choice. Andrea's thoughts turned to Mette. Things must be tough for her there in that big house, alone with Olav and Jon. "Maybe I should give her a call tonight," she thought.

"Are you starting to get nervous?" asked Björn and carried a vase filled with fresh daisies. He put the vase down on the table, took a step back and smiled. "Look, that was the final touch!"

Andrea got up, walked over to Björn, and put her arms around his neck.

"Have I told you how much you mean to me?" she asked. "And how grateful I am to have you by my side?"

Björn hugged her and kissed her on the cheek.

"You've always been there for me, and I think you are the best sister in the whole world," he said.

The doorbell rang. Andrea let go of Björn and stared at him.

"Can you go open the door? They're here earlier than we thought!"

"What does that matter? They are welcome anyhow," said Björn laughing.

"Just go and open, won't you? I'll put some coffee on in the meantime. God, I'm nervous!" said Andrea, wringing her hands.

Björn came back to the kitchen walking stiffly. When she heard his footsteps, she turned around with a smile on her lips. But her smile froze the very moment she saw his face.

"What is it? Has something happened? Nothing has happened to them, has it?" cried Andrea with a high pitched voice.

Björn shook his head and pointed with his hand in the direction of the hall. She threw the kitchen towel aside and rushed out to the hall. There she saw a tall man and a short woman dressed in light summer clothes.

"Oh, what can I do for you?" asked Andrea, staring in surprise at the couple.

"We're looking for your son Verne," said Leif Griffén after showing his police I.D. This is about his friend Jan Kopec, who died as a result of the car bomb. We'd like to ask him some questions."

"I see," answered Andrea, without really having grasped

what this was all about.

"We've tried to reach him on his cell phone, but get no answer," said Detective Sergeant Annika Thorsson in her melodious Norrland dialect. "Can you tell us how to get in touch with him? Or if you could ask him to contact us?"

Annika Thorsson's long ash blond hair framed her face and reminded Andrea of a favorite porcelain doll she had played with as a child.

"My son and his fiancée are arriving soon, so if you can excuse me," said Andrea, taking a few steps in Leif and Annika's direction.

"Is it Verne who'll be arriving?" asked Leif.

Andrea shook her head.

"I have two sons; Kjell is the oldest, and Verne. I'll give Verne the message when he comes home," said Andrea and accepted Leif´s business card.

She stood in the door opening and watched as they climbed into a black Volvo. Kjell happened to turn into the driveway with his Toyota at the same time. Surprised, he stared at the black car that was now in the way and then put his car in reverse to back out.

"Hi, Mom! Who was that?" called Kjell with his head leaning out of the open car window to look at the Volvo as it left.

"Welcome! Come in and I'll tell you," said Andrea waving. "They've come now!" she called to Björn.

He stood beside Andrea and squinted toward the sun. Björn hadn't wanted to admit that he was curious about Isabell. The thought of meeting her made him feel tense, just as he always felt when he had to meet someone new. He studied her as she got out of the car. The first thing he noticed was her beautiful, long legs. She was dressed in white Bermuda shorts, a clear blue top, and comfortable sandals. She had short, fashionably cut ash blond hair and a smile on her moist, red lips as she walked over to meet him and Andrea.

"Welcome Isabell," said Andrea, holding out her hand. Isabell took her hand in a firm grip and said hello. Andrea noticed that her eyes were green-brown and were framed with short, thick eyelashes.

"Thank you for having me," answered Isabell with a light, hoarse voice.

"I'm sorry that Kjell's grandparents couldn't be at home, but they travel a lot and are away now," said Andrea apologetically. In reality, she was thankful that her parents weren't home. Her mother could be quite difficult around Kjell's or Verne's friends. The last time Verne had a girlfriend with him, and Astrid had met her, she had asked twenty questions before Andrea succeeded in re-directing her inappropriate interest.

"And I'm so sorry for your loss," said Isabell, walking out on the veranda with Kjell at her side.

"Yes, it's sad that you'll never get the chance to know Arne," said Andrea. "He would have been so happy …" Andrea couldn't finish her sentence and rushed out to the kitchen. Björn would have to take care of them. She needed to be alone for a minute. When she started to say that Arne would have been so happy for the two of them, the memories washed over her like rain. Grief spread all through her body and felt suffocating. She had lived together with only one man for so many years, and they had shared so much. In the mornings when she woke up and looked at Arne's empty side of the bed, she felt just as empty as the bed was. It was difficult to be suddenly so alone. When life takes a one hundred and eighty degree turn, and you are not ready for it, everything turns upside down, she thought, wiping away her tears. Björn came into the kitchen and hugged her.

"Are you feeling sad?" he asked.

"If you mean am I feeling sad that Isabell and Kjell are here, the answer is no. It was just that I started to think how happy Arne would have been …" and then she started to cry again. Björn went over to the counter and ripped off some paper towel and handed it to her. She took it and blew her nose out loud.

"Enough! I have to pull myself together. We can't let the youngsters sit on the veranda all alone! Even though that could be exactly what they'd prefer," she said with a little smile as she got up.

Andrea went out on the veranda to sit across from Isabell and served the coffee. They sat and talked for an hour. Kjell told them about different episodes from the company where he worked in the USA. Some of them were funny enough to make everyone laugh out loud. Suddenly he turned quiet, took ahold of Isabell's hand, and gave her a searching look. He got a nod and then turned to Björn and Andrea.

"Well, there's a little something we'd like to tell you," said Kjell and lifted Isabell's hand to his lips. He turned toward his mother.

"You are going to be a grandmother!"

Andrea squealed with delight and Björn clapped his hands together in celebration.

"This demands a glass of real champagne!" he said and walked out to the kitchen.

"But I can't drink anything," said Isabell, pretending to sound unhappy.

"Oh, you can have a small glass. The baby won't die from that. It might kick a little more inside your tummy tonight," said Kjell, putting his arm around her shoulders.

"How many months are you?" asked Andrea.

"One week into the fifth month," answered Isabell.

"But you don't look pregnant!"

"I know. Probably because I've always been thin, so now that I've gained almost nine pounds it hardly shows. But I think it's very noticeable," said Isabell and laughed. "I feel like I'm fat!"

"Here's the champagne!" said Björn, passing out glasses from the tray. I'm not just celebrating you and Andrea! I'm going to be a great-uncle!" He took hold of the bottle with an experienced hand, removed the protective foil, and with a soft pop the cork flew off the bottle.

After they had congratulated and made a toast to the lucky couple, Björn went out to the kitchen with the tray.

"What did that big guy and the chick that looked like Marilyn Monroe want?"

"They were from the Serious Crime Division and wanted to talk to Verne," said Andrea.

"What about?"

"Apparently it had to do with the car bomb that killed his friend, Janne," said Andrea.

"But that happened several weeks ago. Why are they coming now?" asked Kjell.

"My guess is as good as yours," answered Andrea.

"I'll bet this has to do with his goddamn gambling," hissed Kjell, getting up out of his chair and pacing back and forth on the veranda.

"What do you mean by his 'goddamn gambling'?" asked Björn, who had come back from the kitchen.

"Just exactly what I said! He gambles in all kinds of ways. His favorite is playing roulette at a casino in Gothenburg," said Kjell. "He's there all the time!"

"What? But when does he do his school work? I mean, I've always thought that he studies properly. What he's said to us is that there are a lot of exams. Has he been lying to me?" asked Andrea and looked searchingly at Kjell.

He shook his head, looked down at the table, and sighed. Isabell grabbed his hand.

"In that case, I've lied too," said Kjell in a low voice. "I've known about his problems with gambling and I haven't said anything to anyone."

"How long has this been going on?" whispered Andrea.

"At least two years I think," answered Kjell. "When I was home last Christmas we talked about gambling and how easy it is to become addicted. Verne didn't agree with me of course. He maintained that he only plays to have fun. I re-member finishing our conversation by saying 'Don't come to me to try and borrow money when you're broke!' Since then we haven't mentioned the word gambling."

Andrea leaned back in her chair and sighed.

"Do you think it was his friend who had loaned him mon-ey?" asked Björn.

"I think it's more likely that some gang loaned the money to the friend and maybe even to Verne. It could be the gang that arranged the bomb. It wouldn't surprise me if that's what happened," said Kjell.

"Do you mean that they could have been out to murder Verne?" said Andrea in a high pitched tone and stood straight up.

"Wouldn't the police have said something about that when they were here?" asked Isabell. "I mean, if someone were in danger, wouldn't they try to protect that person?"

"Please Kjell! Call Verne now! He'll probably answer if he sees that it's you who's calling," said Andrea, clasping her hands and holding them tightly against her stomach.

Kjell got out his cell phone and dialed the number. After four ring signals, the voice mail came on. He hung up, looked at his mother, and shook his head.

"But where is he? He usually always answers his cell phone, doesn't he?" said Björn, patting Andrea on the shoulder.

"No, not always," said Kjell. "Sometimes he's busy playing roulette and then he probably won't answer. That would disturb his concentration."

Andrea sank into her own thoughts. She didn't hear the birds singing their evening songs … didn't feel the smell of vanilla that the honeysuckle spread over the veranda. Kjell interrupted her ponderings.

"Mom, I have another question. It has to do with Dad and Grandma," he said. "When will the funeral be?"

"Jon called … it will be in a week. Both will be buried at the same time in the family grave," said Andrea and fought against the tears that made a lump in her throat. "I can't understand how I'll ever manage that!"

Björn took hold of her shoulders and rocked her in his arms.

"We'll support you the best we can. You know that Mom," said Kjell stroking her on the cheek.

"Thank you. I'm going to need all of you!" said Andrea and patted Kjell on the arm.

Leif and Annika Find Verne

Leif turned toward his colleague Annika. They were in the car driving into Gothenburg.

"Call Matthias and see if his people have caught sight of Verne! They were going to keep him under surveillance," said Leif.

Annika dialed the number, and Matthias answered right away.

"We've been in Gunneby on Tjörn and Verne wasn't at the summer cottage," said Annika. "Have you been able to track him?"

"Wait a minute," said Matthias.

While Annika waited on the phone, she looked out through the car window and saw the flowering meadows and grazing cows and horses. The sights made her miss her hometown in Luleå and her parents' home. She was usually there over Christmas and New Year, sometimes even a week during the summer. At the same time, she was happy with her work in the Serious Crime Division in Gothenburg. Fortunately, she'd been able to buy an apartment on Linnégatan in the same area where Katarina lived. She could understand why Katarina enjoyed living in the Linné area. Everything one could possibly need was readily available there, plus a little more. Lots of restaurants, cafés, a grocery store and the large Slottsskogen park was nearby. "That is a park that the citizens of Gothenburg can be proud of," thought Annika when she heard that Matthias was back on the phone.

"Yes, we've tracked him. Verne Hildeng has been seen at the casino. Get him there," said Matthias.

They passed the gas bell, and Leif moved into the left lane.

"Good thing we weren't too far away," said Leif. "Now that we have the new Göta Tunnel you can end up anywhere if you're not careful when you change lanes."

"Before the tunnel opened I was just getting good at finding my way around," said Annika laughing. "And now you are behind the wheel as usual. Maybe in a year or so I'll want to drive again."

"So you think you won't have to drive for a whole year? What, are you tetig?"

"Tetig? What does that mean?" asked Annika.

"Tetig is Gothenburg dialect, and it means you're nuts," said Leif laughing. "Don't worry, I didn't mean it!"

"It's probably going take me years before I learn all of your weird expressions! But I like them!"

Leif drove up to the entrance of Casino Cosmopol, shut off the motor and turned toward Annika.

"We'll go in and see if we can find him. Let's pretend we are out to have some fun," said Leif. "When we get into the casino, we'll split up and go in two different directions. If you find him before I do, just call me and then ask him to follow along with you."

Annika nodded and got out of the car. They went together up the stairs to the main entrance. There was a guard just inside the doors, and they showed him their I.D.s. The guard wanted to ask them questions, but Leif didn't give him the chance. Annika walked in the direction of the roulette table and caught sight of Verne right away. He was in the middle of a game. She moved silently up behind him and leaned on his back. Verne felt her weight and turned around to ask, "Do you think you could lean in another direction?"

For the second time, an amazingly beautiful woman stood there leaning up against him. He could hardly believe it was true. Mahtab had looked like veiled magic from out of 'A Thousand and One Nights'. This woman was like a warm summer breeze out on the ocean in a boat under the stars, thought Verne and smiled toward Annika.

"Hi, Gorgeous! What can I do for you?" asked Verne.

"I'd be happy if you came with me," said Annika and smiled back.

"Oh, really? That sounds too good to be true, but I'm going to play a little more. So if you go over to the bar and have a drink, which I, of course, will pay for, I'll be right there," said Verne.

"I want you to come with me right now," said Annika and took out her police I.D. to hold up in front of his nose.

His facial expression changed within a half a second. His shoulders sank, and the hand that had a tight hold on his chips opened, letting them fall down onto the roulette table.

"What is it now? Has something happened to my mother?" asked Verne, fidgeting and sounding anxious.

"No, nothing has happened to your mother or anyone else in the family. I just want to ask some questions about the friend of yours who died, Janne Kopec," said Annika.

"I don't know if I'd call him a friend. We met now and then, and never anywhere else except at the Kollgate Restaurant," he said. "To be honest, I don't know what I can contribute to

148

your investigation."

"That's up to us," said Annika. "Come on!"

"Excuse me, but I have to exchange my chips here at the table for cash chips. Otherwise I'll lose my money," said Verne and started to pick up his chips from the table.

"Go ahead. I'll wait," said Annika.

She followed him to the cashier so he could make the exchange for cash and was surprised at the amount that was paid out. "That's more than my take home pay for a whole month," she thought. Unwillingly, she found herself get upset over the fact that such a young person was spreading his money around so nonchalantly at the roulette table.

"Before you take me away I want to visit the gents," said Verne and smiled impishly. "You can join me if you want to!"

"Thanks but no thanks. I'll wait here," said Annika and walked over to a round oak table surround by brown armchairs. Just as she sat down her cell phone rang.

"How's it going for you?" asked Leif.

"Just fine. Right now he's in the gents' room relieving himself," said Annika. "Where are you?"

"I'm standing by the exit just in case he tries to bolt," said Leif and hung up.

Verne was determined to avoid questioning. Right after he left the toilet, he slipped behind some large plants in pots that were further away from Annika and in the direction of the exit. He took off his jacket in the hopes that she wouldn't notice him. But then he ran into a wall in the form of Leif Griffén, who stood imposingly in front of him.

"Are you finished shaking off your dick now?" asked Leif and took a firm grip on Verne's arm. "We're going to take a little ride. You don't have anything against that, do you?" Verne realized that it was meaningless to resist and allowed himself to be led to the car that was parked outside the entrance. Leif gave him a light shove into the back seat. The door was closed and locked shut. Suddenly Annika came running down the steps. Her hair stood straight up in the wind.

"Where'd he go?" she said in a panic. "I lost track of him!"

Leif laughed at her confusion.

"Take it easy! He's not going anywhere. The stupid ass thought he could get away. What an idiot! Now he's going to meet Uncle Greger!" said Leif and jumped into the car.

An impatient Greger sat waiting in the interrogation room together with Matthias. They were trying to decide what was best. Should Matthias handle the interrogation alone, or should Greger do it together with Katarina? Since Matthias was experienced with gang hierarchy and was familiar with a lot of gang members, he could create some surprises for Verne. On the other hand, maybe it would be an advantage for the investigation if Verne weren't aware that the gangs were being followed. That is if he was more involved with them than he wanted to reveal. In the end, they decided that Greger would take the interrogation. Matthias and Katarina would sit behind the mirror and listen without being seen.

Annika and Leif came into the interrogation room holding Verne in between them under the arms. They walked over to the table and put him down on one of the chairs.

"There you go, Verne. Now that's where you're going to sit for the next hour," said Leif and nodded to Greger.

"Do you want us to be present during the interrogation?" asked Annika.

"No, I'll take it alone," answered Greger.

The door closed behind them. Verne looked down at the table, up at the ceiling, and then around the walls.

150

"Well, who's sitting behind the mirror?" he asked with a victorious smile on his lips. "You know that I'm studying law and know how an interrogation is supposed to be conducted?" said Verne as he stuck his hands in his pants pockets and leaned back in the chair. "Go ahead!"

Greger put the tape recorder on and rattled off the necessary information.

"Are you familiar with Heaven's Devils?"

Verne opened his mouth so wide that his chin almost touched his chest. His light eyebrows were raised.

"What did you say they are called?"

"Heaven's Devils."

"I've never heard of them," said Verne.

Greger thought over how likely it was that Verne had never heard of one of Gothenburg's most notorious gangs. That seemed strange. He decided to take another direction.

"Are you addicted to gambling?!

"Why should I be addicted to gambling?" asked Verne. "Just because I play now and then at a casino, does that make me addicted to gambling?"

"Now I'm the one who is asking the questions. Do you think that you are addicted to gambling?"

"No, I definitely do not," answered Verne, pursing his mouth. Greger took out a photo from a red folder and put it in front of Verne.

"Have you met this man?" asked Greger.

The photo was of the man in the red car that Verne had sat together with. But in the picture, the man was alone. He picked up the photo and studied it.

"No, I don't recognize him," he said and put the picture back down on the table. Greger took out another photo, where Verne was standing beside the red car.

"Do you know who is sitting in that car?" asked Greger

and gave Verne the photo. This time

Greger studied Verne's facial expressions to see if he would reveal anything. But Verne had either already learned how a lawyer should behave or else he was simply an innocent passer-by.

"No, I can't remember that I have met them. But maybe it was someone who wanted to have help with directions," said Verne.

The next photo that Greger put out on the table was a picture showing Verne getting out of the red car.

"Did you have to get into that car to give them directions?" asked Greger.

This time it was clear that Verne became uncomfortable. He twisted and turned in the chair and tipped it back and forth. Finally, he leaned against the table and cleared his throat.

"I think this is someone I just met once. But I don't know who he is," said Verne.

"Why did you meet up with him?"

The silence that was a result of the question was evident. Greger, who had interrogated thousands of people, was convinced that it was at this point Verne started to wonder how much the police actually knew.

"Yes, now I remember," he said, leaning backward. "This was a guy who wanted to sell something. When I asked what it was, he asked me to get in the car. Yes, that's what it was," said Verne and put the photo down on the table.

"Oh? What was it that he wanted to sell?" asked Greger and smiled inside himself.

"An iPod."

Matthias and Katarina sat behind the mirror and chuckled. It was going to be interesting to see how Greger would tackle that answer.

152

"I wonder if he even knows what an iPod is," thought Katarina.

Greger opened his folder, bent his head down and read the documents there with interest. Verne squirmed in his chair.

"You know Verne, from what I can see in my papers no such object has been mentioned. However, traces of narcotics were found in the car."

Matthias made a theatrical "Hat's off" gesture behind the window.

"That was talented," he said and patted Katarina on the hand. "Very smart!"

"Yea, but it's a lie," said Katarina. "We haven't brought that car in."

"True, but apparently Verne doesn't know that, judging from his expression," said Matthias.

"All I know is that he wanted to sell the iPod to me and I said no thank you. That was the end of it," said Verne.

"Since you are studying law, I should think that you would know better than to fall for something like that," said Greger. "If a complete stranger offers you a product from a car, you must have understood that it's been stolen?"

"Of course I did," said Verne with an offended tone. "And for that very reason, that I am studying the law, I wanted some direct experience of how criminals do things. In that way I get another type of experience than what I get through lectures at the University," he said and snorted.

Greger had to admit that Verne was smart. That irritated him. And he had no idea what an iPod was. Something that he guessed both Katarina and Matthias were having fun about behind the window. He knew that they knew what it was. The mere thought of having to sit in front of a computer was enough to make him feel anxious. He hated it. It was so difficult for him to keep up with all of the new electronic devices that arrived in a constant stream. Just learning how to use the damn cell phone took him a whole week, he remembered, still angry about it. Stefan Kronfeld, on the other hand, worshiped any new techniques that were available on the planet and even learned how they worked! Greger shrugged his shoulders.

"How well did you know Jan Kopec?"

"As I pointed out to the other police, I only met him at the restaurant where he worked. It wasn't as though we played golf together," said Verne.

"Did you borrow money from Jan Kopec?"

"Absolutely not! Why would I borrow money from him? It was the other way around. I was the one who loaned him money," said Verne, sounding offended again.

"Oh, really? How much did he borrow from you?" asked Greger.

"A hundred crowns now and then, not more. Why don't you talk to the personnel at the restaurant instead of me? They knew him much better than I did," said Verne.

"Was he also a gambler?"

"What do you mean by also? I told you that I'm not a gambler. What I do is called entertainment, nothing else!"

Greger mumbled and looked down at his papers. He couldn't think of any more questions.

"Can I go now? Or have you got more photos that you want me to look at?" asked Verne with a satisfied grin.

"You can go," answered Greger. "Just see to it that you don't end up getting into the wrong cars in the future!"

Verne got up, and Greger opened the door. They went out at the same time. Verne turned around to Greger and said,

"Cheer up, it wasn't that bad, was it?"

Greger felt like he wanted to say a thing or two but knew that there was no point to it. Instead, he gave Verne a big

154

smile for an answer before he turned his back to him and stepped in with Matthias and Katarina.

"What was that thing he was talking about?" asked Greger.

The question made both of them burst out in laughter.

"Sorry Greger," said Katarina, who couldn't stop laughing. "We actually made a bet that you didn't know what an iPod is!"

Greger just stood there and acted as though his feelings were hurt. But in the end he couldn't help smile since they seemed to be having so much fun. "What kind of a boss am I if I can't provide the opportunity for those working for me to have a good laugh once in a while?" he thought.

"An iPod is a little device that looks something like a cell phone. The great thing about it is that you can download and listen to thousands of songs," said Matthias. Greger's chin dropped, and he stared at Matthias.

"Did you say thousands? How does that work? No, never mind; don't try to explain it to me. I'm not going to buy one anyway," said Greger shaking his head. "I'm happy with my CD player that I have at home and in the car. That's good enough for me!"

"What do you think we should do about Verne? Should I have him followed?" asked Katarina.

"No, we know where he lives and since he's studying at the University, he won't disappear. But he was lying. I'm convinced of that. It's just that I can't prove it!"

When Verne walked out of the Police Station, the sun was shining on him. It was warm, and he threw his jacket over his shoulder. "I guess I'll just have to use my legs to get back to the casino," he thought and started walking in the direction of Heden. Fifteen minutes later he stood waiting for a green pedestrian light at the intersection. From where he stood he could see his car. He crossed the street and started walking toward it. Suddenly a black car drove up beside him. Verne stopped abruptly and was almost run over. Two men jumped out of the car and in two seconds they had thrown him into the back seat. A gloved hand covered his mouth, and both men pushed him down with his head against the seat. He was terrified. It felt like an eternity before the car stopped. During the whole ride, no one said a word. Verne closed his eyes and even though the car stood still he didn't dare open them. Someone pulled him out of the car and threw him down on the ground. Intense pain shot through his hip when he landed on the hard surface. Verne opened his eyes. They were on a wooded road. Wherever he looked, he saw evergreen trees growing tightly together. He had no idea where he was. In front of him were two men in black hoods with holes cut out for the eyes drawn over their heads. One set of blue eyes and one of brown looked at him in silence. Verne got up and stood frozen to the ground without saying a word.

"Have you thought about the offer you got?" asked the man with the blue eyes in a black hood.

"What offer?" asked Verne.

A strike in the stomach made him lose his breath. Verne fell over, groaned and held his stomach.

"What's your answer?" asked the same man.

The kick in his back made Verne lose consciousness for a second. Thoughts like "Now they're going to kill me" raced through his mind. How could he give them an answer if he could hardly breathe? Verne managed to wave his hand. One of the men bent down close to his face. He could smell his aftershave, and it smelled terrible.

"Do you want to say something?" asked the man. His breath stank of tobacco.

"I'll take it," groaned Verne.

One more kick in the stomach and Verne tasted blood in his mouth. Suddenly his trousers felt wet. The shame over having peed in his pants from fright made him forget the pain for a brief moment.

All of a sudden he heard the car drive away. He opened his eyes and discovered he was alone. His cell phone beeped from receiving a text message. It was in his jacket that they had thrown on the ground beside him. Verne turned carefully over and crept over to the jacket. The message was short. "We'll be in touch." He didn't need much time to figure out who "we" was. Slowly he stood up. It hurt all over. He leaned toward a telephone pole and tried to feel if anything was broken. Every time he took a breath, it hurt. They had probably broken one of his ribs. Verne wanted to call Kjell and ask him for help, but then he remembered Kjell's opinion of gambling and this attack was of course connected to his gambling. Besides, he had no idea where he was. He had first to try and figure out his position. Since there were telephone poles there must also be houses in the area, he thought and started limping off in a Westward direction.

After about a half an hour of difficult walking, Verne found a house. He walked through the entrance gate and caught sight of an elderly woman. She was bending over in what seemed to be a vegetable garden. Verne mustered his strength and tried to walk as normally as possible, at the same time waving and calling. The woman stopped her weeding and stood up.

"Hi … can you help me?" yelled Verne with a big smile.

"What do you need help with?" asked the woman, taking a few steps toward him.

"It probably sounds ridiculous, but my girlfriend and I had a fight. She threw me out of the car and drove off. I don't even know where I am!" said Verne and put on a sad facial expression.

The woman wiped her soiled hands on her red apron and chuckled.

"Sure, I can help you. You are in Norra Aggetorp. I have my car behind the barn. I'll drive you as long as you're not going to Borås!"

"No, I'm going to Gothenburg," said Verne, happily surprised by this woman's willingness to help.

"Well then, that's only thirty kilometers; Borås would have been seventy! Come along; you probably want to get back to your girlfriend, in spite of it all!" she said, laughing.

Verne spread out his jacket on the car seat, climbed in on the passenger's side, and sat down. Every move hurt, but he tried to look cheerful. He nodded to the woman and managed to attach his seat belt. During the trip to Gothenburg, he desperately tried to figure out how he was going to get out of the grip of these men. That they wanted something from his father's company he had understood. And that it was probably narcotics he also realized. The question was what they expected of him. He really didn't want to have to pay any attention to the whole thing. Verne took a deep breath and put his hand up against his chest when the pain got to be too much. Thirty minutes later, the woman dropped him off outside the casino.

"You'd better see to it that you don't make your girlfriend mad the next time you're out for a drive," she said laughing and drove off.

Verne stopped smiling the minute she left him. He limped over to his car and sank down in the driver's seat. The sound of his phone ringing made his heart jump. It was Kjell.

"Hi, Kjell! How's everything with you?" asked Verne.

"With me? That's what I'm asking you! We've been trying

158

to reach you the whole day, but you haven't answered. Where are you? When are you coming to Gunneby?" asked Kjell and sighed.

"Not today anyway," answered Verne. "I'm going home to Hovås and we can meet up tomorrow, ok?"

Kjell thought Verne sounded down and didn't protest. Maybe one of his girlfriends had broken up with him, he thought.

"Okay, but promise me you'll call tomorrow," said Kjell. "Mom gets worried when she doesn't know where you are and you know why!"

"Sure, I get it," said Verne. "I promise I'll call tomorrow. So what did Mom say about Isabell?" Verne thought it might be a good idea to talk about Isabell since he knew that she was the woman in his brother's life. That was a good way to draw attention away from himself.

"Everyone loves her, of course," said Kjell with pride in his voice. "We've also told everyone about her being five months pregnant, which made Mom and Björn both overjoyed!"

"Congratulations, Bro! So now you're going to be a father!" said Verne, hiding a cough.

"Yea, thanks! And you're going to be an uncle!" said Kjell. "Bye now, and take care!"

Verne turned the key, and the car started without difficulty. It would be wonderful to get home, take a warm shower, and lie down on a soft bed, thought Verne as he carefully turned the steering wheel and backed out of the parking place.

When Verne woke up later, he was in his bed. He looked at the clock. It was a quarter to six in the morning. What was it that woke him up or did he just get enough sleep? He slowly got out of bed, supporting himself with the help of a golf club and pulled away the curtains. The early morning sunlight flooded the room. He hobbled into the bathroom. The large towel he'd used after his shower yesterday was still on the floor. He fished it up with the help of the club and hung it over the heated towel rail. It felt tight across his chest and on his thigh he had a Charley Horse as big as the palm of a grown man's hand. Maybe he should get some medical attention this morning. If they asked how he had been injured, he could lie and say he fell off a ladder. He heard his cell phone ringing softly and looked around the room. Where was his jacket? It was under the covers!

"Hi! Are we going to meet tonight?" asked Mahtab. Verne blinked twice before he remembered the text message she had sent.

"Of course!" he said. "Where do you want to meet? Shall we go out for dinner? My treat!"

"Nine o'clock at Palace," said Mahtab. "Is that alright?"

"Perfect. Let's meet outside," said Verne.

"I'd rather not … can't we meet inside at the bar?" asked Mahtab.

"Okay, nine o'clock inside at the bar," said Verne and felt the beginnings of joy in his body, in spite of the pain.

In the Assignment Room

Matthias and Greger were in the assignment room. In front of them they had about twenty photographs taken on Blendas Gata and Norra Hamngatan.

"What do you think the motive could be for these shootings?" asked Greger as he studied a picture of one of the murdered men.

"So far we haven't got much to go on. By testing the bullets, we've found out that two different weapons were used. But we haven't found any weapons. Nor have we found any connection between the two victims, and neither of them is in our records. This appears to be crimes of insanity. On the other hand, it seems strange that two crimes of insanity would take place on the same day with just a few hours in between. I've always had a hard time swallowing that kind of coincidence," said Matthias.

"I agree with you," said Greger. Should we bring in the National Force? Or do you think it's too early?"

"To be honest, I've already been thinking about that. The only thing that's preventing me from getting in touch with

161

them is that I would like to investigate a little more with SI and with the help of your team. We also have Massoud under surveillance. The question is whether or not that will give us anything," said Matthias, making a grimace.

"Okay, we'll take it one day at a time and see what comes in," said Greger.

Katarina came into the room together with Leif and Annika. She walked over and gave Matthias a quick kiss on the cheek.

"Uh huh, so here you both are doing nothing of value. Did you get a report yet on the body behind the dumpster on Packhuskajen?" she asked.

"No, but we should get it any day now. It's been a week since the lab got the samples from the body. Maybe that answer will take us a step further," said Greger with a touch of hope in his voice. A call came for Matthias, he waved to Katarina and stood over by one of the windows. She watched him while he talked on the phone. Katarina felt lucky to be a part of his life. Deep inside, she also hoped that Agneta, Matthias' sister, was, in fact, pregnant. It would be fun to become a 'bonus' auntie. The thought of being able to spoil a baby with everything from love to lots of Christmas presents appealed to her. Suddenly Matthias started motioning to her, gave a thumb up, showed four fingers and put his hand on his stomach, all the while smiling broadly. It wasn't hard to understand what he meant. Agneta was pregnant and in her fourth month. "Hurrah!" thought Katarina to herself.

Verne Looks Forward to Meeting Mahtab

Verne stood waiting at the bar with a glass of beer. It felt tight over his chest from the bandage the doctor at the medical center had found time to wrap around his ribs. He looked around but couldn't see Mahtab anywhere. Then he looked at his watch; it was five minutes past nine. From behind the bar, one of the bartenders walked toward him and called out his name. Surprised, he put up his hand.

"Here, there's a phone call for you," said the bartender and handed over the phone along with a small package.

Verne took the package and the telephone and looked at both with raised eyebrows and an open mouth. The bartender turned around and disappeared out of sight. Verne stared at the display, but it just said "unknown caller." Carefully he raised the phone to his ear.

"Hello, this is Verne."

"Listen carefully. Mahtab isn't coming! Don't interrupt me! The telephone you're holding in your hand is the only connection we're going to have with you. The package contains a charger. It's important that you don't lose anything.

163

When we're finished with each other, you can throw everything away. Have you understood?" Instead of answering, Verne nodded. The second after the person on the other end screamed at him, Verne answered clearly that he understood what they wanted. The conversation lasted two minutes, but it felt like an eternity. Sweat ran down his neck, and the only thing he wanted to do was to get out of there and get some air. Since he hadn't checked any jacket, he could hurry out. He stood on the sidewalk just outside the entrance and remained still there, taking deep breaths of air into his lungs. Finally, he regained balance enough to start walking toward the taxi station. During the ride home, he thought about calling Mahtab but regretted it and put his phone away. Even she must be mixed up with all of this somehow, he thought and sighed.

Since Kjell and Isabell had decided to be with the rest of the family at Gunneby on Tjörn, Verne had the house in Hovås all to himself. He kicked his shoes off as soon as he came through the door. It was such a release to walk on the cool ceramic tiles in the hall. Verne walked into the library and started to look for the brandy. He knew that his grandfather used to hide it behind the books. There was usually more than one bottle hidden. All of that was to avoid having his grandmother discover him. Verne laughed to himself. He found a bottle behind the Bible. "Typical Grandpa!" he said out loud. Verne poured the brandy into one of the crystal glasses that was on a tray on the desk. With a sigh of relief, he sank into one of the armchairs. He took a big gulp and felt the warmth of the alcohol spread through his body. How in hell would he solve what that bastard talked about on the phone? In order to find out which trucks from the manufacturer that contained narcotics to be transported to the warehouse for distribution to the pharmacies, he would have to contact the head of the warehouse. That would look suspicious! After two more glasses of brandy, he had solved the problem. But in any case, he would have to wait until after the funeral. The man on the telephone had given him two weeks to get all the information. That should be time enough, thought Verne as he drank up the remaining drops from his glass.

Arne Hildeng`s Last Will and Testament

After the funeral for Arne and Elsebeth Hildeng, both families were present at the office of Lawyer Örjan Grund. They
were gathered to be informed about matters of the estate.
Four hours had passed since the coffins were placed in the
family grave. Björn sat beside Andrea and just like all the others, they were dressed in black. The chairs had been arranged
in three rows in front of the lawyer's desk. In the first row
sat Björn, Andrea and her two sons, Kjell and Verne, with
Isabell in between them. Olav Hildeng sat together with Jon
and Mette in the middle row and in the last row sat Knut and
Astrid Caling, Andrea and Björn's parents. Shortly before the
burial, Astrid had turned to Andrea and asked if it would be
appropriate for her and Knut to be present when the will was
read.

"Of course, you should be there. I might need your support
after all that's happened," had Andrea answered.

Örjan Grund stood in front of them in a dark gray suit.
He ran his hand over his bald head, adjusted his steel framed
eyeglasses on his long, narrow nose and cleared his throat.

"Arne Hildeng has asked me to carry out his last wish and I will start with that right away."

With those words, he took out a DVD from its case, put the disk in the player and put on the TV. Andrea looked at Björn in surprise, but his gaze was fixed upon the television. Chairs scraped against the floor, coughs and throat clearing spread in the room, but as soon as Arne Hildeng appeared on the screen and started to speak, it became silent. Arne sat in a chair and spoke straight into the camera. After Andrea figured out that Arne had recorded the DVD at this lawyer's office, she started to listen to what he had to say.

"First of all, I want to say that when you are watching this film, I will no longer be with you. That was the point of this recording. No one is to find out about what I am going to tell you before or after my death." Arne made a pause, got up from the chair and walked over to the camera. After that the TV screen went black. Everyone turned their attention to the lawyer who was sitting on a chair to the left of the television. But he calmed them with a hand motion. Exactly ten seconds later Arne came back on the screen. He wiped his eyes with a handkerchief, put it away in his pants pocket and looked back into the camera.

"I had to take a break. It was difficult to sit here and talk, knowing that the day you look at this film I won't be with you anymore."

Andrea got a stomach ache from Arne's visible difficulties and felt like her throat was stuck in a clamp.

"First I want to talk to you, Andrea. I have always loved you, no matter how many times we've fought. I want you to know that. But there is one thing that made me very disappointed, and that disappointment ate away at me for twenty years. In the end, I felt compelled to find out the truth. I was able to do that without anyone in the family finding out about

it. But before I reveal what I did I want to say a few words to my sons."

Andrea leaned forward with trembling lips. She smiled encouragingly toward her sons, and they smiled back. The situation was undeniably absurd, thought Andrea. It felt as though everyone was sitting in a movie theater and in a few minutes Arne would come in through the doors and ask them what they thought of the movie. She shook her head and turned back to the TV screen.

"Kjell and Verne, I don't know if you have always thought that I was a good father, but you should know that I did everything in my power so that you could have the safest and most loving childhood possible. I know I have been away traveling a lot because of my work. But as you already know Kjell, that is a must if you want to build a career and have a decent income. Perhaps there isn't always time or space for the family in all situations. And you, Verne, have probably also noticed that time goes fast and that things don't always turn out the way we want them to. I'm thinking especially of your education. You didn't choose to study law of your own accord like your mother did long ago, but instead were threatened and tricked into that choice. But, just like your mom, you'll of course also become an excellent lawyer. Even though I know that you would have preferred to become a doctor. In spite of what you will soon hear, I want you to know that I love you both."

At this particular moment, Arne straightened up in his chair and stiffened his posture. *"Andrea, I want you to listen very carefully to what I have to say. I know that you have been unfaithful."*

Directly after those words, Björn got up from his chair and ordered the lawyer to immediately shut off the television. Everyone else stared with wide-open eyes at his abrupt

168

behavior. Örjan Grund put the film on pause and looked in surprise at Björn with his clouded, grey-blue eyes.

"I want a time-out," said Björn and gave Andrea a meaningful look. She stared at him with an open mouth and could feel her face turning red. Andrea avoided looking at her parents even though she could instinctively feel their stares burrowing into her back. The lawyer asked everyone to stretch their legs for five minutes. For Andrea, it sounded like they were at a conference and not a funeral. Björn stretched out his hand, and she took it thankfully. He more or less dragged her through the corridor up to a door. He opened it and in just a few seconds they had managed to leave the others, who he knew had quite a few questions they wanted to ask Andrea. She looked around. They were standing outside in a landscaped garden. In the middle was a fountain surrounded by large, red, sweet smelling roses. The sound of the trickling water had a calming effect on Andrea and she sat down on the white painted bench beside the fountain.

"My God, what will the children think of me after this?" sighed Andrea.

"Do you mean it's true?" asked Björn and sat down beside her. "Mom's going to skin you alive!"

Andrea looked at Björn for a few seconds and started to laugh a little. She covered her mouth with her hands and finally started laughing out loud. Björn joined in, and soon the two of them sat there giggling like a couple of kids.

"Okay, we have to pull ourselves together," said Andrea taking Björn's arm. "What if someone came out here and found us laughing at Arne's funeral. What if Mom ..."

The mere thought of her mother forced Andrea to have to hold back more laughter.

"Right now I'd really like a cigarette," said Björn.

"But you've never smoked," said Andrea.

"Well, it was a long time ago. You wouldn't remember. I didn't smoke for very long; about a year I think. Then I got tired of it! Lucky for me," he said. Björn leaned forward on the bench and rested his elbows on his knees. "Would you tell me what happened when you were unfaithful? I mean … only if you really want to, of course."

Andrea took a deep breath. Suddenly the door opened behind them, and the lawyer cleared his throat.

"The others want to continue. Can we do that?"

Björn looked at Andrea, who nodded.

"Give us a minute, please," said Björn.

The lawyer mumbled something impossible to hear and closed the door.

"Now don't let Mom attack you with a million questions. You are, in fact, a grown woman! It's no secret that Mom has been on Dad's case for all these years and who knows why? And we've all witnessed more than once how hurt he has been by it," said Björn and put his arm around her shoulders.

"What do you think Mom and Dad are going to say? They certainly won't think their daughter has behaved as would be expected," said Andrea and looked Björn in the eyes.

"It worse having to deal with Mother than Father," said Björn and patted her on the cheek. "Come on, let's go. I'll support you!"

They stepped into the office and Andrea consciously chose to look straight ahead. She sat down at her place and nodded to the lawyer who pushed the button to let the film continue.

"I don't know who you have been unfaithful with, but since I have proof that Verne is not my son, you can't deny facts."

After that sentence, Astrid Caling fell out of her chair. Knut Caling called for help and Verne stood up to stare accusingly at his mother. Kjell sat as though he were stuck frozen to his chair and didn't react when Isabell tried to

170

whisper something in his ear. Björn took Andrea's hand in a firm grip. It hurt, but she didn't dare move. The lawyer stopped the film one more time and looked wide-eyed upon this group of very hysterical persons in grief.

"Perhaps we should take a proper break for some coffee?" he asked, notably raising his voice.

Astrid Caling had regained her composure and stood upright beside her husband. She stared at Andrea, and her eyes were harsh.

"I would like to speak with my daughter alone now," said Astrid.

"You're not the only one," said Verne with a sharp voice. "I'd also like to know what this is all about!"

Andrea stood with her head bent down and didn't dare to look anyone in the eye. Björn still had her hand in his. If he hadn't, Andrea might have fled the room. The only ones who hadn't said a word were Jon and Mette. They seemed to be mostly in shock over everything they had heard and seen.

"Who is my father?" yelled Verne. "I have the right to know!"

Björn positioned himself in front of Andrea and looked out over the various members of the family.

"I'm also shocked, but has anyone thought that perhaps even Andrea is in shock? Can't you give her ten minutes to collect herself? In that way maybe we can get an explanation for what we've heard without cutting each other's throats?" asked Björn in a mild tone of voice. He nodded toward everyone and led Andrea away for the second time within the space of a few minutes, back to the landscaped garden. He sat her down on the bench and then went over to the fountain to collect some of the cool, running water to put on Andrea's warm face. She jumped from the cold water.

"Oh my God, how am I going to explain this?" she said

with tears running slowly down her cheeks. "I never thought … I didn't know … how could I be so stupid?

"We all do stupid things when we're young. And we don't think our mistakes will be a problem when we get older," said Björn and sat down beside her.

"How could Arne be so mean that he didn't first give me a chance to explain to Verne?" said Andrea, and for a second there was a flash of anger in her eyes. "Of course there were times when I suspected that Verne wasn't Arne's son, but time passed and sometimes I even managed to forget that I had been unfaithful. It only happened once!"

"Once is unfortunately enough," said Björn and stroked her cheek over and over. "Who is Verne's father?"

"It can only be one person," said Andrea in a low voice. "It's Jon!"

Björn's hand went limp and fell onto his knee.

"Jon," repeated Björn. "Does he know about it? I mean, does Jon know that Verne is his son?"

Andrea shook her head.

"But now that he's heard Arne in the film maybe he understands. Jesus, what a mess! How am I going to get out of this?" said Andrea and sat wringing her tightly clasps hands in her lap.

"You can't get out of this," said Björn. "You have to tell the truth. That's the only way. If nothing else, for Verne's sake."

"But what about Mette? How do you think she's going to react? I've slept with her husband and even conceived a child with him. Which we all know is her biggest dream, or at least it was her biggest dream to have a child. She's going to kill me," said Andrea and bent her head down toward her chest.

"The one she ought to kill is Jon," said Björn with disgust. "He is a first class asshole in all categories; that's what Arne always used to say!"

172

"Did he? How did he know that?"

Björn turned away and started to fiddle with one of the roses that was hanging over the bench.

"Maybe this is the time for the truth to be spoken," said Björn and pulled off one of the petals from the rose.

"What do you mean?" asked Andrea.

At that very moment, the door was pulled open, and Astrid stormed out into the garden. She rushed over to Andrea and with a hand on each side of what used to be a waist, positioned herself broad legged in front of her.

"It's time you got yourself back to the rest of us," she hissed. "We want to hear the rest of the story about your life with Arne. You have apparently not been the adoring wife that you've always made yourself out to be."

Andrea got up slowly from the bench and brushed off her dress.

"Well, you know Mom, if all wives were like you there wouldn't be any men left on the planet," said Andrea, glaring her right in the eye as she walked past. "They would have preferred to hang themselves instead of getting married! Poor Dad, that's what I say!"

Astrid gasped for air. With a gaping mouth and wide open eyes, she stared at her daughter who walked off in front of her with a swish.

"Björn, why aren't you saying anything?" asked Astrid.

"Because I have nothing to add," he answered and followed after Andrea.

On the way back into the room, Andrea's and Jon's eyes met. Andrea was surprised to discover an expression of pleading in his eyes. She didn't stop by his chair and just walked quickly over to her spot. The lawyer stood beside the TV, wiped the sweat from his forehead and stuck his finger in between his shirt collar and neck in an attempt to create some air. His face has taken on a reddish look. With a look of desperation, he stared at Andrea hoping that this time Arne Hildeng would be able to finish speaking. Andrea sat down, and Björn followed shortly after. She nodded toward the lawyer. He put on the DVD and chose to stand up this time.

"I hope that, for Verne's sake, you know who his father is and that you explain to him why you chose to be unfaithful. That is if you have an answer to that."

Everyone could see that he had tears in his eyes and Andrea felt very uncomfortable.

"I have also carried a secret all these years and it is with a heavy heart that I confess my secret to everyone. I have always been bisexual!"

The lawyer had somewhat of a glassy expression in his eyes as he quickly looked back and forth over the family. His white handkerchief waved in his hand as he hurriedly wiped off his forehead. But much to his relief, nothing happened. No one shouted that he had to stop the film. Everyone sat still in their seats, and he let out a silent sigh.

"Forgive me Mom! I know that this is a shock for you. I don't think I was the son you were hoping for. But you'll always be well taken care of by Dad and Jon. They are men who can be trusted." Arne wiped away the tears that were running down his cheeks.

Björn took hold of Andrea's hand and gave it a squeeze. She answered by squeezing back. In a way, it was good that Elsebeth didn't have to experience this, thought Andrea. If she'd been alive, she would probably have had a heart attack if she had heard what Arne just said.

"Now I'm going to tell you who will be getting my shares of the company."

Arne paused and looked toward the window that was to his left. Everyone could see that he was breathing heavily.

174

Finally he turned back toward the camera.

"Everything I'm telling you is also on paper with all of the necessary signatures. So there is no point in anyone trying to nullify the will," said Arne with a determined look. *"I have seen with my own eyes how people can change from ordinary, timid persons to hungry vultures willing to do almost anything just to get a piece of the game. I hope and am convinced that I have succeeded in preventing that with this will. I would like to start by saying that the distribution of the shares has nothing to do with what has just come forth. This is simply my last wish, and I want it to be respected,"* said Arne and stared into the camera. *"Since I own fifty-one percent of the shares of the company, I have the right to transfer the largest post of thirty-six percent of the shares to Mette."*

A hush passed through the room, and everyone looked at Mette. She sat with her mouth wide open and shook her head. This time the lawyer paused the film without anyone asking him to. He understood that what Arne had said had caused a lot of confusion.

"Do you have any idea why Arne gave you shares?" asked Jon and looked at his wife as though he had seen her for the first time in his life.

Mette just shook her head again.

"You probably had an affair with him behind Mom's back," said Verne with a hateful look. "No wonder Mom was unfaithful!"

"I think you just passed the limit for what is common decency," said Björn getting up. "Did you listen at all to what Arne just said? You are acting with complete disrespect right now! I suggest we all keep quiet and listen to what Arne has to say."

Mette gave Björn a look of gratitude. Inside her, it was chaos. Jon had already revealed through his body language what was going to happen when they got home. It would probably be a good idea to ask Björn if he would come along with them. But how could she do that without Jon hearing? Why had Arne given her all those shares? She didn't understand. How could she explain this to Jon? Nor would he believe that she didn't have an explanation.

"The remaining fifteen percent of the shares I leave to Kjell. I know what you are thinking Verne. But this has nothing to do with that you are not my biological son. I love you just as much as your brother. This decision was made a long time ago. I feel that Kjell is better equipped to run the company, and that's all. And now to Jon. What I want to say to you is that if you hadn't been my brother, I would have put an end to our acquaintanceship. The reason is the terrible way you treat Mette. You may have thought that no one knew. But I did! Above all, the last years have been hell for her. How do I know? I'm not going to reveal that. That secret I'm taking with me on my journey."

Jon sank into his chair. His head fell toward his chest, and Mette saw tears running down his cheeks. She neither wanted nor dared to touch him at the moment.

Björn had been watching Jon after Arne's revelation and had a feeling of satisfaction. He was the one who had told Arne how badly Jon treated Mette. Once, about two years ago, Arne told Björn that he had received a letter from someone who had been employed at the Pharmacy. In the letter, the woman wrote that she had been sexually molested by Jon more than once. Finally, the situation had become so difficult that she had been forced to look for work in another town. Arne had gotten in touch with her and discovered that she hadn't been the only woman who Jon had molested, and that this had gone on for several years. Björn remembered how

176

angry Arne had been when he spoke about this. He also sent thoughts of gratitude to Arne, wherever he was now, for not revealing to everyone that it was Björn who had been Mette's guardian angel at Arne's request. Not even Andrea knew!

"For you Verne, I have arranged monthly support for the amount of fifteen thousand crowns that you will receive until you graduate and find work. To Andrea, I leave all that we have purchased together. You have always been a wonderful wife, in spite of having been unfaithful, which I believe only happened once, but even one meeting can create a child. I also want to apologize for the way I have treated you the last month. That was revenge. I know that I've always said how uncivilized it is to want to get revenge, but I couldn't help myself."

All of a sudden there was a knock on the door. The lawyer paused, looked at the clock, and nodded. The door opened, and Greger and Katarina walked into the room.

"Welcome," said Örjan Grund and introduced himself. "I'll get some chairs for you."

He then stood by the television in front of the surprised group and cleared his throat.

"Chief Inspector Greger Thulin and Inspector Katarina Linde have come here at the request of Arne Hildeng. We will now conclude Arne's last wish," said the lawyer and turned toward Greger and Katarina.

Greger nodded and wondered to himself what the rest of the group was thinking about right now. He had received a telephone call from Örjan Grund, who informed him that in accordance with Arne Hildeng's last wish, he wanted the police who had investigated his death to attend this particular occasion. That was why he was sitting there together with Katarina, just as questioning as everyone else in the room.

"The idea to arrange my death to look like a murder didn't

come to me just as a result of finding out that Verne was not my son. Even though finding out about that made it all seem much simpler. I don't know how many nights I paced back and forth, swearing at you Andrea. I finally decided how I would do it. It wasn't difficult to get hold of the morphine. I own several pharmacies! But it was difficult to pick a time to do it. Still, it felt as though I didn't have any choice."

Once again, Arne paused and looked out the window. He chewed on his lower lip, and you could see that the knuckles turned white on his hands that were holding on to the arms of the chair.

"I hid the amount of morphine that I knew would be enough on board the boat a long time ago."

Now tears ran down Arne's face but he didn't bother to wipe them away.

"All I knew was that I wanted to die with you, Andrea, by my side. Even though I knew you might be suspected of murdering me, you would know ... that I ... have always loved you."

Andrea let out a small scream and Björn was able to grab her just as she fainted. The lawyer shut off the video and sat down behind his desk.

Björn stroked Andrea over her hair and whispered comforting words. Greger looked with wide open eyes at Katarina.

"Well, it looks like the Arne Hildeng case is closed," said Greger and nodded in the direction of the lawyer.

"But why did he do it? Did he give any explanation?" asked Katarina, addressing the question to any one of the members of the family.

"None whatsoever, I would say," mumbled Jon.

"I don't understand anything," said Kjell. Dad loved Mom, loved us, wasn't sick, but still chose to take his life. Can it have something to do with him saying he was bisexual? Did Dad have HIV? But that would have shown up when you did the autopsy ..." said Kjell and turned to Greger.

With one eyebrow lifted in an arch, Greger looked at Katarina. She shrugged her shoulders.

"I don't remember whether or not an HIV test was taken," said Katarina. "We'll have to check that when we get back to the station."

"Yea, and we only have about a thousand documents to go through," said Greger. "Hope that the four people who sit and register our information haven't lost any papers along the way!"

After Katarina and Greger left the lawyer's office and came out into the summer sun, Greger stopped a minute to take a deep breath.

"Are you okay?" asked Katarina.

"The atmosphere in there was suffocating and the expression on Verne's face made me wonder. I'm going to call Örjan Grund tomorrow because I think I want to see the whole film," said Greger.

"I noticed Verne too. He looked truly hateful, and it seemed to be directed towards his mother. I wonder who Verne's father is? It would be interesting to see the whole film. If you get the opportunity to see it, I'd like to come along," said Katarina.

"Do you think Arne Hildeng could have had HIV? As far as I know, there are only three places in Sweden where tests are always taken, and that is Stockholm, Lund, and Uppsala. But we can always hope that Sara still has blood left from Arne's body. That way we'd be able to find out," said Greger.

"What I think is strange is that Andrea didn't tell us about her husband's bisexuality. If she knew about it, of course," said Katarina. "By the way, wasn't it you who said that you recognized the name Hildeng and had heard it in some other context?"

"Yea, I remembered what it was when we were sitting in there. The story was told to me when I was fresh out of police school. One of my bosses told me about a case he had had. It was about the body of a child. It had been discovered by a gardener, who at the time worked for old man Hildeng, Jon and Arne's grandfather. The gardener had started to dig a hole to plant a cherry tree but instead he dug up the corpse of a child," said Greger.

"Whose child was it?"

"If I remember correctly, the mother was never found. In those days there was no DNA testing, which would probably have revealed whose child it was, that is if it was someone in the family who was the father," said Greger.

"But if the child was found on Hildeng's land, someone in the family must have been responsible, said Katarina.

"I think that the Hildeng family had a lot of power at that time. No one dared to risk their career," said Greger.

"What happened to the child?" asked Katarina.

"No idea! But it would be interesting to ask Olav if he remembers anything about that event."

"What year was that?"

"I think it was at the end of the fifties, or maybe the beginning of the sixties. Olav must have been around twenty and should remember the case if he lived at home," said Greger.

Katarina shrugged her shoulders, shook out a cigarette, lit it and took a drag.

"The criminal statute of limitations on that case has passed a long time ago. We'll never find out about that. We have more recent crimes to figure out. Let's get back to the others at the Station, tell them what has happened, and then we'll see if we've got any answers on Black Pete," said Katarina.

"Black Pete?"

"Yea, the charcoal burned body from Packhuskajen," said Katarina and walked toward the car.

Where's Mette?

Still at the lawyer's office, Björn sat and held Andrea. Astrid Caling sat in silence and stared into a wall. Isabell and Kjell were talking softly with one another. Knut Caling had left the room, and Verne paced back and forth. Jon sat stiffly on his chair with his arms crossed over his chest. Olav winked at Mette, their eyes met, and she bent her head down quickly. The lawyer sat at his desk, going through documents. He took a peek at the family members now and then to see what was happening, and then cleared his throat loudly.

"I have only one document left and that is Elsebeth's last will and testament. Nothing unusual actually since everything goes to her husband, Olav. I do have one letter which is to be handed over to the members of the family in the event of her death. Therefore the letter should be given to you Olav," said the lawyer holding a yellowed envelope.

"Who is the letter from?" asked Jon.

"The letter is from your grandfather, Ingvald Hildeng," said the lawyer and handed it over to Olav.

"But are you certain the letter should be left to Father and

182

not to us, I mean me?" asked Jon as he stood up and bent over his father's shoulder to get a closer look at the letter.

"No, I am not certain, but the instruction was that when Elsebeth passed away, the letter should be given to those who survived her," said the lawyer with a mouth that looked like a straight line.

"How is it that you have this letter?" asked Jon.

"My father was Ingvald Hildeng's lawyer and it has been kept in our safe, until it was time to be delivered."

"Could you please open the letter?" said Jon, staring at his father.

"No, I think I want to open it at home in peace and quiet when I am alone," said Olav and put the letter in his jacket pocket.

"Enough is enough!" yelled Verne. "Is there anyone who cares about what I've had to listen to? Is there anyone who understands how I feel? I've live my whole life thinking that Arne Hildeng is my father, and now it turns out that I have been living in a lie! What do you have to say about what you've done?" said Verne and positioned himself in front of Andrea.

"Please Verne," said Andrea and took his arm. "I didn't know. I never thought ..."

Verne pulled his arm away.

"You weren't aware that having sex with another man than your husband could result in a child? I thought you were an educated woman," said Verne, turned abruptly around, pulled open the door, and left the room.

"Wait, Verne! Please let me explain!" said Andrea with a weak voice.

"I don't think there is any point in trying to explain this to him right now," said Kjell. "It's better if he gets a chance to calm down. He'll probably go to the casino and lose a few thousand crowns and blame the bad luck on you!"

"I think you owe us an explanation here and now," said Astrid Caling, staring at her daughter.

"She doesn't owe us anything," said Björn, holding a protective arm around Andrea. "Why should she have to turn herself inside and out in front of us? The only one who needs an explanation is Verne, nobody else. Right now the best thing would be for everyone to go back to their own homes."

"I want to talk with you before you go home," whispered Mette.

Andrea jumped at her words, but let out a sigh of relief when she realized Mette was talking to Björn. Andrea looked for Jon and noticed that he and Olav had gone off to the side to discuss something with the lawyer. Björn left Andrea and started walking over toward Mette, who signaled with her hand that she didn't want Jon to notice. Björn got the hint and strolled slowly in her direction.

"Could I come home with you?" asked Mette, bending her head down and pretending to look for something in her handbag.

"It's better if I give you the keys to my apartment. I'm going home with Andrea and stay with her a few nights. Then you can have the apartment all to yourself," said Björn, slipping her his key ring. "I'll call you when I need them."

Mette put the keys quickly down in her bag and closed it. She gave Björn's arm a quick squeeze and looked at him with gratitude as she quietly walked out the door unnoticed. He nodded, smiled and then returned to Andrea, who stood waiting for him. Kjell and Isabell came over to Andrea and hugged her before they left the lawyer's office. Astrid and Knut Caling got ready to follow along with them, but when they stood in the doorway, Astrid turned around and glared at her daughter.

"I hope it won't be too long before you get in touch," said Astrid. Andrea stared back, but didn't say a word. She turned toward Björn and gave him a meaningful look. He nodded and without a word, they left the room.

"Why did my grandfather give your father a letter?" Jon asked the lawyer, noticeably irritated.

"I can't answer that. I've already carried out the instructions associated with the letter and can't do more than that," said Örjan Grund and ambled back to his desk.

"Why is the letter important to you?" Olav asked his son.

"I'm curious, that's all," answered Jon. He suddenly noticed that Mette and the others had left the room. The only persons left besides himself were the lawyer and his father.

"Did you see when Mette left?" asked Jon.

"No ... there was no goodbye for me either," said Olav looking around the room. He had hardly finished his sentence when Jon rushed out of the room. He could hear Jon calling Mette's name. Finally he heard the outside door close and understood that even Jon had left without saying goodbye. He turned to the lawyer and apologized for his son's behavior and thanked him for the day's proceedings. After that, he walked slowly out of the office. It would be great to get back home, put on the computer and enjoy in mid daylight, thought Olav. He walked with light steps out onto the street in order to get a taxi that would take him to Central Station.

Casino Cosmopol

Verne walked with determined steps into the Casino in Gothenburg. For every step he took, he felt more and more angry. What made him most angry was not inheriting an equal part of the Pharmacy chain shares, an inheritance that he had always viewed as his own. But thanks to his mother, he had been robbed of that treat. He didn't believe for one second what his father, or rather his step-father, had said about his last wishes. "If I had been his biological son, I would of course been given my equal share," he thought angrily. Now Kjell and Mette had them! And why in hell had he given such a large amount to Mette? This ruined his whole plan for getting rid of his debt. At the same time, he felt deeply bitter towards his mother. She had destroyed his life! How could she? Verne exchanged money for a box of chips and went over to his favorite roulette table. Absent mindedly, he laid out some chips on number thirteen. Now he would have to lie to Kjell again. Not that it mattered that much. He had lied to him many times before, especially about how he managed to get money to gamble with. The difference this time was that now he would, against his will, become involved in transactions that were illegal and perhaps even dangerous, thought Verne. Suddenly someone gave him a powerful shove in the back, and he tried to turn around, but a hand on his spine held him in a grip of steel.

"Shouldn't you be doing something else than standing here gambling away our money?" said a muted voice right into his ear. Verne stiffened and began to pick his chips back up again mechanically. He changed them to cash chips, put them in the box and walked over to the cashier. He didn't even dare turn around. He recognized the voice all too well. It was the same voice that had beat him up on a dirt road. Verne rushed out of the casino and walked quickly over to his car, got behind the wheel, backed out of the parking lot and put the pedal to the floor, leaving several millimeters of rubber behind on the asphalt.

Amir Is Showing His Face

Mahtab had arranged to meet her brother Massoud at Cafer Yapisan on Hammarkulle Square so that their parents couldn't hear their conversation and ask questions. She felt uncomfortable about having lured Verne into a trap and wanted to confirm that her part of the agreement was completed. No longer did she want to be a part of this game. Massoud seemed tense when he sat down across from her. He kept looking around in different directions.

"Are you scared of something?" asked Mahtab.

"No, why do you think that? I just don't want any of my friends to see us sitting here," answered Massoud.

"I've ordered two cups of gehve," said Mahtab and smiled at her brother. She loved him and wanted Massoud to free himself from the horrible gang she realized he had gotten involved with. In the emergency ward at Sahlgrenska Hospital where she worked, she had seen far too many gang members come in with knife and bullet wounds. Most often the patients hadn't dared say a word to the police, fearing that the next time they would come to the hospital they would end up

188

dying there on a medical stretcher.

"So you're mixing Iranian with Swedish?" said Massoud and laughed a little. Mahtab brought her hand up to her mouth to hide a giggle.

"It just pops out sometimes," she said. "Probably because Mom and Dad hardly ever speak Swedish at home."

Massoud reached forward and took an ashtray from the table beside them. His long sleeved shirt was pulled up and revealed parts of a bandage.

"What have you done to your arm? Have you hurt yourself?" asked Mahtab.

"Hi, Massoud! Hi, Mahtab!"

They froze in their chairs and looked up at the voice that had just called them by name. Amir stood by the table, smiling broadly. His black hair was combed back and shined in the sunlight. The white shirt he was wearing was unbuttoned at the chest and revealed a two-centimeter thick gold chain around his neck. Just behind him was a young, blond girl. The first thing Mahtab noticed was the bulge on her stomach. Simultaneously, Mahtab tried to form an opinion of what this girl looked like, but since she had sunglasses with mirror reflection glass, it was impossible to see her eyes. And yet there was something familiar about her appearance, thought Mahtab.

"Here you are sunning yourselves," said Amir, pulling up one of the empty chairs to sit down. The pregnant girl still stood behind Amir.

"Wouldn't you like to sit down?" asked Mahtab. She got up, went over to the table beside them, took a chair and placed it demonstratively beside her own. Mahtab caught a glimpse of the anger in Amir's eyes when he looked at Massoud. But almost instantly, as soon as Amir and Mahtab looked at each other, his facial expression was blank again.

The girl sat down and brushed aside her long blond hair with a shaking hand.

"Would you like something to drink?" asked Mahtab.

The girl shook her head.

"What's your girlfriend's name?" asked Mahtab and turned toward Amir with a smile.

Inside, she was nervous. She thought Amir's behavior was contemptuous, since this young woman was obviously his girlfriend. At the same time, she didn't dare to criticize him for fear of Amir's anger hurting Massoud or herself.

"Her name is Emelie," answered Amir, who got up and walked into the café.

"Hi, my name is Mahtab," she said and stretched out her hand.

Emelie took Mahtab's outstretched hand with uncertainty and Mahtab was surprised to discover that Emelie's hand was ice cold. Emelie let go of her hand, leaned back in her chair, and didn't say a word. Mahtab gave her brother a questioning look, but judging from his expression he didn't want to get involved with her attempts to get Emelie to talk. Amir came out with a glass and a Coca-Cola bottle in his hand. He sat down and poured the soda into his glass. Finally, Mahtab couldn't remain silent, pretending that everything was normal.

"Why don't you introduce Emelie to us? Here we are, sitting together, and you act as though Emelie is practically invisible," said Mahtab, gesticulating eagerly with her hands to emphasize what she was saying.

"Hasn't your sister learned anything?" hissed Amir through clenched teeth. "Tell her to shut up 'cuz I don't think you would want me to tell her," said Amir, staring at Massoud. He put his hand on one of Mahtab's arms in an attempt to calm her. But she shook off his hand and got up.

190

"What kind of a beast are you? Who do you think you are? A little gangster who runs around with a knife and a pistol and frightens people! So you think that's respect?" yelled Mahtab and left the outdoor restaurant walking rapidly. Behind her, she heard someone following her, but she didn't dare to turn around and kept walking faster. Then someone grabbed her arm, and she was prepared to start hitting.

"Mahtab, you're crazy!" cried Massoud and stopped her from moving forward.

"Oh, is it you! I'm sorry, but I can't stand Amir," said Mahtab and felt how her heart started returning to its normal rhythm.

"We're going to go back there, and you are going to say you're sorry to Amir," said Massoud, still holding her arm.

"Are you kidding? I'm not going to apologize to him," said Mahtab.

"You have to! He'll get angry if you don't, and I'll have to take the consequences. You wouldn't want that, would you?" said Massoud pleadingly.

"You have to leave that gang! If you don't, no one knows what will happen to us!" said Mahtab. "What if Mom and Dad will find out what you're up to?"

"You're not going to tell them, are you?" whispered Massoud and let go of her arm.

Mahtab sighed out loud and looked at her brother. Massoud could see in her eyes that she had softened. The dark brown eyes had a soft glow and the wrinkle on her forehead that signaled she was angry was gone. She shrugged her shoulders and started to walk back in the direction of the café. Massoud breathed out in relief and walked by her side. They were at the café again and on the way to their table when Mahtab was surprised to see a stranger sitting beside Amir. Mahtab gave Massoud a look filled with questions, but he just shook his head and made his way over to the table.

"Hey, Hazim!" said Massoud and sat down.

Hazim said hello back, but his eyes were following Mahtab. She took hold of a chair from another table and sat down beside Emelie. The conversation between the men died, and Amir looked at Mahtab. He gave her a disciplinary cock of his head. Mahtab looked quickly at the man who had just appeared and saw that he, like Amir, also radiated something unpleasant. "I wonder if they belong to the same gang?" thought Mahtab and took a deep breath.

"Excuse me, Amir. I behaved without respect towards you and your fiancée. It won't be repeated," said Mahtab and had to restrain herself from showing her anger.

"Good, then that's handled," said Amir, lifting his glass and drinking up the last of the Coca-Cola.

Mahtab could see that Massoud had a stupid smile on his lips now and that he was sucking up to Amir. It was a disgusting sight. She got up and said that she had to go. Stepping away with an ingratiating smile on her face and hating herself all the while that she did it, she convinced herself that this was for the sake of her brother and her family. There had to be a way to get Massoud out of Amir's grip.

"Now we can talk," said Amir and bent forward over the table toward Hazim. He raised his eyebrows and nodded quickly in the direction of Emelie.

"You don't need to worry about her. Just make like she doesn't exist," said Amir and smiled to Hazim. Those words sent shivers up Massoud's spine, but he forced himself to think of something else.

Back at the Police Station at Ernst Fontells Place

Greger stood leaning over his desk. With squinting eyes, he tried to read a document from Chief Coroner Sara Kronfeld. He was swearing at himself for having forgotten his glasses in the assignment room but didn't have the energy to go and look for them. He was far too curious and wanted to find out right away what detailed findings she had discovered about the charcoal burned body discovered on Packhuskajen. In Sara's report, it said that the corpse was male and that he had already been dead when the fire broke out. His airways had not contained any soot. If he had been alive, he would have breathed in soot, and that would have shown up in the autopsy. His blood contained traces of amphetamines, which could either mean that he was an addict or that he was murdered by being given an overdose. Sara had sent some samples to the National Board of Forensic Medicine. So far, the Board had not reported what type of amphetamine it was, which would reveal if it was a type they had dealt with earlier. The corpse had not yet been identified. They had DNA and were searching through all of the registers, but it always took about a

193

week, thought Greger and felt hopeful.

Katarina walked into the room with a coffee cup in each hand.

"Well, do we have anything?" she asked and put down one of the mugs beside Greger.

"It depends on how you look at it," answered Greger and took a sip. "So far we have no name for your Black Pete, but we know that the body is male and that it contained traces of amphetamine, so with a little luck … Have you spoken with Matthias today?"

"Yes, we're getting together tonight. His sister Agneta has invited us over for dinner. Is there something in particular you're thinking about?" asked Katarina.

"I was wondering if the SI group had found out more about the gangs and the impending fighting," said Greger.

"You already have that information. Look!" Katarina walked over to the computer and pushed the enter key, found the email and put the printer on. One minute later, Greger had five documents in his hands.

"I see, that's great," he said and put the papers on his table.

"Aren't you going to read them?" wondered Katarina.

"Yea, but the print is too small. I have to get my reading glasses. They're still in the assignment room."

They walked together to the assignment room, and Greger was thankful to find his glasses just where he had left them. He chuckled, and Katarina looked at him.

"What are you laughing about?"

"That I, for a second, actually thought someone might have taken my eyeglasses. But then I remembered where I am," said Greger.

"Are you saying that just because we're at the Police Station that that is some kind of guarantee no one would rob us?" said Katarina. "Boy, are you naïve!"

194

"Well, at least not in this room," said Greger and put on his glasses to start reading the document prepared by the SI group. "Have you read this?"

Katarina nodded.

"This is good news in a way, and then again, not," said Greger. "Striking at several places at the same time usually gives results, but now three weeks of planning have already passed, and for every week that passes, the risks expand. Not that I'm saying we're sitting in a boat full of holes, but in the past a leak here and there has been known to occur ..."

"Yes, Matthias is also a little concerned about that. But since they've had to coordinate the action with the Narcotics Division, it's taken more time to plan," said Katarina. "I've asked Matthias if I can participate in Operation Saffron.

"Shouldn't you have asked me first?" said Greger and pouted.

"It was better to find out whether or not I could participate first; then I'd ask you!" said Katarina and patted him lightly on the arm.

"Well, what did he say?"

"Matthias wouldn't promise anything. He's going to take it up with Håkan Pedersén, head of the Narcotics Division, and then get back to me," said Katarina.

Greger shook his head without thinking about it. He remembered all the times that he had had to sit and wait. Wait to storm a house or an apartment. It wasn't that he participated in the action itself ... the Task Force took care of that. He never went in until the area was secure.

Suddenly Greger heard someone running in the corridor, voices shouting, his telephone rang, and Katarina's phone rang a few seconds later. Both picked up their cell phones at the same time. Looking each other in the eyes, Greger realized that Katarina had received the same message he had.

Her eyes were dazed, and her mouth hung open.

"Oh, God! Think positive! This doesn't have to mean that he's dead!" said Greger and was already on his way out of the room together with Katarina.

She didn't answer. Her lips were tightly pressed, and the dash to the garage was made in record time. Greger was just a few meters behind, alternately running and trotting. He was breathing heavily and sounded like a broken bellows when he jumped into the passenger's seat. Katarina pushed the gas pedal to the floor.

"Now you have to think professionally," said Greger and held the handle on the inside roof with his left hand while struggling to get the seat belt on with his right.

"How professionally did you think when it was Johanna?" asked Katarina and kept her eyes on the road.

A motorist with the side windows pulled down had to drive up on the sidewalk when Katarina came speeding along with the flashing blue light and screaming siren.

"Fucking idiot! How difficult is it to look in the rearview mirror instead of grooving to loud music," hissed Katarina and made a sharp turn to the left.

"You're right, I wasn't particularly professional when my daughter died, and that's why I'm pointing this out to you. Don't make the same mistake I did," said Greger and put his hand on Katarina's arm. "Let's not think the worst!"

She didn't answer and just continued to focus one hundred percent on driving the car to Fridhemsgatan up toward Mariagatan. The street was narrow and cars were parked all along the whole street.

Already in the round about when she drove past Mariaplan, she could see the fire engines, police cars and crowds of people. Katarina had no idea how she managed to stop the car. But she jumped out of it, ran over to the blocked off area, and straight to Charlotte, who had her protective clothing on. Suddenly she was just standing there, and somewhere within a foggy field of view she noticed that Charlotte was talking to her. Katarina saw that Charlotte's lips were moving, but she didn't hear what she said. Her eyes had fastened on what had once been the entrance to Matthias' house. Parts of the door lay spread out within a radius of one hundred meters. What remained was a large hole, and it was still smoldering from different spots on the exterior of the building. A chilling thought ran through her mind. Was it possible to survive such a powerful explosion?

"Listen to me Katarina!" screamed Charlotte. "Matthias is okay! He's at Sahlgrenska Hospital and is unhurt! But his sister is not!"

"Sister?" repeated Katarina. Why had she been here? Then she remembered Agneta's unborn child. "What's happened to her? And the baby?" she screamed, grabbing Charlotte's shoulders and shaking her. Two strong hands grabbed Katarina's shoulders and pulled her away from Charlotte. It was Greger, and he turned toward her.

"Listen carefully! In just a minute we're going to Matthias and his sister. Right now you have to pull yourself together and let the bomb and forensic technicians do their job! Are you listening Katarina?" asked Greger without letting go of her shoulders.

Charlotte was still standing there, and Greger noticed the sad expression in her eyes above the mask covering her mouth. Katarina relaxed, and suddenly tears began to run down her cheeks like a quiet summer rain. Greger took her in his arms and led her to the car, opened the passenger door, put her in the seat and attached her safety belt. Greger took her in his arms and led her to the car, put her in the passenger seat and attached her safety belt.

"I'll be right back. I have to say a few words to Charlotte," said Greger and stroked her on her cheek.

"Do you have something for me?" asked Greger, bending over Charlotte, who was on her knees scraping off something from the ground.

"We don't know anything yet. The bomb technicians had to get in first, and that took a few hours as you can imagine," said Charlotte and nodded in the direction of what was left of the house.

"How many were hurt?" asked Greger.

"Four altogether. Matthias' sister was the most seriously injured, as well as two people walking outside who got knocked over from the shock wave, and the fourth was Matthias' neighbor, who got his bookshelf blasted over him. All four were brought to Sahlgrenska Hospital. Matthias went along with his sister in the ambulance for obvious reasons," answered Charlotte.

"We'll have to get the Nationals involved immediately. The bomb wasn't designed for Matthias' sister; it was aimed at him!"

Verne Confronts His Mother

Andrea parked the car on the gravel yard in front of one of the four garage doors. One door was open, so she knew that Verne was home. His blue BMW was sloppily parked, as if he had been in a rush. Björn got out from the passenger side, and they walked toward the main entrance in silence. The gravel crunched under their shoes. The path up to the front door was lined with bluish purple lavender blossoms that spread a powerful aroma. Every year when she breathed in that smell through her nostrils, she remembered how her grandmother had sewed small linen bags about the size of matchstick boxes and then filled them with dried lavender blossoms. She laid the small bags between the clothes in bureau drawers and every time you opened a drawer to take out a pair of stockings or a jersey, you were enveloped by a mild aroma of lavender. "No one bothers to make those little bags by hand anymore," Andrea thought with nostalgia. "Everyone is so busy! Why are we all in such a rush?" She shook off her musings and returned to the now. It felt so good that Björn had time to be with her for a few days. She needed his support for what was to come.

"If you want I can put some coffee on," said Björn with a loud voice while nodding in the direction of the living room. Andrea understood his nod meant that Verne was sitting in there, waiting for an explanation; an explanation that he should have gotten many, many years ago. She took a deep breath and let her shoulders fall.

"Why am I so tense?" she thought and wrinkled her brow.

Andrea stepped into the salon and looked at the sun shining in through the rectangular panes of the window. The panes created a pattern that looked like bars on the rug. "Strange, it feels like I'm entering a jail even before I've received my sentence," she thought. In her work as a lawyer, she was always prepared and well-read, but no one could possibly prepare her for what she was about to go through. It had never even occurred to her that she might have to defend herself in front of her son.

Verne sat curled up in his grandfather's green, worn leather armchair. He had his arms wrapped around his legs and his head resting in between his knees. As a child, he had always sat in that position when something was wrong. Now he was a grown man and probably very angry, thought Andrea as she went closer to her son with determined steps. She sat down on the sofa across from the armchair, leaned back, and looked quietly at Verne. He didn't look her in the eyes and just stubbornly stared down at the rug. Without thinking about it, Andrea starting drumming with her fingers on the arm of the sofa.

"Are you nervous Mom?"

Her whole body stiffened from Verne's voice and she stared at him. Verne smirked at the same time as his eyes were filled with hatred.

"Not nervous, more afraid," she answered.

200

"You ought to be," he said and stretched out his legs to their full length. "Do you realize what you've done? My whole life I've thought that Arne was my father, and now I find out that he wasn't. Can you understand how that feels?"

She shook her head, but still looked at him. A shiver of fear crept over her when she looked into his eyes.

"If I had been Arne's biological son, I'm convinced that I would have gotten as big a share of the Pharmacy chain as Kjelle," said Verne. "Now he gave most of his shares to Mette. Don't you think that was strange?"

Andrea was surprised about what Verne just said. He wasn't grieving about Arne; he was grieving about his inheritance! How had Verne become so cold? She didn't understand. He hadn't asked her again about his biological father. In one sense that was a relief ... maybe he didn't care, thought Andrea and started to relax.

"I don't know why Arne gave most of the shares to Mette. Maybe he was disappointed in Jon if we are to believe what he said in the film."

"You know what? I don't believe that for a minute! Arne gave her the shares as payment for having fucked her. His own brother's wife. Goddam," said Verne and suddenly got up from the chair. He walked over to one of the windows and stood there with his hands in his pockets, overlooking the park.

"Do you know who my real father is?" he asked, still standing with his back toward her.

"Yes, I do," said Andrea, holding her breath.

"Well, who is it then?" said Verne and turned toward her.

"Here I am with the coffee!" said Björn, loudly and clearly, smiling toward Andrea.

He walked over to the table and put the tray down. Giving Andrea a meaningful look, he started to arrange the coffee cups and saucers.

"Thanks, Björn, a cup of coffee would be nice," said Andrea. "Verne, do you want a cup too?"

He nodded once, turned his head away and continued to look out the window. She gratefully took the cup that Björn offered her but didn't dare look at her son. Andrea felt that she needed a break before she was going to answer Verne's question and hoped he would calm down after he sat down to drink his coffee. Having Björn with them at the same time she would give her answer made her feel more secure. The only noise in the room for a few minutes was the sound of cups being lifted off and put down on their saucers, and the clinking of stirring spoons in coffee cups made of fine porcelain.

"Mom, I want the answer to my question," said Verne and put his coffee cup carefully down on the table.

"Jon is your father," answered Andrea.

Björn was watching Verne and noticed that his hands holding on to the arms of the chair had started to shake. Suddenly, he jumped up out of the chair, lifted his arms up toward the ceiling, threw his head back and laughed out loud. Andrea had tried to prepare herself for a variety of reactions, but this one she was totally unprepared for. What could Verne be thinking about right now? He jumped over to Andrea and stood in front of her. He put a hand on each arm of her chair and leaned forward toward her. She pulled back and could feel that her head was pressed up against the headrest in the armchair.

"How certain are you that it's Jon who is my father?" he asked, staring into her eyes.

"One hundred percent," answered Andrea and stared back.

"Why hasn't Jon said anything?" wondered Verne and let go of her chair.

"Because I haven't talked with him about it," said Andrea.

202

"When had you planned to tell him that he was a father?" Verne went back to his chair and threw himself down in it with a thud. He leaned back and put one leg over the other. "Since Jon and Mette have been together for over twenty years and still don't have any children ... which we all know has been Mette's great wish ... shouldn't you have told Jon that he has a son? Don't you think so?"

Andrea bent her head down and mumbled something that not even Björn, who was sitting beside her, could hear.

"What did you say?" asked Verne sounding stern.

"I thought I would wait until I spoke to you first," said Andrea. "I didn't know ..."

"How I would react you mean? Well, now you can see that I'm really happy about it. It suits me perfectly to have Jon as my father. He has been a part of my life, is no stranger and owns the next largest part of the shares in the company. And Mette's thirty-six percent of the shares is only an advantage for me. Since Mette and Jon are married and hopefully don't have a prenuptial agreement, this could mean that Jon owns half of the shares that Mette has inherited from Da ... Arne," said Verne, smiling broadly.

Andrea jumped up from her chair. "The only thing that's important to you is the money! Is that how I am to understand your reaction? You don't care at all that my beloved husband is dead!" screamed Andrea with tears pouring down her face.

Björn hurried to put his arms around her and gestured with his head to Verne that he should leave the room. With a shrug of his shoulders, Verne stepped past his mother and went out into the hall. Andrea clearly heard the outside door close. The paintings hanging on the wall shook slightly from the bang.

"Sit down here," said Björn and led her back to the armchair. I think the best thing to do right now is to call Jon and ask for a meeting before Verne drops this news at their front door. Think what a shock that would be for Mette."

Björn didn't tell Andrea that Mette was in his apartment staying out of Jon's reach. It was best that Andrea didn't know about that when she spoke to Jon, he thought.

"Yes, you're right. I'll do that right away," said Andrea. Björn got the telephone and gave it to her.

"Hey Jon, it's Andrea. Would it be possible for you to meet me right away?"

"I'm on my way home right now, but sure," answered Jon. "By the way, did Mette go home with you?"

"No, why do you ask? Wasn't she with you?"

"Yes, but I stood talking with the lawyer and Olav. After that, everyone had disappeared. I thought she might have gone home with you," said Jon.

"If she shows up, I'll tell her you are on your way," said Andrea and hung up.

"Well, is he coming?" asked Björn.

"Yes, he'll be here in fifteen minutes. He wondered if Mette had come with us," said Andrea. "Do you know where she is?"

"Nope, no idea," said Björn, crossing his fingers behind his back. "I hope she can forgive me lying," he thought.

Björn stood in the hall when Jon came in through the door. The look in his eyes was glassy, and he was breathing heavily. Before Jon had arrived, Björn had planned to leave him and Andrea alone. But as soon as he saw what shape Jon was in, he changed his mind.

"Were you on your way out?" asked Jon.

"Just to get some bread and cheese," said Björn. "I'll be back in five minutes. Andrea is in the kitchen.

"Has Mette arrived?"

"No, was she going to?" wondered Björn, raising his eyebrows and looking surprised.

"I don't know," mumbled Jon. She's just vanished … I can't understand where she is."

"I'm leaving now," called Björn over Jon's head. "Did you want Philadelphia cheese?"

Andrea came out into the hall with a surprised look on her face and then she saw Jon.

"Yes, get that cheese, I like that kind," said Andrea and gave Jon a stiff smile. "Come in, let's sit in the living room," she said turning around and walking in front of Jon.

They sat down in separate armchairs. Jon looked around the room and after a while a smile appeared on his lips.

"It's been awhile since I sat in this room," he said and tried to muster the courage to hear what she was going to tell him.

"Verne isn't Arne's son. He's your son," she said.

"Is he my son?" yelled Jon and practically lifted out of his chair. "Is it true?"

She nodded, still with her head bent down. She didn't dare look him in the eyes. Jon stood in front of her and grabbed her arms. He shook her a little.

"But this is wonderful!" said Jon. "That was the best news I've had today!" He let go of her arms and squatted down on the floor in front of her chair.

"Are you sure I'm his father?" he asked with a tense voice.

"Yes, I'm sure! But, of course, you should both do a paternity test," said Andrea and was surprised at the strength she heard in her own voice.

"How do you do a test like that?" wondered Jon and went back to his chair.

"The National Board of Forensic Medicine has a homepage and you just click forward to the Forensic Genetics

Department. That's where you can print out all the documents that are necessary for a paternity test," answered Andrea looking steadily at Jon.

"Does Verne know that I am his father?" asked Jon, rubbing his hand over one day's growth of his beard. Andrea nodded. "How did he take it?"

"Actually, about the same way you did. He was happy," said Andrea. But she didn't mention Verne's happiness about being an heir to the Pharmacy chain. That would have to be a later discussion.

"Hi, now I'm back," said Björn and stepped into the room. "They were out of the cheese you wanted, so I got another kind."

Andrea gave Björn a smile and he understood that she had things under control. He had taken the chance to call Mette while he was away from the house. She had shut off her cell phone but answered Björn's landline telephone when she heard him leaving a message for her. Björn told her that Jon was with Andrea but didn't tell her why.

"Where is Verne, by the way?" wondered Jon and got up out of his chair. "I'd like to see him."

"I don't know, but you have his cell phone number, so just call," said Andrea and followed him out to the hall. "I'm driving out to Gunneby! I need to feel the smell of freshly cut grass, drink elderberry juice and just breathe," she said and stretched out a hand to Jon. "I want to remain friends in spite of everything that has happened, and I hope you won't make me sound like a bitch when you talk to Mette. I was young and thoughtless. Had I known what I know today, I would have never done what I did," said Andrea.

Jon took her outstretched hand and caressed it. She let him do that even though she felt some resistance.

"I wonder what our lives would have looked like now if I

206

had known that Verne was my son when he was a baby," said Jon. He lifted her hand up to his lips and gave it a kiss.

Andrea had to keep herself collected to avoid pulling back when she felt the tip of his tongue in the palm of her hand. Björn stood beside them and could see from looking at his sister that something was wrong. He pretended to lose his balance and bumped into Jon, who had to drop Andrea's hand.

"Oh, I'm so sorry!" said Björn, stretching his hand out toward Jon. "Hope to see you soon again," and secretly crossed his fingers behind his back one more time. They shook hands, and Jon stepped outside, turning around with a smile toward Andrea. Björn's narrow hand rested on the door handle. He waved goodbye to Jon, closed the door, and locked it.

"He took it well," said Andrea. "But the question is how Mette is going to react." Tears ran down her cheeks, and she felt awful about Mette. Would she have been able to forgive if the roles were reversed? She hardly dared think about it.

"I hope you're coming with me to Gunneby," she said, looking at Björn.

"Of course I am! You don't think I'd leave you alone with Mom do you?" he said and took her in his arms.

Katarina and Matthias at Sahlgrenska University Hospital

This was the second time within a short period that Greger and Katarina had to visit Sahlgrenska's Emergency Ward. Greger walked up to the first nurse that he caught sight of. He tapped the young, dark-haired beauty on the shoulder.

"Excuse me, can you help us?" he asked, looking around.

"Of course I can," she said and turned around.

Greger noticed the name tag that was pinned onto her coat. It said Mahtab.

"What kind of help do you need?" asked Mahtab and smiled at him.

"We are police officers from the Serious Crime Division and are looking for one of our colleagues who arrived with an ambulance," said Greger, waving his I.D. in front of Mahtab's eyes.

The smile disappeared, she couldn't speak, and her face got white. The ground started to spin. The police had discovered that her brother was a criminal! What she had feared all along had happened, thought Mahtab.

"Hello, there!" called Greger. "We're looking for our

colleague who came in with his badly injured sister. Where are they?"

Mahtab woke up from her thoughts and rushed over behind the information desk. She logged into the computer and turned around with a stiff smile at Greger. "What was the name of your colleague?" she asked.

"His name is Matthias Brodd and his sister's first name is Agneta. I don't know her last name. Greger turned around to ask Katarina, but she was gone. He looked around but didn't see her anywhere.

"Follow me," said Mahtab and walked off. Greger hurried after her and kept looking around for Katarina at the same time.

Katarina stood at the beginning of the corridor and saw Matthias before he noticed her. "My God, he's a mess!" she thought, dismayed. His facial color was ash gray, and he had dark purple rings under his eyes. He sat on a bench, leaning forward with shaking, clenched hands. His clothes were spattered with blood. Suddenly, he turned toward her. For one second, Katarina stood still, staring into Matthias' eyes. Then she ran and threw herself on her knees in front of him. He took her hand, held it hard, and their crying echoed in the corridor.

"Agneta lost the child," he wept. "She lost her baby! I can't handle this! It's too much! It's not worth it! Her dear child is gone! Dead! Murdered by those goddamn gangs!"

"Has anyone talked with Agneta?" asked Katarina, trying to sound calm. But inside she felt raging anger and powerlessness. "Her husband? Where is he?"

"Agneta is unconscious, in a coma. Her husband is on a business trip and is coming home tonight," said Matthias.

Katarina became frightened when she heard the sudden

monotone in his voice. He sounded completely apathetic. The words were dead. They came out just because they had to, not because he wanted to say them.

Greger caught up with them and stood beside Katarina. She recognized his shoes.

"How are you doing?" asked Greger and put his hand on Matthias' shoulder.

"I'm alive, but I should be dead. Agneta is alive and breathing with a respirator. The child is dead, and I'm quitting now," answered Matthias with the same apathetic voice he had before.

Katarina and Greger looked at each other. She shook her head ever so slightly so that Matthias wouldn't notice. She glanced at Greger and signaled that she wanted something to drink.

A door opened in front of them and a woman in a white doctor's coat came out. At first she seemed confused by what she saw, but then she picked out Matthias and approached him.

"Matthias Brodd?" asked the doctor.

He nodded.

"Are you also Agneta's relatives?" she asked, looking at them questioningly with her green-blue eyes. Her eyes were half covered by a pair of eyeglasses framed in red plastic.

"No, we are Matthias' colleagues," answered Katarina. "How is Agneta?"

"Will she be able to get pregnant again?" asked Matthias with a hard tone of voice.

"We can't say yet, but we want to see that the first twenty-four hours of her healing process yields positive results," said the doctor, avoiding looking at Matthias when she spoke.

"Agneta has internal injuries, and we just have to hope for the best. She's had a traumatic experience and been through

210

several hours of surgery," said the doctor while she shook their hands, and then left them with a mountain of unanswered questions.

Mahtab had hidden behind a wagon filled with linens and watched them. Her breathing went back to normal when she understood that the police weren't after her brother. She couldn't go any closer without revealing herself, so she couldn't hear what they were talking about, but she knew that Matthias Brodd's sister was in critical condition. The question was if she would live through the night. Mahtab sneaked back and walked into one of the linen storage rooms. She got her cell phone out, put it on, and saw that she had a text message from Verne.

"Want to meet and talk! Where and when?"

She sent a message to Amir. Their agreement was that if Verne got in touch she wouldn't answer until she had first spoken with Amir. She kept her part. Within seconds, she got an answer from Amir, who told her where and when she should meet Verne.

"Dress sexy" was the last thing Amir wrote. Mahtab answered Verne's text, and it only took a minute for her to get an okay. Trembling, she got ready to leave the storage room. The very moment she pushed on the door, someone else opened it. Mahtab tumbled out and ran into one of her colleagues.

"Oh, so that's where you were. I've missed you," said the blond woman.

"I thought I'd forgotten something in the linen storage, but I was wrong," said Mahtab and rushed past her. She walked along the corridor that opened out into the Emergency Ward. She suddenly saw a thin girl with long, blond hair fall onto the floor. Several of the personnel rushed over to help her.

They lifted her up and laid her on a stretcher. At that very moment, Mahtab remembered why Amir's pregnant girlfriend had seemed familiar! She had come to Emergency about two months ago heavily bruised in the face around her eyes and with bare spots on her scalp. The personnel felt that this was a clear cut case of physical abuse, but Emelie claimed that she had fallen off a bicycle. The hospital staff had tried to get her to say what had really happened, but Emelie had stubbornly maintained that her injuries were from an accident. They couldn't do any more than dress her wounds and send her home. Emelie was getting back into her clothes and had her back to the door when Mahtab came into the room pushing her wagon filled with test tubes. She couldn't help but gasp when she happened to see Emelie's back. It was covered with scabby sores and bruises as if she had been whipped. Emelie quickly pulled down her jersey and turned around. Their eyes met, and Mahtab could see the panic in this girl's eyes. She nodded, put her finger to her lips, and then backed out of the room with her wagon behind her. That was why Mahtab had the feeling she had met Emelie before when they met at the café. But since Emelie's sunglasses covered half of her face, she hadn't been able to see her eyes. Mahtab was sure that it was Amir who had abused Emelie. Her brother was obviously involved in a very messy situation. "How am I going to get him out of Amir's grip?" she asked herself in desperation.

Greger stood leaning over Matthias and Katarina was still kneeling in front of his legs. After the doctor had left them, no one had said a word. Katarina felt drained after the shock from the phone call about the bomb and realized that it had been too much for her. Where would Matthias find the strength to fight against these gangs? Right now she didn't

212

want to have to think at all. On the other hand, her job required first and foremost her ability to focus, not her ability to sympathize. Katarina got up and stood beside Greger. His facial expression was filled with worry and sadness. Greger took a firm grip on Matthias' arm and pulled him up from the bench. Katarina took Matthias under the other arm, and they walked out of the hospital supporting him from both sides. On the way home to her apartment, she sat beside Matthias in the backseat and talked to him. But she talked about nothing of any importance since anything else was impossible at the moment. She didn't dare to let silence do the talking. Greger helped Katarina get him into the elevator, into the apartment and over to the bedroom.

"I'm going to ask Stefan to send a doctor," said Greger before he disappeared out through the door. "I'll be in touch!"

"Do you want to take a shower?" asked Katarina. "It might take an hour before the doctor comes. What do you think? Do you feel strong enough to walk to the shower?"

Matthias sat hunched over on the edge of the bed and showed no indications of wanting to move. Katarina wished that she could do more than just stand there and watch him suffer. But she knew from her own experience that there wasn't much more she could do right now. Just being there was sometimes enough for the person grieving. Suddenly Matthias lifted his head and stretched his hands up toward the ceiling.

"Katarina, help me! I can't take it!" he screamed and wept at the same time. She took him in her arms and held him without words. Her cell phone rang, and she loosened one hand to answer.

"Hi, Katarina, it's Stefan. Are you alone?"

"No, I have Matthias here with me," she answered. "Hello, are you there?"

"I'm sending someone," said Stefan and hung up.

Katarina stood with the phone in her hand and stared at it. She was used to Stefan Kronfeld being very brief as well as cutting off his sentences, but this was too much. What did he mean by that? She put the phone away and gave Matthias her complete attention. First she led him into the bathroom, got him undressed as well as herself, took him into the shower and turned on the water. To an outsider, lathering Matthias' body with soap would look like a sexual act, but for her it was a way to show him love. He stood apathetically in the shower and the suds began to run down into his eyes. Katarina took a sponge, washed his eyes, and rinsed off the soap carefully. They got out of the shower, and she rubbed him dry with a bath towel, dressed him in a clean T-shirt and underwear, led him back to the bed and tucked him in under the blankets. She lay down gently beside him and stroked him over his hair.

It Was Not Just a Bad Dream; This Is for Real

Katarina woke up to the sound of the doorbell. She got out of bed quickly and glanced at Matthias, but he was still sleeping. On her way to the door, she grabbed her bathrobe, hurried out to the hall and opened the door. She was surprised to see three of her colleagues standing outside the entrance. One of them coughed and looked off to the side with embarrassment. "Can we come in?" asked Stefan and took a step past her. Greger and Charlotte walked in along with him. Katarina noticed that they seemed to be nervous.

"Where's Matthias?" asked Stefan and went out to the kitchen.

"He's sleeping, but if we keep making noise he'll probably wake up," said Katarina and followed Stefan. He took Katarina by the shoulders and put her down on one of the kitchen chairs. Greger and Charlotte placed themselves alongside and stood in silence.

"This isn't going to be easy, but someone has to say it. Agneta is dead," said Stefan in a low voice while looking

215

her in the eyes.

Katarina bit her lip to keep herself from crying out loud. Hot tears stung her eyes. She got up, walked over to the kitchen sink and turned on the faucet. Bending her head down, she let the cold water run over her face.

"How do you want us to handle this?" asked Charlotte, giving Katarina one of the kitchen towels that hung beside the refrigerator.

"I don't know," she said through the tears. "I didn't know Agneta very well. I've met her husband a couple of times and the same with her parents. The only one I know well is Matthias, and I think best would be to bring the whole family together. Has anyone gotten in touch with her parents?" asked Katarina.

"I asked Leif and Annika to get in touch with Agneta's husband and her parents. They promised to see to it that all of her relatives would be informed and given assistance to get to Sahlgrenska," said Greger.

"Perhaps it's just as well to wake Matthias so we can drive him there too," said Charlotte.

Katarina nodded and walked into the dark bedroom. She sat down on the edge of the bed and shook Matthias gently. He groaned and turned over. She shook him a little harder and whispered some loving words in his ear. He sat half way up and looked at her sleepily.

"What is it?" he mumbled. A second later his sleepy brain woke up enough to remember what had happened. He groaned and started to cry out loud. Greger stepped into the bedroom and cleared his throat.

"I think you have to get dressed," he said and walked over to the bed.

"What are you doing here?" asked Matthias and looked up at him.

216

"We've come with bad news," said Stefan and took four steps over to Matthias. "Your sister died three hours ago. Your parents have been told and even your sister's husband. We'd like you to help us and come along to the hospital. The idea is that the family will gather there. Can you manage?"

Stefan's voice was filled with sympathy and yet an authority that made Matthias take a deep breath, get up and start dressing himself slowly. Katarina could see Matthias clenching his jaws and heard him grinding his teeth.

"Weren't you going to send a doctor?" whispered Katarina to Stefan out of the corner of her mouth.

"I couldn't get ahold of one. You know what the situation is! Where are we when people need us?" said Stefan and opened the door.

Greger and Charlotte remained standing on Nordenskiöldsgatan and watched them drive off to Sahlgrenska Hospital in Stefan's car. Greger put his arm around her shoulders and kissed her on the forehead.

"God, I know how that feels," sighed Greger. "He's going to have a tough time for quite a while. The question is whether or not he will find the strength to hunt down the gangs again."

He took a stronger hold of Charlotte's shoulders as if he wanted to reassure himself that nothing bad would happen as long as she stood tightly right next to him.

"We have to get whoever is behind this," said Charlotte.

"How far have you come in looking for evidence at the site of the bomb?"

"We've collected broken glass, parts of the door, and especially the material that surrounded the lock. We think that someone has broken into the apartment, arranged the Semtex on the inside of the door and left a detonator in the lock. We suspect the idea was that Matthias would come home, put the key in the lock, turn it and boom!" said Charlotte. "But then it wasn't Matthias …"

"Do you know why Agneta went to Matthias' place?" asked Greger.

"No, I have no idea why she went there," answered Charlotte. "But since she had a key, she might have done that now and then. Matthias was in the USA for two months. Maybe she watered his plants and took care of his mail."

"I'll ask Katarina if she knows anything about it when she comes back from the hospital. I'm going to the station to contact the National Police. Coming with me?" Charlotte nodded. "I can't wait until Matthias can do it, and who knows when he'll be back working. The gang leaders and their hatchet men never take a vacation," said Greger and started walking in the direction of his car that was parked by the café down at the end of the street.

Mahtab Takes a Shortcut

Verne stood to wait for Mahtab on Kungsportsplatsen. He was on the stairs by the statue of King Karl IX, known as Kopparmärra by the people of Gothenburg. He kept looking at the clock that hung on the gable of the house.

"She's late again," he muttered. The cell phone that he'd been given by the Palace bartender was in his pocket, but it had been quiet. He still had one more day before he had to give them an answer. Today he was hoping to get some kind of explanation from Mahtab about what was going on. Suddenly he felt a hand on his shoulder and turned around with a smile on his lips. The smile disappeared when he saw who it was.

"Hi, Verne! What's up?" asked Kjell and smiled. "At first you seemed happy to see me, but then your smile disappeared. Maybe you were expecting someone else?"

Verne nodded to Isabell and patted his brother on the arms. He looked over Kjell's shoulder for Mahtab, but couldn't see her anywhere. Now he had to get rid of Kjell and Isabell as quickly as possible without awakening their suspicions, thought Verne.

Mahtab stood watching from one of the covered stops by the trolley tracks. Amir had given her orders only to meet up with Verne if he was alone. As she observed the persons who were talking with Verne, she had the feeling that he knew these people well. The woman appeared to be pregnant.

"It's so strange that every time I see a pregnant woman I feel such a strong longing to have children," thought Mahtab. These were such stupid thoughts since she didn't even have an apartment of her own. She still lived with her parents. Thank God, she didn't need to share a room with anyone. But just because she had her own room didn't mean that she could bring home anyone she wanted to, thought Mahtab sadly.

"Do you have time to go and have a cup of coffee together?" asked Isabell and hoped that he would say no.

"Sorry, I can't," answered Verne and looked at his watch again.

"How are you, by the way? I'm thinking about everything that Dad talked about," said Kjell and put his hand on Verne's shoulder.

"Oh, don't think about it! I'm fine! Sorry if I seem a little stressed, but I have an important meeting in a minute. So if you don't mind … can't we be in touch?" said Verne and smiled broadly at his brother.

"Sure, no problem Brother. Call me if you want to talk," said Kjell. He put his arm around Isabell's shoulders and started to walk slowly away.

"There is something strange going on with Verne," said Kjell when they were no longer within earshot of his brother.

"In a way, I understand him. To have to find out after you have buried your father that he wasn't your biological parent can't be easy. But I'm glad that you are only half-siblings," said Isabell. "I don't like Verne's overbearing manner."

"I think it's connected to his addiction to gambling. He has a sickness. Unfortunately, I am not the right person to help him," said Kjell. "I just hope that he's not going to get into trouble."

"What do you mean? If he has an addiction to gambling, he's already in trouble," said Isabell. "Are you thinking about loan sharks?"

Kjell nodded.

It was those last words, about gambling addiction that Mahtab heard when she passed Kjell and Isabell on her way across the street to meet Verne. She started to understand her role in this whole game and felt a shiver run along her spine. Mahtab met up with Verne with an artificial smile on her lips. She let him hug her, but when his lips started to get close to her mouth, she pushed him away.

"Can we sit at the café that's behind us?" asked Mahtab, pointing.

"Sure, we can sit outside," said Verne.

They both sat down with a cup of coffee. Mahtab looked around. She had the feeling that they were being watched. But looking at everyone she could see, she couldn't see anyone that she recognized. Maybe Amir didn't trust her anymore after the incident with Emelie at Cafer Yapisan at Hammarkulle Square. She forced herself to let go of the thought that they could be watched and decided to concentrate on Verne instead. Her instructions from Amir were to dress sexy, and it seemed to work. Verne could hardly take his eyes off her low cut blouse. Mahtab felt ashamed but tried to sound self-assured when she spoke.

"What did you want to talk about?" she asked.

"We can start with why you didn't show up at Palace. Instead, I was given a cell phone, and a threatening voice gave me orders about certain things. What do you know about that? Are you involved?" asked Verne.

"In what? I have no idea what you are talking about! I was fifteen minutes late and when I got to Palace you were gone," answered Mahtab and succeeded in sounding offended.

"How did that man know your name?" wondered Verne.

"Half of Hammarkullen knows my name," said Mahtab and felt a drop of sweat run down behind her ear.

"But how did he know that you wouldn't come on time?"

Mahtab was trying to figure out how she was going to explain away the situation. The problem was that she always had difficulty lying. She made herself move her chair closer to Verne and leaned up close to him.

"Don't you think we should just forget everything that has happened and concentrate on doing something more enjoyable?" said Mahtab and smiled broadly toward Verne.

He felt the smell of her perfume and put a hand on her thigh. Mahtab stiffened, took a deep breath and put her hand on his thigh. She squeezed it lightly and looked into his eyes.

"What do you say? Shall we go somewhere where we can have more privacy?" asked Verne and tilted his head to the side.

"I think so too," said Mahtab, lying.

In actuality, she had no desire to go off somewhere with Verne. She was a virgin, and no man had succeeded in getting involved in her life. To allow a man who she didn't have any feelings for wander over her body with his hands was unthinkable. Mahtab wanted to help her brother, but not by selling her body!

"I've parked the car in NK's parking garage," said Verne and got up.

Mahtab suddenly got an idea. There might be a way to get out of this situation, and she was almost sure she'd found the solution. They started walking in the direction of Gamle

Port, and they happened to walk along the roads toward the garage she was hoping for. Mahtab stopped suddenly, cried out, and pointed to one of the shops on the street.

"Oh, I just remembered what I should have bought a week ago!" she said enthusiastically.

"Really? What's that? Can't it wait another week?" asked Verne.

"No, now that I am here I just have to go and buy that book," answered Mahtab and started walking toward the shop.

Verne stood where he was and looked frustrated but didn't make any moves to go along with her. And that was exactly what she was hoping for. Before she stepped into the shop, she turned around and blew a kiss to Verne. He responded with a smile. Once in the shop, she approached a woman who worked there. While talking to her, she gesticulated wildly and hoped that Verne could see her through the shop window. At first the woman looked concerned but then broke out into a smile and waved with her hand for Mahtab to follow her further into the shop. Verne walked closer to the shop window, but could no longer see Mahtab. He shrugged his shoulders and thought that it could hardly take very long to buy a book.

The shop worker showed Mahtab the way to the personnel room. The corridor in the back was lined with boxes of books. They walked up to a double door, the woman punched in a code, opened the doors and showed Mahtab what direction she should take. She hurried along and ended up running all the way through NK's first floor. She went out through the main entrance, crossed the street, ran up Kungsgatan and turned on to Fredsgatan. As she was running, she kept looking quickly over her shoulder to be sure that she wasn't being followed. It wasn't until she crossed Kyrkogatan that she gradually started to slow down. It was fortunate that the shop worker had believed her story. She'd told her that she was being followed by an ex-boyfriend. Thank God there are kind people in the world, she thought. Now she wanted to have a serious discussion with her brother. Things just couldn't go on this way. She wanted to have her calm, structured and above all secure life back. There must be better ways for Amir to get what he wanted from Verne without having to keep her in constant fear.

After waiting twenty minutes, Verne's patience ended. He went into the shop and tried to find the woman who had assisted Mahtab, but without success. Another shop worker came up to him and asked if he would like some help. It turned out that the other shop worker had left work for the day, and no one knew where Mahtab had gone. Slowly but surely, Verne started to realize that she had tricked him, and that meant that she was indeed involved in this whole scheme one way or the other, he thought with irritation. He had one day left and then it was time to deliver, thought Verne.

"Time to talk with Dad," he said quietly and smiled at the thought of it.

The National Police Force

Two days after the bomb explosion, the mood in the assignment room was somber. Greger had contacted the National
Police and now sat waiting for two persons who were going to
help them catch these madmen. Katarina's eyes were swollen,
and Greger realized that she had been crying. Matthias was
sick listed for the time being and temporarily staying with his
parents. Everything was turned upside down for all of those
who had been involved. The burned corpse had been identified and was a man who belonged to Hazim's gang. Since they
had found Massoud at the same location, and he belonged to
Amir's gang, Greger came to the conclusion that this must
have been an inside settlement. But being able to prove it
was something else entirely. Massoud could just as well say,
if they could ever get him to talk, that he passed the area,
saw the flames, and tried to extinguish them, and that was
why he had light burns. Maybe it would be better to focus on
Verne Hildeng. If they put people on him twenty-four hours a
day, maybe he would lead them straight to the gangs, thought
Greger.

"I think we should concentrate on Verne," said Katarina, sounding as though she had read Greger's thoughts.

"We've put together a great presentation of what we have so far, to give to the guys from National. They'd better be satisfied with it!" said Leif and smiled broadly.

"Let's hope that we are," said a man with a base voice.

Everyone's eyes turned toward the entrance. A woman and a man stood there looking at them.

"Yes, we're from the National Police Force," said the man as he stepped into the room. "We received excellent directions from Stefan Kronfeld as to where to find you, and, of course, we want to help with whatever is needed to put as many gang members in prison as possible."

"And I'm not a 'guy' but maybe that'll be alright anyway?" asked the woman, looking at Leif.

He nodded. The woman in front of him was about forty and had short hair dyed blond with dark highlights. Her gaze was sharp, and her lips thin and narrow. Women with narrow lips are real bitches, just so you know, had Leif's father always said and pointed in his mother's direction. Leif grinned at the memory of his father.

"Did I say something funny?" asked the woman.

"No, excuse me. I was thinking about something else," said Leif and noticed how arrogant he had sounded. He got a kick in the shin from Katarina and jumped from it.

"As you may know, we've been removed after what happened to our colleague's family when a bomb was detonated," said Greger as he got up and went to greet them.

"Of course," said the man and held out his hand. "My name is Per Nyström and am called Pelle."

The woman also shook Greger's hand and introduced herself as Birgitta Rand.

"And they call me Gittan," she said with a smile.

Four hours and two liters of coffee later they had everything into context. While they had been sitting in the assignment room, personnel from the Narcotics Division also came to provide them with information. Every document was registered and placed in notebooks that lay on the table. Greger sat with one of the notebooks in front of the group and brought them up to date about the current situation. After that report, everyone seemed satisfied with their assignments, and one by one they left the room.

"We're staying at Hotel Opalen. Here are our telephone numbers," said Pelle and put a note down on the table in front of Greger before they left the room.

Katarina sat quietly and looked out through one of the windows. Greger accompanied the couple from National Police to the door. He stood looking after them.

"I wonder how Matthias is doing right now?" he thought and sighed. "What a crazy life we lead when you think about it. Death threats are a part of everyday life. Why do we put up with this?" he wondered.

Greger walked over to Katarina and put his hand on her shoulder. She jumped, looked up at him, and put her hand over his. Her golden-brown eyes were wet.

"Will you see Matthias tonight?" asked Greger.

"No, I can't handle it. I know this sounds egotistical, but right now I don't have the strength to meet all of that family's grief," said Katarina.

"You don't need to explain. I understand," said Greger and patted her lightly on the cheek.

"I want to get the bastards who are responsible," she said. "Preferably before it happens again, because I know it will. The people in those gangs have no scruples!"

The House in Strömstad

Olav was standing by the mailbox and saw to his surprise that Verne had come for a visit. The car drove past him and disappeared around the bend going at a very high speed.

"He always drives too fast," thought Olav as he put the mail down in his bag and trudged back to the house. Ten minutes later he walked through the front door. The sight that awaited him was unexpected. In front of the stairs in the hall, Jon and Verne stood hugging each other. Jon saw his father and the smile on his lips was broader than it had been in a very long time.

"Hi, Dad! I have fantastic news I want to tell you!"

"Really? How's that?" said Olav and started to go through the mail on the hall table.

"Verne is my son," said Jon and held his arm around Verne's shoulders.

Olav dropped the letters on the floor and stared at them with an open mouth.

"I realize this comes as a shock to you. It was for me too, but a happy one," said Jon.

"Well, that's the least one can say," mumbled Olav. "How does Mette feel about her new role as stepmother? You've told her I hope?"

"I haven't seen her since the funeral," answered Jon and his smiled disappeared.

"But where is she? As far as I know, she doesn't have any friends left," said Olav and looked at a grinning Verne. "How does it feel for you to have a new father after all these years?"

"For me it's only positive," said Verne. "Of course, at first I was angry when I found out that Mom had been unfaithful, but then fortunately it was with the right man! I've known Jon my whole life and been with him almost as often as I've been with Arne."

"What do you mean when you say that she doesn't have any friends left?" interjected Jon. "Just what I said! The only people she's been socializing with for the last ten years are Andrea, Björn, Elsebeth and me. Now we can count out Elsebeth," said Olav and his upper lip trembled. "Don't tell me this is news for you … if you do, you're lying!"

Jon stared at his father but then turned back to Verne.

"Mette knows where she lives and when she comes home we'll tell her. I've tried to call her, but she won't answer," said Jon.

"Well, everything will probably be all right," said Olav. He picked up the mail from the floor and headed toward the salon.

"Jon, there's something I need to talk to you about," said Verne.

"You can call me Dad if you like … I have nothing against it, but I can understand if it feels strange in the beginning," said Jon.

"Of course, I'd like to call you Dad," said Verne and felt that he was less nervous. It didn't seem to be at all difficult to steer Jon onto the road that he had already mapped out, thought Verne with pleasure.

They went out onto the terrace and sat down in the porch chairs. Jon had a good look at Verne and couldn't understand how he had missed all the signs. Verne's profile was so similar to his own. The dark blond hair, the light blue eyes, and the cleft chin. It had all been there the whole time, and yet Jon had never noticed it until now. He could hardly stop looking at his son. A feeling of happiness flowed inside of him that was difficult to put into words.

"Well, Dad, I would really like to become acquainted with how the Pharmacy chain works," said Verne and bent his head down, feeling tense about what the answer would be. He wanted Jon to think that his interest in the company was genuine.

"That's great! Of course, you'll get to learn everything! In what department would you like to begin? Economy? Research?" asked Jon and looked at his son with eyes overflowing with love.

"What about distribution?" asked Verne, breathing out a sigh of relief.

"Sure, if that's where you want to begin," said Jon. He looked a little surprised. "When were you thinking of starting?"

"Right away, today, if it's possible," said Verne.

"Well, it's not impossible, but why are you in such a rush?" wondered Jon.

Verne had to remain calm he thought to himself. He must prevent Jon from becoming the slightest suspicious.

"All these years Arne cared more about Kjelle. He forced me to study law, but I wanted to become a doctor. Kjelle was allowed to choose whatever profession he wanted. I always felt neglected," said Verne, letting out a big sigh and putting his head down again.

"Let me arrange it so you can be in touch with the head of the Distribution Department right away," said Jon and picked up the telephone.

During the phone conversation, Verne walked around the terrace. He took a deep breath and looked out over the ocean. He noticed the grill and thought he would have it changed for a gas grill and have some new teak furniture bought while he was at it.

"All of this is going to be mine one day, anyway," he thought, enjoying his new position. His thoughts were interrupted by the cell phone. The message was short.

"Call now." Verne wrote down the number and looked at Jon, who was still talking. He positioned himself up against the railing, dialed the number and focused his eyes on Jon.

"Come to Järntorget, Folkets Hus tomorrow at three p.m. You'll receive more instructions," said the voice and hung up. Verne stared at the telephone and felt he would like to throw it into the ocean.

"Has something happened?" asked Jon and looked worried.

"No, not at all," answered Verne. "Did you get a hold of the boss?"

"Sure, no problem! Robert says that you are welcome to get in touch. Here is his direct number. He'll help you with everything you need to know," said Jon and put his arm around Verne to hug him.

"Thanks, Dad! Would it be okay if I move out here? I'd rather live here in Strömstad than in Arne's house in Hovås," said Verne and smiled ingratiatingly.

"Of course you can live here if you want to," said Jon.

"Don't we have to ask Grandpa first? He might think it's

not appropriate," said Verne.

"Why would he think that? He loves you just as much as I do," said Jon. "Come, we'll go to him. He's going to be really happy about this, I promise!"

Olav sat in the salon and read the newspaper. He heard voices coming closer and understood what was going on. In a way, it was great that Jon finally had a child of his own, a son. But at the same time, Olav was disappointed about his son's behavior toward Mette. In the space of one day, it seemed as though Mette had ceased to exist. That was terrible! She had always stood by her husband's side. Olav was also well aware of the cruel way Elsebeth had treated Mette during the greater part of their marriage. Everyone had noticed it. Deep inside, he felt that Kjell had always been his favorite grandchild. Perhaps that wasn't fair, but that's the way it is, thought Olav. He put his paper down and let it rest in his lap.

"Dad, Verne wants to live here in the house with us. You have nothing against that, do you?" asked Jon with his arm around Verne.

"No not at all, but shouldn't you ask Mette as well?" answered Olav.

"I can't think that she would say no," said Jon and a deep wrinkle appeared on his forehead between his eyebrows.

"That's not what it's about. Of course, she wouldn't say no, but she's your wife and should be a part of your decisions," said Olav and lifted up his newspaper again.

Jon shrugged his shoulders and took a firmer grip around Verne and left the room. Olav looked after them and shook his head.

"I'd better buy myself a little house and let the rest of the family live here on their own. Everything would probably be much calmer," he thought.

232

A Secret Meeting

Mahtab was outside the entrance to her work and was on her way home when her cell phone rang. She looked at the display, but the number was unknown.

"Hello, this is Mahtab," she answered.

"Don't say anything … just listen. This is Emelie," said a whispering voice.

"I snitched your number from Massoud's telephone in case you wonder. I need your help! Come to the Hard Rock Café on Kungsportsavenyn tonight at nine p.m. Go to the ladies' room and wait until I come. I'll explain more when we meet," said Emelie and hung up.

Mahtab stood with the telephone in her hand and looked around at the people who were nearby. But everyone seemed to be behaving in a normal way. Did Emelie remember their meeting in the Emergency Ward? Mahtab started to become nervous. Good thing she was off this evening and didn't have to change shifts! She would have to give her parents a little white lie. What could Emelie want help with? It was courageous of her to call me, thought Mahtab and hurried in the direction of her trolley stop. If she were lucky, she would just make it in time for the number eight streetcar.

It was five minutes to nine when Mahtab sneaked down the stairs to the ladies' room at Hard Rock Café. In front of the mirror, two women stood putting their make-up on. They didn't seem to notice her. She went into the smaller toilet area and locked the door. After a while, she heard the other two women's voices fade away. Five minutes later the door to the ladies' room opened, a male voice gave some commands, and the door was closed. Mahtab waited a few seconds before she opened her door. She met Emelie's blue eyes. She lifted her hand, put it over Mahtab's mouth and pointed to the door to the ladies' room.

"He's standing outside," whispered Emelie in Mahtab's ear.

She nodded.

Emelie pulled Mahtab into the same toilet area that she had just left. Emelie unbuttoned her pants and to Mahtab's surprise she took out a plastic bag that she'd hidden there and gave it to Mahtab. She took the bag and saw that it contained four small cassette tapes, numbered one to four.

"What am I supposed to do with them?" whispered Mahtab.

"Hide them in a safe place. Next Thursday I want to do this again, but you need to give me four new tapes," whispered Emelie back. "But not nine p.m., nine thirty instead! I want to you listen to the tapes too! Promise me!"

Mahtab nodded.

Emelie buttoned her pants, flushed the toilet, and gestured for Mahtab to remain. Mahtab put the bag with the tapes in her handbag and waited five minutes before she sneaked out again. When she was back on Kungsportsavenyn, she walked in the direction of the Art Museum. "Once I'm at

234

the Public Library I can take the bus to Brunnsparken," she thought. "Where can I get ahold of a tape recorder so I can listen to these, and where do I buy new tapes?" she thought. It wouldn't be smart to ask Massoud, so she decided instead to ask someone at work the next day.

Five days later Mahtab sat in the personnel restroom and listened to the tapes. What she heard made her freeze with fear. What should she do with this? Should she go to the police? My God, what if Amir would find out that she sat listening to conversations between him and Hazim? Conversations where they were planning murders and discussing who they would pick to do the killing? If Amir found out about this, he wouldn't hesitate to murder her too. That was obvious to her when she heard how nonchalantly they decided who was to be killed and how it should be done. And now she realized who was behind the police officer's sister's death. Someone pulled at the door, and Mahtab thought her heart would stop.

"I'm done in a minute," she said with a disguised voice. The person outside stopped touching the door and left.

In two days, she would meet Emelie again, get perhaps four more tapes and give her the four new tapes she had bought. The mere thought of sneaking into the Café again and seeing Amir sitting there with his friends, laughing and joking at the same time that she knew he was a murderer made her shake in her whole body. When she would meet Emelie, she would try to convince her that the best for everyone would be to give the tapes to the police. She would even say that she didn't want more tapes to hide. Then the police would be able to help Emelie too. There was witness protection; Mahtab had read about that in the newspaper. She forced herself to think positively. She would gather the little courage that she had and meet Emelie for the second and last time, thought Mahtab.

Mahtab Has a Talk with Massoud

Massoud sat quietly on the bed in Mahtab's bedroom and waited. She had asked him to come to her after dinner. Her parents had looked at her in surprise when she told them what she wanted. It was unusual for brother and sister to be in each other's bedrooms, but she had promised to keep the door open during their conversation. Her father had stared at Massoud, but he skillfully avoided his father's eyes. Her mother had gone to the kitchen sink to wash dishes, and acted as though nothing unusual had happened. Their family was strict and there were a lot of rules about what the children were allowed and not allowed to do. Mahtab's behavior wasn't against the rules, but it was obvious that they were worried, she thought. In an attempt to calm her father, she smiled at him, but he didn't smile back.

"I want you to leave Amir's gang," said Mahtab with a low voice, looking at Massoud.

"You know I can't," he whined. "You know what will happen if I try. By the way, you don't have to have any more contact with Verne. Pretty soon we'll have him where we

237

want him," said Massoud and stretched.

"You'll have him where you want him? What do you mean by that?" asked Mahtab and forgot to keep her voice down.

"Oh, never mind! Forget about it! You've done your part," said Massoud and looked over toward the door.

"Don't you understand what I'm saying to you?" said Mahtab. "I want you to leave Amir's gang. They are dangerous! Don't you understand that?"

"Of course they're dangerous! That's why you have to be careful what you say!" whispered Massoud.

Mahtab thought back to her second meeting with Emelie. She had panicked when Mahtab had used the word 'police'. Emelie grabbed Mahtab's arms and shook her. She looked deeply into Mahtab's eyes and spoke each word slowly and deliberately.

"If you go to the police, I'm dead. Do you understand? Dead!"

Mahtab had nodded and repeated the sentence: "I promise! I won't say anything." Emelie let go of her arms then and left her alone in the toilet. Mahtab sat down on the toilet seat and shook for several minutes before she dared to leave the place. Now her brother was sitting in front of her and threatening her! He seemed to enjoy being a gang member!

"Cool down now Sis! Nothing's going to happen to me. As long as you stay calm," said Massoud, got up and sashayed out through the open door.

Mahtab got up slowly and closed the door after him. She went back to her bed, lay down on top of it, and let the tears roll down her cheeks. It was a good thing she'd never had time to tell Massoud she knew how he'd burned his arm, she thought.

Guilty Thoughts

Greger was alone in the assignment room. He'd just found out that Verne Hildeng had met someone at Järntorget, and that person had given him something. The trackers weren't sure, but judging from the objects size, it could easily have been a gun. Unfortunately, they'd lost Verne even though they had put someone to watch his car parked on Linnégatan. Verne never went back to his car and disappeared into the crowds. Greger had called Katarina in as well as the Special Investigations Department's secondary leader. He had even asked for personnel from the Narcotics Division and called Charlotte as well to let her know what was going on.

"When did this happen?" asked Katarina as she sat down. She seemed to be out of breath.

"Did you run here?" wondered Greger.

She shook her head.

"I was at Matthias's parents' home when you called, and you said to get here right away," she said.

"How is he?"

"He's taking one day at a time. He is crying every time

I'm there; it's terrible," said Katarina and sank down over the table. "I don't know if I have the strength to see him cry anymore."

Greger patted her lightly on the head. It hurt inside when he heard how badly Matthias was feeling.

"I can go along with you the next time if you want me to," said Greger. "That might help."

Katarina shook her head. She straightened up and wiped her tears away with the back side of her hand.

"Tell me now, what's happened?"

"Four days ago, Verne Hildeng met a man at Järntorget by Folkets Hus. It looked like this person gave him a gun," said Greger.

"Four days ago! Why didn't we find out about this before now?" cried Katarina. "Where is Verne now?"

"The trackers have more than just our case to handle, and Verne has disappeared into thin air. But they are looking for him," said Greger.

"Shit! Stefan's going to blow up," said Katarina and sighed.

"Only if we tell him," said Greger.

"Tell me what?" asked Stefan and stepped into the room. "What was it you wanted to tell me?"

Charlotte came in at the same time as Stefan. She brought her team of forensic technicians with her, so altogether they were six persons. She looked at Greger, lifted her hand up in a small wave, and winked at him discreetly. He sighed out loud and glared at Stefan.

"Well, it's hardly good news, but, of course, we'll let you know what's going on," he said and smiled stiffly at Stefan.

Katarina was lost in her own thoughts while Greger outlined the crazy situation for Stefan. What if it had been her instead of Agneta who had been taking care of Matthias' apartment while he was in the USA? She had offered it, but

240

Matthias had said don't bother, it was easier for Agneta to take care of the plants and the mail. She already had a key and drove past his place on her way to work. If I had insisted, I could have been murdered instead of Agneta. She shuddered at the thought. At the same time, she felt guilty that it was she who was alive and Agneta who was gone. Was that something that Matthias thought about every time they saw each other? Was that the reason that he cried every time they met? But why had Agneta been at his place that particular day? Matthias had already come home and been home for several days. Had he asked her to go there? Katarina hadn't dared ask him why Agneta went to his home that afternoon. Was he feeling guilty because she was dead? If I had had a key to his place, maybe he would have sent me instead of Agneta, that is, if he had sent her? All these if's, thought Katarina.

At the Summer House

At the house in Gunneby, Björn and Andrea sat in the hammock with their arms around each other. In front of them sat Kjell and Isabell on the other side of the table. Astrid and Knut Caling had left the house after they had heard the whole truth about Andrea having been unfaithful. The conversation had escalated and was completed in a crescendo, not unlike the times Astrid would play those terrible pieces by Bela Bartok on her piano, thought Björn and smiled inside of himself. As if Andrea didn't have enough problems as it was! No, our dear mother would, of course, pour gasoline on the fire he thought and looked at his sister with tenderness. He still hadn't said anything about Mette staying at his apartment, but he didn't think that was something that Andrea needed to worry about for the time being. That was Jon's problem.

"We might as well have a drink," said Björn. "Would anyone else besides me like to have a gin and tonic?"

"Thanks, that would be great! You'll have to stick to elderberry flower juice," said Kjell and stroked Isabell over her hair.

242

Björn went out to the kitchen to mix the drinks and called Mette at the same time. It was probably time to bring her up to date. Astrid might run into Mette somewhere and, in that case, it was better that he tell her than his mother.

"How are things with you?" asked Björn. "Are you feeling lonely?"

"Yes, actually," answered Mette, and sat down on the broad window sill. "Are you in Gunneby? How's Andrea? Has Jon been in touch?"

"To take your questions in the right order, yes, I am in Gunneby. Andrea is feeling terrible, and Jon has been asking for you," said Björn. "But now you have to listen to me. What I'm going to tell you now will make you feel sad. I wish I didn't have to tell you, but it's better that you hear it from me than anyone else," said Björn. He took a deep breath and started.

Mette didn't say a word during the whole of Björn's monolog. He could hear her breathing over the phone. Andrea came into the kitchen suddenly and looked at Björn with surprise. She mimed, Who are you talking to?

"So if you can direct your anger toward Jon instead of Andrea, I'd be thankful," said Björn and winked at her.

Andrea stood frozen to the ground when she realized who Björn was talking to. She started to feel faint and grabbed the kitchen counter with one hand. Björn went over to her right away and took hold of her shoulders. At the same time, he held his head next to Andrea's so she could hear what Mette was saying.

"I only feel sorry for Andrea. You two have always been supportive of me. That's more than I can say for Jon," said Mette with a bitterness in her voice that couldn't be hidden. "You can tell Andrea that I feel absolutely no hate towards her."

"If you want, you can stay in the apartment a few more days. I'm not coming home before Monday next week at the earliest," said Björn.

"Thanks so much … I might stay, but I'm not quite sure. If I leave before I'll leave the key under the flower pot, just like we agreed," said Mette.

After the conversation, Björn stood still watching Andrea. "Strange; all the trials and tribulations that we human beings have to go through, and to what purpose?" he thought.

"Do you think that Mette is telling the truth about not being angry with me?" asked Andrea.

"Yes, I do. You heard what she said. It's Jon who is the scoundrel. During all the years that Mette wanted to have children, he did nothing to help out. She was examined, and they found nothing wrong. But he refused to provide a sperm sample and then there was nothing more that could be done," said Björn. "Why do you think he refused? I think he was scared … scared that the test might show his sperm was worthless. Now we know that there was nothing wrong with his sperm, at least one time, but something might have happened later to make him sterile."

"Poor Mette, can she really go home knowing that Jon has a child, a child that she wanted but couldn't have? Good God, how could one foolish mistake in my life cause all this suffering?" said Andrea and started to cry. "Why didn't I tell Arne? Why?"

"There are too many why's in our lives, but what's done is done. Instead, we'll have to concentrate on making the best of the life we have," said Björn while he held and comforted her.

Verne Gets His First Lesson in Pharmacy

Verne was at the company's pharmaceutical warehouse in Oslo and trotted along after Robert. He had arrived three hours ago and was already tired of Robert's lecturing.

"How is the medicine transported to our drugstores?" asked Verne pointing to boxes in different sizes.

Robert jumped, turned around and wrinkled his large nose. His brown bangs stuck out in all directions.

"Since we handle large amounts of narcotic medicines, we also have restrictions," said Robert.

"I see. What kind of restrictions?" asked Verne and finally started to get interested.

"All of our drivers go through a control in our Security Department. In the morning, when the drivers come to work, they punch in a code. The system gives them a computer generated choice of their route for the day as well as the person who will pack their truck. In that way, it's never the same people who work together. It's foolproof!" said Robert and flashed a huge grin at Verne. But Verne had a hard time returning the smile. Thoughts were moving through his head one after the other. How would he communicate this information? They would never accept it. There must be some way to crack this foolproof system, thought Verne. But how?

"Where do we get our deliveries from?" asked Verne.

"From Germany; the company is called Celecio and is one of the larger wholesalers in Europe," said Robert. "They deliver on time and are almost always able to fill our orders."

"How often do we get deliveries from Celecio?" wondered Verne and chewed on his lower lip in irritation.

"Several times a week at different times of day," answered Robert. "You see, we've protected ourselves against possible robberies. The sale of narcotics generates a lot of money in certain circles. That's why we want to protect our personnel from temptation and threats. If the people who work for us don't know which medicines will be driven when or where, it's difficult for gangsters to plan a robbery."

Verne had to agree. This was really bad news. Now he'd have to invent another lie when they would call him for an answer. He might be able to hold them off one more day, but then he was done for, he thought with desperation. Asking Kjell for help came to his mind again. After all, the situation had changed for both of them. To approach Jon and ask if he could borrow one hundred thousand crowns wasn't an option. That would awaken his suspicions immediately, so soon after it had come out that he was his son. Jon would think that Verne was just after his money.

"Hello, are you with me?" said Robert in a loud voice and put a hand on Verne's shoulder.

"Yes, I am!" he said and continued to tag along after Robert.

The plan was that Verne would spend four days with Robert and then go home. He still had a few exams to take before it was time for semester break. Postponing taking the exams was a possibility, but he didn't want to do that because of his current situation.

"Goddamn!" he thought. "How in hell am I going to get out of this?"

"Suddenly an idea came to him. Why hadn't he thought of this before? He started whistling a tune, and Robert stopped to stare wide-eyed at him.

"Robert, I think this is enough for me right now. Thanks so much," said Verne and held out his hand. Robert took his hand, shook it up and down and watched with surprise as Verne walked briskly out of the building. Verne got into his rental car and took out his cell phone. He dialed the number and waited for an answer. Two minutes later he smiled a victorious smile, put the car into first gear and stepped on the gas pedal.

Amir sat at Hard Rock Café with a smile on his lips after finishing his telephone call. So far everything was going as planned. He kicked Emelie on her shin. She winced from the pain.

"Did that hurt?" asked Amir, leaning closer to her face. She shook her head and gave him an artificial smile. "I didn't think so! Go get a café latte for me," said Amir and gave her a shove.

Verne remained in Oslo for the agreed upon four days. He called Jon every day and reported on his progress. The only remaining concern had been calling the anonymous man with the deep voice. Verne had sworn on his father's grave that he would do what they asked him for. He would pay back the ninety thousand plus interest that he had borrowed and then hope that the problem would be taken care of. The anonymous voice's reply was short:

"I'll get back to you."

Verne had been biting his nails for two days while waiting for the call that finally came.

"We have an agreement. The same time and place as before."

Verne took a deep breath and sighed with relief. The heavy weight on his shoulders felt lighter, and life started to look brighter again.

The Search for Verne

"Katarina, can you call Andrea Hildeng and find out if she knows where Verne is?" asked Greger. "We don't have much else to choose from! Make up a reason for the call."

Katarina woke up from her ponderings and nodded. She took her phone out and made the call with her back towards the group.

"Hi Andrea, this is Katarina Linde from the Serious Crime Division in Gothenburg. Do you possibly know where Verne is? This is nothing serious; we'd just like to ask him a few simple questions," said Katarina.

"Unfortunately I haven't spoken with him for over a week. Try calling Jon. He may know more," said Andrea.

"What about Kjell? Does he know where Verne is?" asked Katarina.

"No, Kjell and his girlfriend have been with me here in the house on Tjörn the whole time," answered Andrea.

Katarina went back to the group and gave them a report from the call. Shortly thereafter Greger's cell phone rang. As he was talking, he gave them a thumbs-up.

"The trackers have caught up with Verne again. An hour ago he picked up his car on Linnégatan. They've promised they won't lose him again.

"How are you doing?" asked Charlotte as she moved closer to Katarina. "You look sad. Have you seen Matthias?"

"Thanks for your concern," said Katarina and put her hand on Charlotte's arm. "I was with Matthias when Greger called. He's still living with his parents. It's not certain that he'll move back to his place after the renovation. I doubt that he will. It seems as though he's lost his will to live. I talked with his mother and she said that he just lies on his bed all day, staring at the ceiling. She's tried to talk with him, but he says very little. I want to speak with Stefan about connecting him with a psychologist. Matthias will probably get angry, but if it's Stefan who requires it, he'll probably give in."

"I think that's the right thing to do," said Charlotte. "Given the state he's in, Matthias needs professional help."

"I heard my name mentioned," said Stefan and smiled toward Katarina. "Is there something you want to talk about?"

Katarina gave him a short description of the way Matthias was acting and Stefan came rapidly to the conclusion that it would be best to call in a psychologist.

"I'll arrange it, don't worry," said Stefan. "Now there are a few other things we need to attend to," he said and turned toward the group. "Do we have anything to go on for the shootings on Blendas gata and Norra Hamngatan? Do we know anything in addition to the victims being shot with two different weapons? Any DNA evidence?"

Charlotte shook her head.

"I hardly need to mention that the media is pressing me for more information," said Stefan. "Have you read the papers this past week? Did you see all the strange sources they quoted? Chief Prosecutor Marianne Konttii is calling me once a day, and these aren't cheerful conversations, I'll tell you that." His brown eyes that usually looked focused appeared to have a layer of tiredness over them.

"As things are now we don't have anything that will hold up in court," said Greger. "We have to keep tracking a while longer before we can make a move," said Greger. "I just hope nothing else happens in the meantime!"

Mette Arrives and Verne Leaves

Mette's determined steps echoed as she walked into the house, and she thought the place felt deserted. During the time she'd stayed in Björn's apartment, she had felt safe in spite of the loneliness. She glanced at the paintings that hung in rows on the walls; portraits painted in dark colors of the entire Hildeng family, all the way back to the sixteen hundreds. "What a pompous bunch," thought Mette and started to walk up the broad stairs that led to her room. The silence was unpleasant and created a cold atmosphere in the house.

"Elsebeth's spirit is probably hanging over us," she thought and got the shivers. She opened the door to her room and stopped on the doorstep. What in hell was this? She stared at all the boxes there were spread out all over the room. She took a look into the carton that stood closest but didn't recognize any of the things there were in it. Who did these things belong to? She walked over to one of the closets and opened the door. Her clothes were gone. Instead of her dresses, blouses and skirts, shirts, jackets, and suits were hanging there. She rushed over to the large brown stained bureau

252

and pulled out the top drawer. Men's underwear and socks lay where her lingerie used to be. She stood in the middle of the room and looked around. All of her personal things were gone! Her framed photographs that used to hang on the wall! In the bathroom, there were only men's toilet articles. She felt anger build up inside of her. Every article she saw that wasn't hers made her heart beat faster. "Where the hell is Jon?" she thought. She walked over to the open door and listened, but everything was quiet. She left her room, closed the door and walked over to Olav's part of the house. Looking into his room, she could see that the computer screen on his table was dark. Then she walked back to her part of the house. Suddenly she heard happy, cheerful voices. Mette rushed ahead toward the stairs that led down to the hall. She stopped on the first step and tried to locate where the voices were coming from. They were in the salon! As she hurried down the stairs, the thick carpet muffled the sound of her high heels and she sneaked along the wall that led to the salon. If someone had asked why she was tip-toeing around in her own home, she wouldn't have been able to give them a reasonable explanation ... she just had a feeling. "But since my room looks the way it looks that feeling is not without a reason," she thought and could feel more anger brewing inside of her.

"Sit here," said Jon to Verne and pointed to one of the armchairs. "I want you to tell me how things went for you in Oslo. One short call a day didn't give me the whole picture. Was Robert helpful enough?"

Mette couldn't hear Verne's reply, but she knew that it was him. His voice couldn't be mistaken for anyone else's, she thought with irritation. In a flash, she realized who had taken over her room. "That does it ... I've had enough!" she thought and walked into the salon with clenched fists. She stopped in front of the armchairs.

"Who the hell gave you permission to take over my room?" hissed Mette. Some drops of saliva landed on Verne's shirt. He looked at her with raised eyebrows and the beginning of a smile twitched on his lips.

"Oh, how nice! Welcome home dear stepmother. I'm fine, thank you!" said Verne.

"Calm down Mette," interjected Jon when he saw her green eyes narrow and darken.

"I'm supposed to calm down? You must be out of your mind! I've been gone a few days and when I get home, Verne has moved into my room. Would you mind explaining to me how that happened?" she yelled and put her hands on her hips.

"Well, as you most likely already know, Verne is my son and as my son he has the right to come live with his father if he wants to … which I am of course both proud and happy about," said Jon and raised his voice.

"As if it weren't enough that you were unfaithful when I believed we were happiest, and then you refused to give me the chance to have children. And now you're sitting here, you bastard, posing with your son. Thank God I didn't have any kids with you, considering the lousy genes you deliver!" Mette spit out.

Just at that particular moment, Olav came into the room, walked over to Mette, and put his hand on her shoulder. She jumped, turned around, and became silent.

"Come with me, Mette, so you and I can have a talk," said Olav. "I have a few things I want to tell you." Olav put his arm around her shoulders and led her out of the room. Jon could hear her weeping and shrugged his shoulders.

"Don't worry about her tantrum. In a few hours everything will be back to usual again," said Jon and smiled at Verne.

"Don't worry, Dad. I know that you love me," said Verne and hugged him. "By the way, I have to drive into Gothenburg. I have a few things to attend to."

"Does it have to do with school?" asked Jon. "Or is it something I can help you with?"

"Another student has borrowed some of my books, and I need them for the exam the day after tomorrow," said Verne. "I'll probably be back late."

"Do you want me to arrange some dinner you can warm up when you get home?"

"No thanks, Dad. I'll eat out. It's simpler," said Verne. With those words, he left his new home. All the way into Gothenburg, he hummed the tune "Money makes the world go around" from the musical "Cabaret". Verne was in a wonderful mood when he swung his car into the parking area at Packhuskajen. He got out, looked around and caught sight of the people he was looking for. Ten minutes later he had one hundred thousand crowns in his pocket. He went back to his car and watched as the green Volvo left the parking lot. It was a done deal. Verne didn't have to pay back his new loan for a week. Now he could finally get rid of one debt, he thought with satisfaction. Another thought popped into his head simultaneously. If I gamble with this money, I can double the profit. Then I'll be free from debt in two directions. That shouldn't be much of a problem, thought Verne. He opened the car door and walked with determined steps toward the Casino. The very moment that Vern walked into the Casino, the green Volvo returned to the parking area.

While Verne was standing at the roulette table, Greger was talking with the trackers to get the latest information.

"Should we pick him up at the Casino?" asked one of the trackers.

"No, I think it's better that we wait. Something's going to happen for sure. He got money from someone out of Amir's gang. The license plates from the green Volvo are registered to a young woman who doesn't even have a driver's license, but we know that her brother is a Xantino's member," said Greger. "I'm sending one more car to follow the Volvo!"

The roulette ball bounced in the wheel, jumped down into slot fourteen, but bounced up again and finally landed in slot number thirteen. Verne breathed out, stretched his hands up in the air and cheered. He had succeeded in doubling his winnings in just three hours. "The game goddess is finally with me," he thought with satisfaction. "If I can double it, I can triple it," he thought victoriously. One more time he managed to win with number thirteen and the other players around the table groaned with displeasure. Suddenly, a man in a black suit walked up to the dealer and whispered something in his ear. Verne wasn't happy about the break in the game and wrinkled his forehead in a frown. After the conversation with the man in the suit, the dealer turned to the public, apologized and said that the table had to be closed temporarily. He directed them to the roulette table placed beside them. Verne could hardly believe what he was hearing.

"What the hell?" he said out loud and immediately felt a hand on his shoulder. The hand belonged to the man in the black suit.

"Could you please keep it down?" asked the man.

"Excuse me, but I got upset about the table being closed down with no warning," said Verne and took a step away from the man.

"But that doesn't prevent you from playing at one of the other tables," said the man and smiled.

Verne nodded and without looking around he walked slowly over to one of the tables positioned nearby. He convinced himself that since the game goddess was with him, it wouldn't matter what table he played at. She would, of course, be with him wherever he played at the Casino. He lost the first bet, felt discouraged, but then won the second and even the third. "Now I'm on a roll again," he thought and started to hum his favorite song.

The trackers sat in their car and tried to make themselves comfortable. The hours never went by as slowly as they did when on a tracking assignment, thought the man behind the wheel and struggled to keep his eyes open.

Verne's eyes were shiny and his face sweaty. In only two hours, he had lost over half of his win. He talked himself into believing that the chance of winning was still in the air. If he just won one more time, he would pull it off! He held his breath as the ball rolled around on the wheel. When it finally fell into slot number thirteen, he took a deep breath and got the adrenaline kick he needed. "Yes!!!" he thought. "Now I'm back in business! Nothing can stop me!" Verne doubled his bet and stood relaxed by the table. The ball rolled into slot number thirteen and adrenaline streamed through his body. "Life is fantastic," he thought. But the second after the ball bounced out of the slot and landed in the next one. Verne refused to see what he saw. It couldn't be true! There must have been something in slot thirteen, something that made the ball bounce up again! He leaned over the table and was immediately reprimanded by the dealer. Drops of sweat poured from his hairline and ran down over his forehead. Verne put his hand in his pants pocket, but there were no bills left. He put his hand in the other pocket, only to realize that it was just as empty. The dealer looked at him with sympathy and shook his head. He walked over to the bar and sat down on a chair.

257

The bartender came over, but Verne waved him away. He didn't even have money for a light beer. No matter what way he looked at it, there was only one solution to his problem, and that solution could give him the space that he so desperately needed. He would have to involve Kjell. And yet Kjell wouldn't have to know the whole truth, he thought. "I'll have to put some bait on the hook and hope that he bites," thought Verne to himself.

The sun had already been up two hours when Verne came out of the Casino at six in the morning with drooping shoulders and a hanging head. He took a few steps and looked around. There wasn't much traffic at this time of day, he thought and walked to his car. When he had five meters left to the car, the door to the green Volvo opened and a man climbed out. He walked toward Verne. At the same time, the trackers started the motor in their car, and raced toward Verne. Frozen to the spot, Verne stared at the black car that came toward him full speed. The man from the Volvo ran back and jumped into his car and burned rubber as he drove off. The trackers stopped their car one meter from Verne, looked at him, put their car in reverse and took off in the same direction as the Volvo. Verne just stood there and felt his heart's anxious beats. "What the hell was that?" he thought and walked unsteadily over to his car, hopped in and locked the doors. As he backed the car out of the parking lot, he looked nervously around. Driving in the direction of Tjörn, he kept looking into his rear view mirror as he tried to think about what he was going to do. Who was in the black car? Were they members of Heaven's Devils? The guys in the Volvo were with Xantinos, he knew that. Now that he had debts to both gangs his situation was not the best, and his hands got very sweaty as he held tightly onto the driver's wheel. Skit! Why did Lady Fortune abandon me? So fucking typical that this should happen now!

Verne turned off the highway toward Stora Höga. At the department store, he looked around for a good place to park the car. What he needed now was a few hours of sleep, then into the department store bathroom to freshen up and after that head full speed out to Gunneby, he thought with satisfaction. A truck was parked at the back of the store parking lot. He couldn't see the driver anywhere. Verne parked his car beside the truck to use it as camouflage so no one could see his car from the road. He adjusted the car seat into a more comfortable position and pulled his jacket up over his shoulders.

Suddenly someone knocked on the car window. Verne jumped and looked up sleepily at the face staring at him. A man smiled at him. Verne raised the seat up, turned the key, and pushed the button to bring the window down.

"Are you okay?" asked the man. I noticed that your car has been here for hours and just wanted to check to see if you were alright."

Verne looked at the clock mounted on the dashboard. It said eleven thirty-eight. Good god, he had slept for over five hours.

"Eh, my wife kicked me out," said Verne, cleared his throat and smiled at the man.

"Sure, skit happens," sighed the man. "Well, I just wanted to check up on you," he said and walked away.

Verne felt the foul taste in his mouth and opened the glove compartment to see if he could find some chewing gum or breath mints to improve it. He was surprised to find a wrinkled hundred crown bill there and got out of the car to walk into the department store. He found the men's room and washed his face. Then he sauntered into Adenmark's, let a stick of deodorant find its way into his pocket, and bought a tube of toothpaste as well as a toothbrush. After that, he had money left for a cup of coffee and a newspaper. That would take care of another hour. It was one forty-five when he decided that the time was right. The air in the car was stale, and it was hot as hell. The sun had been pouring down on the car, and Verne put the air conditioner on right away. As he drove out to Gunneby, he sat talking to himself. He was testing different tones of voice as he made up the story he planned to tell his brother. It was necessary to sound as convincing as possible so Kjell would take the bait, thought Verne.

Chief Coroner Sara Kronfeld

This particular morning Greger felt unusually perky when he stepped into his office. The night reports from the trackers lay on his desk, and he read them with increasing interest. Katarina joined up and started to read over his shoulder.

"What do you think?" asked Greger and leaned back in his chair.

"That Verne is in a hell of a mess," she answered and sat down across from Greger. "The question is how we can use this situation without putting Verne's life in danger? I'm wondering why he's driving out to Tjörn all of a sudden. According to the tracker, he's slept in his car at Stora Höga. It looks like he's on his way to say hello to his mother. Strange, especially since he just moved in with his new father in Strömstad."

"Yea, that was quite a turn of events," said Greger. "But then again, things happen when we least expect them to. By the way, we should have the DVD from the lawyer today. It'll be interesting to see and hear the whole contents of Arne Hildeng's last will and testament. Who knows, maybe it will let in a little light in our otherwise very gray sky."

"Yesterday I was with Matthias and noticed a change. He wants to come back to work," said Katarina abruptly. "Maybe the psychologist that Stefan sent has managed a shift. What do you say? Do you think he's up to it?"

"I'm not the right person to make that decision. Since Stefan is in touch with the psychologist, he's the one who decides whether or not Matthias is ready. Strange that Stefan hasn't walked in yet when we're talking about him. He's done that the last few times," said Greger boasting and raised his ringing cell phone to his ear. The bushy eyebrows raised during the conversation. He said "Uhuh, uhuh," and nodded. Katarina sat waiting expectantly to find out who he was talking to.

"Well, who was it?"

"Sara Kronfeld. She wants to see us. It's about your Black Pete that was found on Packhuskajen. They've got an answer about the amphetamine that was found in the body. People from Narcotics are on their way too."

Thirty minutes later everyone stood waiting for Sara Kronfeld in the meeting room at Forensics. Suddenly they heard steps approaching from the corridor outside. Sara came into the room walking briskly and looked resolute. She nodded quickly at Greger and Katarina when she went past their chairs. Walking to the short end of the table, she put down a whole pile of notebooks, put on her eyeglasses and finally looked up at the whole group.

"Thanks so much to all of you for getting here on such short notice. As you already know, for this particular case we've used the LC-MS technique. First we did a screening analysis of the sample that we managed to get from the badly burned body. Since the screening yielded a positive result, we were able to determine the type of amphetamine. We now know where it's been found earlier. The same type of amphetamine was discovered in the body that floated ashore near the Stena Line wharf. That body was identified as Hasan Al Mani, a political refugee from Palestine," said Sara and looked at Greger.

"I remember him," he said. "He was only nineteen years old and had come to Sweden six months earlier. Unfortunately, we had no records for him. Through the Migration Agency, we found out that he had arrived in Gothenburg together with another gang of Palestinians. They all just stood there one day at the entrance to Streteredsvägen in Kållered and were seeking asylum. Not one of them had any documents to prove who they were. That they had been brought here by traffickers was obvious, but we couldn't get any of them to tell us the truth. Six months later, Hasan Al Mani's body showed up at Masthuggskajen," said Greger and snorted.

"Since there were no indications that Hasan had been an addict, our first reaction was that he had committed suicide, but perhaps we need to re-think that," said Sara and gave her husband,

Chief Super Intendant Stefan a questioning look.

"Well, perhaps it's worth more analysis," said Stefan. "Hasan could have actually bought the amphetamine in order to take his life, but we should look more closely at this. We have to get our hands on Heaven's Devils and Xantinos, make some searches and find the evidence that we so desperately need. But it depends on how alert our colleagues are," he said and looking at Greger.

Greger squirmed in his chair and cleared his throat.

"Speaking of colleagues, I can share some good news. One of our employees whose had a tough time of it lately is coming back tomorrow. Matthias Brodd returns to his position as head of the Special Investigations Department," said Stefan and looked at Katarina with a smile.

She nodded and looked victoriously at Greger. Finally, thought Katarina. Her last meeting with Stefan had hinted that this could be possible, but she hadn't dared hope that it would be this soon. Her heart jumped for joy when she thought about Matthias. Maybe now they could get closer again. The distance between them had become greater than what she could have ever imagined. Since she didn't have any brothers or sisters, she didn't know what it felt like to lose one. The deepest grief she had known was when her husband Lennart died of cancer and shortly thereafter her mother. Those experiences had ripped her heart apart, but in time the grief faded. Matthias was at the beginning of his grieving. The family had chosen to have a private funeral for Agneta and Katarina was the only person outside of the family who had attended. The thought that gave Katarina comfort was the Matthias had quickly received professional help, and it seemed to have been effective.

Verne Visits Gunneby

When Andrea opened the door and saw a smiling Verne standing at her doorstep, a lot of different emotions raced through her mind. Verne and his first words, his first shaky steps, when he learned to ride a bicycle, and his happy laughter when he finally managed to stay afloat in the water. All these sequences fast forwarded before her eyes. But even though Andrea felt love towards Verne, she also was also afraid of her son.

"Hi Mom, can I come in?"

"Verne! Of course, come in!"

Andrea took a step backwards and left room for him to step in. She didn't dare stay in the hall and instead walked briskly out onto the veranda. Björn looked up from the grill and when he saw Verne he squeezed out a smile.

"We're going to eat in a minute. Would you like to stay and have dinner with us?" said Andrea wringing her hands nervously.

"Absolutely," answered Verne. "Where are Kjell and Isabell? Are they coming too?"

"Yes, they are on their way. Kjell and Isabell have been at Liseberg* today and they also saw Universeum** since they were in the vicinity," said Andrea and could hear how nervous her voice sounded.

"Will you be spending the night?" asked Björn. "In that case you can have a beer. There are some cold ones in the refrigerator!"

Verne nodded and started walking in the direction of the veranda doors. Andrea stopped him with her hand.

"Stay out here on the veranda. I'm going to get some plates anyway and can take your beer out with me," she said and hurried off.

"Boy, Mom sure is nervous," said Verne and sat down in a chair that was close to the grill.

"Yea, and you have no idea why," said Björn. Flakes of charcoal swirled in the air when he used barbecue tongs to grab one of the pork fillets.

"That's history now! I got a new Dad and I think Mom made a good choice," said Verne and put his legs up on the table.

"No feet near the food, please," said Björn and shoved Verne's feet from the table. "Even though the table isn't set,

---

* Liseberg is an amusement park located in Gothenburg, Sweden, that opened in 1923. It is one of the most visited amusement parks in Scandinavia. The park itself has been chosen as one of the top ten amusement parks in the world by Forbes magazine.

** Universeum is a public science museum in Gothenburg, Sweden that opened in 2001. Universeum is divided into six sections, each containing experiment workshops and a collection of reptiles, fish and insects. Universeum occasionally gives Swedish secondary school students a chance to debate with Nobel prize-winners and professors.

266

this is the table we're going to eat on and I don't want to see any of your footprints there!"

Verne smiled broadly at Björn. At the moment, nothing could disturb his good mood. He was convinced that Kjell would back him up. But he would have to handle things in a smart and clever way.

"Sorry Björn, that was careless of me," said Verne and brushed the table off with his hand.

Björn grunted but didn't say anything. There was something about Verne's manner that didn't jibe; his good mood, for example. He was usually always sullen and whiny. Did the fact that he now knew Jon was his father change him? Or was it the thought of getting a share of the Pharmacy Chain that attracted him? Most likely the latter, thought Björn. They heard voices and Andrea came out on the veranda together with Kjell and Isabell.

"Hi, Bro!" said Verne, got up and gave Kjell a pat on the shoulder and hugged Isabell. "I came by to see how things are. Mom invited me for dinner. It looks like it's going to be delicious!"

Kjell had been warned by Andrea that Verne was sitting on the veranda and it was with mixed feelings that he met his brother.

"I got a call from Robert in Oslo. You spent a few days there," said Kjell and sat down in the hammock. Isabell hurried over to sit beside Kjell and spread out so that Verne would have no room to sit. Caught off guard by her gesture, he pulled over a chair and put it beside the hammock on Kjell's side.

"Really? And what did good old Robert have to say? I just went there to learn a little more about the company, which I also have a share of these days. It was very interesting," said Verne and poured his beer into a glass.

267

"Why was it that you wanted to learn everything about distribution? I would have thought that the Economy Department would have been more along your line of interest, in view of your education," said Kjell.

"Actually, the Distribution Department has to do with economy. It's about what goes to waste."

"What waste? I've never heard anything about that," said Kjell and raised his eyebrows in surprise. "Dad always used to say that they had a water-tight system. Spot checks for the personnel, never the same routines for the drivers, everything has run perfectly as far as I know," said Kjell.

"They've become more sloppy," said Verne. "I could see several holes in the system. This is what I thought you and I could talk about.

By putting the emphasis on "you and I", Verne hoped that the rest of the family would understand that this was something he wanted to talk with Kjell about *alone.*

"No problem! Of course, we should eat and enjoy our dinner first! Never talk business at the food table, that's rude," said Verne and grinned at Björn.

"Do you think that we'll make it without getting rained on?" asked Andrea and walked over to Björn. "It looks threatening." She looked out over the fields and to the west lay dark clouds approaching.

"I don't think it will rain until later this evening," said Björn. "I hope we get lots! The garden needs a real soaking!"

The conversation during the meal was somewhat stilted. Andrea talked about her petunias that she had in pots on the veranda, and about the elderberry blossoms that she wouldn't find time to make juice of this year either. Isabell said uh huh and nodded at appropriate times. Verne ate quite a lot and tried to joke with Kjell. Björn thought the whole thing was bad theatre and kept wondering what the real reason was for Verne's visit and his exaggerated pleasant manner. When Verne offered to help with the dishes after they had eaten, Björn pushed him out of the kitchen saying that enough was enough and act the way you usually do so we can all relax. Verne had left laughing and gone back to the others on the veranda.

"I'd like to take a walk with you," said Verne and turned toward Kjell. "You don't need to worry Isabell. I'll have him back within an hour!"

Isabell smiled toward Verne, but she was actually angry inside. There was something about Verne that irritated her. His whole behavior was artificial and slippery. And she had heard that people who have a gambling addiction would do anything to get ahold of money for their gambling, and that worried her too. Isabel shook her head and tried to think in more positive directions. She would simply have to trust that Kjell stood firmly with two feet on the ground and that he wouldn't allow himself to be fooled by Verne.

The two brothers walked along the paths that led away from the house and down to one of the few bus stops in the area. Neither of them noticed the bird songs, the smell of the woods, nor the dark clouds building up on the horizon to warn of bad eather. At one point, Verne was about to put his arm around Kjell in order to emphasize his good intentions, but stopped himself at the last minute. He noticed that Kjell was already suspicious and that would simply have strengthened his suspicions.

"Well, what do you think about my idea?" asked Verne.

"I don't really know how it could be carried out," said Kjell. "Robert thought your suggestions were too hasty, not well thought through, and totally confused, as he put it."

"Oh, really? So that's what he thought? What did he base his conclusions on?" asked Verne and cheered to himself. Everything was going according to plan!

"Robert can't understand how you can disapprove of the distribution. Nothing has happened in thirty years, they update the procedures continuously, and he feels safe with the security system," said Kjell. "By the way, are you thinking of starting to work for the company in Oslo?"

"Maybe. I think the branch is very interesting. It's probably not going to be long before Sweden lets go of its pharmaceutical monopoly and we'll need to be prepared when that day comes."

Kjell was surprised about his brother's interest in the company. During all the years that they thought they had the same father, Verne had never shown any interest in it. Now, all of a sudden, he was acting as though he wanted to be head of the company and run it in his own way. Was this due to Jon, together with Mette, having the largest number of shares? If they decided that Verne should run the company, he wouldn't have much to say about it with the smaller amount of shares that he owned. Should he perhaps ask to buy Mette's shares, without first mentioning it to Jon or Verne? Would that work?

"Are you listening to me?"asked Verne, raising his voice.

"Of course I'm listening," said Kjell, without knowing what Verne had just said.

"Good. Then maybe you could do me the favor of talking with Mette. Find out how she feels about selling her shares. You don't need to say that I'm the one who's going to buy them. Say that I t's you who wants them," said Verne and flashed a large, toothy grin. Kjell nodded. For the first time during their conversation, he felt as though he had the upper hand and grinned back at his brother's cunning smile.

"Great, Bro! Now I'd love a beer. Shall we walk back home

again? It's going to rain and then it would be nice to be back indoors," said Verne.

Isabell was happy to see them walk back up the path to the house, especially since Kjell seemed to be relaxed and in a good mood. Maybe the conversation with Verne hadn't been as serious as she first thought. And Andrea was happy that her sons seemed to be having a good time together. She welcomed them with open arms and gave each one a hug. The only one who didn't buy the brotherly love was Björn. But he maintained a positive appearance, mostly for Andrea's sake. He wanted her to feel good. There hadn't been much happiness in the family for a long while he thought as he walked into the kitchen to get some cold beers. The first drops of rain fell on Andrea's face when she got out the rain cover for the hammock. Just a few minutes later, raindrops pattered on the roof. Now and then, the dark skies were lit up by lightning followed by thunder. They lit some candles and put the candlesticks on the table in the living room. By the light of these candles, the persons sitting around the table seemed to be enjoying each other's company.

The Raid Is On

In a wooded area just outside of Biskopsgården, Katarina and Matthias waited in a black van along with two other persons for the signal. Rain pounded down on the roof of the car and having a conversation under those circumstances was difficult. In the weak light from the dashboard, Katarina could see Mattias clenching his jaws. She could also hear the sound of grinding teeth. They had still not gotten close again to talk openly about Agneta's and her unborn child's death. All focus had been on the operation that they were now waiting to start.

Police intelligence had gathered information, and that had then crystallized into four groups. Katarina glanced out through the window pane and saw that the weather was, for once, on their side. The sky was dark gray and the wind tore through the tree tops. The bulletproof vest that Katarina wore was uncomfortable, and she groaned softly. Their van was parked about one hundred meters from the target area and tension levels in the van rose steadily the closer the clock got to the designated time for the raid. According to what had been discovered, this farm was owned by Xantinos and was

272

their hiding place for a weapons arsenal. The farm lay in an isolated location and was owned by a man who was a resident at Lillekärr's home for the elderly. According to the doctor they had spoken with, that man had become senile three years ago and had no relatives. They had learned about the farm thanks to someone who had tipped them off. If everything went according to their planning, they would seize the five men guarding the weapons on the outside. After that, the remaining eight persons inside the house would be overpowered and removed of their weapons. The other three groups would attack simultaneously at different addresses spread out through Bohuslän. Chief Prosecutor Marianne Konttii had been informed, and everyone was looking forward to obtaining crucial evidence that could knock down any of the defense lawyers' arguments for their clients.

The first thing that came towards Katarina and Matthias when they ran in the direction of the house was the smell of gunpowder. About twenty shots had been fired, but to their surprise there were only two members of the gang inside the house, both with handcuffs on and broad smiles decorating their heavily tattooed faces.

"Where are the others?" asked Matthias and walked over to one of the men.

"What others? Have you got bad eyesight? Do you see any more than two of us here?" answered the man and spit down in front of Matthias feet.

"Take them to the Police Station and let them have nice, cozy separate cells there," said Matthias. "In the meantime we'll have a look around at your nice place!"

"Go ahead!" hissed the other one as he was being led away by one of the policemen.

"I've sent people out to the barn and the rest of us will take the main building," said Charlotte who had arrived already dressed in her protective clothing. "It'll be interesting to see what we find!"

"We're driving to the Station and meet the others. But they didn't get that many either, oddly enough," said Matthias. "Altogether we have seven people instead of the thirty we had anticipated. Strange," he said and rubbed his chin.

"Can someone have warned them?" asked Katarina.

"Sure, and the next question is who? I trust everyone in my troop one hundred percent. But it's always difficult to get everyone to keep their mouth shut when we are such a large group involved in a raid," he muttered. "To hell with it; we'll have to do the best we can with what we have. One of these bastard gang members might make a mistake and then I will put the son of a bitch away for eternity," said Matthias.

Katarina was surprised to hear the rancor in Matthias' voice. Never before had she heard him be so filled with hate. When one of the gang members spit on his feet, she had held her breath for fear of what might happen. Then he had kept cool and professional, but now it seemed as though anger was taking the upper hand. Katarina didn't dare to protest and just nodded at him. They left the house and trotted in the direction of the van. The wind and the rain tore at their clothes. Halfway to the van one of the forensic technicians called to Matthias.

"Can you come in here for a minute?" he yelled in the wind and stood waving them over to the entrance of the barn. Matthias and Katarina hurried back and both felt increasing excitement. What had the technicians found? They stepped in and saw rigged spotlights that cast strange shadows over the rotten planks holding up the rickety barn. There was a mini-excavator on the middle of the cement floor. Matthias walked over and inspected the machine.

"This looks like it's been used recently. Do you think they've rented it or stolen it?"

Katarina followed one of the other technicians who pointed at a cement mixer and piles of sacks with mortar as well as several empty sacks that lay spread out on the floor.

"I doubt that anyone from this gang is studying to become a farmer. Looks more like it's going to be used for new crimes of some sort," said Katarina.

"Dig up the whole goddamn garden! Every millimeter of the house needs to be examined! There is something or someone buried here," said Matthias with a hard voice. "We're going back now, but can be reached on our cell phones at any time in case something interesting shows up."

With those words, he stepped out of the barn closely followed by Katarina. She was pondering over how she could get Greger alone without Matthias suspecting anything. The happiness over Matthias being back had been exchanged for fear. His behavior had changed, and it wasn't for the better. Maybe he had come back to work too soon? It seemed as though the grief over Agneta's death had been exchanged for limitless hate toward the possible offenders. That could result in almost anything if they succeeded in arresting the right people, thought Katarina as she sat own in the van beside Matthias.

The assignment room, which normally held about twenty-five people, had suddenly filled with double that many. Stefan Kronfeld stood by the short end of the table and to his right sat Greger. Katarina walked into the room and realized that the conversation with Greger would have to wait. She went to stand by the window closest to the whiteboard. On the way there she'd managed to step on two person's toes and spill some drops from the coffee cup she was holding in her right hand. A few of those drops landed on a pair of shoes belonging to Pelle from the National Criminal Police. He smiled at her, and she smiled apologetically back.

"Well, these were meager results," growled Stefan, after having welcomed everyone. "Where did this go wrong? Does anyone here have a decent explanation? We had hoped to arrest at least thirty people, and all we got were a lousy seven. Do I need to say that their lawyers are already banging on my door? So what happened?" asked Stefan, sticking his hands into his pants pockets and rocking his lanky body back and forth.

"We had received information that Hazim and his gang would be at their farm in Utby. We judged the source to be reliable, but when we got there, we only found one person in the house. He lay snoring in a sofa. My men had to shake him to wake him up. We still don't know what he'd taken to sleep that deeply, but all the necessary tests have been taken," said Håkan Pedersén, head of the Narcotics Division, and responsible for one of the four groups that had participated in the raid.

"Does anyone know what the technicians found or if they found anything of value?" asked Greger. "How did the house searches go?"

"Everything seemed as though it had been cleaned recently if you ask me," said one member of the SI group. We were in Uddevalla and it seemed as though they had hired a whole cleaning patrol. I don't even have it that clean at home!"

"At least we've left Xantino's farm looking like a place where they test missiles!" said Matthias.

Katarina listened to his voice and thought it sounded metallic and impersonal. But the distance between them prevented her from seeing his facial expression.

"Really? What made you take that decision?" asked Stefan.

"The number of machines and other tools that were in the run down barn! A mini-excavator stood right in the middle of the floor and seemed to have been used recently," said Matthias. "And there were sacks of mortar piled up beside a cement mixer, as well as empty sacks spread out over the floor."

"Then it will take several days before we'll know if there is anything of interest on that farm," muttered Stefan. "I think we can say that we have a disaster on our hands. The press is going to love this! And Chief Prosecutor Konttii is going to be pissed off for several days. What the rest of us are thinking and feeling we can just keep to ourselves," said Stefan as he gave everyone a short nod and then left the room.

Katarina tried to get over to Greger, but it seemed impossible. People from different divisions were practically standing in line just to exchange a few words with him. Even Matthias was hanging over Greger's shoulder. She decided to write her report and then go home. There wasn't any point in doing more. The few hours of the night that remained she might as well spend in her bed. Tomorrow is another day, as Christer Björkman sang in the Melody Festival, thought Katarina, but she couldn't remember what year. Pretty good song she mumbled and went to her room.

A Truck with Pharmaceuticals Disappears

Two days after the failed raid, Stefan Kronfeld walked into Greger's room. This was not usual procedure and he looked up at Stefan in surprise. It was more common for Stefan to call and with a few words order personnel to come to his office. Charlotte called at the same time and wanted Greger to come over to her room. At one of the gang's farms, they had found some interesting objects. During Greger's conversation with Charlotte, Stefan sat down in the chair in front of his desk.

"Has anything of interest come up for this investigation?" asked Stefan.

"If you're referring to my conversation with Charlotte, I don't know yet. But anything that we find is of interest at this point," said Greger. "What can I do for you?"

"I wanted to ask what you thought of Matthias' performance during the last raid," said Stefan clearing his throat.

"Something wrong?" asked Greger.

"Yes and no. Katarina has spoken with me, and I also wanted to hear your point of view," said Stefan.

"Isn't he going to the psychologist anymore?"

"Yes, but it's only a matter of time before his treatment is considered complete; that is if we should rely on what the psychologist is saying," said Stefan.

"I don't understand why Katarina went to you and not to me," said Greger and felt disappointed. "She usually talks with me about most things."

"She tried to directly after the raid in the assignment room, but there were so many people around you that there was no opportunity to ask the questions she wanted an answer to," said Stefan.

"I don't know if I'm the right person to answer your question," said Greger. "During the meeting he was alert and seemed to have things under control. His presentation about what his group had succeeded and not succeeded with I can't complain about. The only thing, if it's a problem, was that his expression was apathetic when he talked about the raid. Matthias usually makes a lot of jokes, even when he is being professional."

"Have you seen him like this before? I mean, before this happened with his sister?" asked Stefan.

Greger became quiet as he thought. He didn't want to say anything that might jeopardize Matthias' job. He knew that Matthias was a skilled police officer. And police officers are human beings with the same strengths and weaknesses as any other line of work, thought Greger. That Matthias could ever jeopardize his colleague's lives was something he couldn't imagine. Of course, Matthias had been depressed and out of form a while, but who wouldn't be after surviving a bomb explosion?

"No, I can't see anything that would require Matthias to be taken off duty," said Greger and looked Stefan in the eyes.

"Okay, that's good Greger. That was all I wanted to hear,"

said Stefan and got up to leave the room.

Fifteen minutes later Greger was in Charlotte's room. After a kiss and a hug, they stood leaning over two photographs of objects that confused both of them.

"A white shirt button and a plain gold earring," said Greger and looked at Charlotte with an expression that said, what the heck is this?

"We found blood on the button, and there were remains of skin on the earring. We've sent it all away for analysis," said Charlotte.

"Where was this found?" asked Greger and pointed to one of the photos.

"Both objects were found on the farm at Utby. They were wrapped up in a dishtowel and were found in a hole well hidden behind a board in the house."

"Why would someone hide a shirt button and an earring? That seems strange," said Greger. "We'll have to hope that the analysis tells us who they belong to. If the samples were enough for a DNA test, that is."

"Sara Kronfeld was convinced that they were good enough. So all we can do now is keep our fingers crossed," said Charlotte. "How are things with Matthias and Katarina, by the way?"

"Before I came over to you, I had a visit from Stefan, and he was concerned about Matthias. But I think he'll feel better working than sitting home alone with his thoughts.

"I remember what it was like when I was attacked with a knife by that young, crazy woman in my apartment," said Charlotte and a shiver went through her body as she remembered what happened. "What a stroke of luck that you came earlier than expected. And even luckier that you'd forgotten to return your service weapon and could use it to save my life. After that scare, I was happy to come back to work.

It helped me forget and it was easier to process what had happened together with my workmates," she said and gave Greger a kiss on the mouth.

"But I don't know how things are with Katarina. Apparently she had wanted to talk to me about Matthias right after the raid, but I wasn't available. So she went to Stefan instead," said Greger.

"When you see her, can't you invite them both home for dinner over the weekend?" suggested Charlotte. "We might be able to all have a calm weekend together for once. Ask her anyway."

"Yes, I will. Sometimes a change of scenery is all that's needed to get back into harmony with one's mind," said Greger. He lit up at the thought of a good dinner and a nice wine to go along with the meal.

When Greger got back to his room, Katarina was sitting on a chair waiting for him.

"Why didn't you call and let me know that you were sitting here waiting?" asked Greger.

"It's not that important. I just thought we could work on what's happened in Oslo," said Katarina. "It might have ramifications for us."

"What do you mean Oslo? What's happened there?" Greger remained standing in the door opening, and his eyebrows jumped up and down.

"We found out about it an hour ago. A truck went into a skid, couldn't straighten out the trailer and went over. It happened last night. When the ambulance came to the scene, the driver had disappeared. Police were sent out to search the woods in the area, but they couldn't find him.

Here's the interesting part. The truck was stolen and contained large amounts of narcotic medicines. The value of what has been stolen, in the wrong hands is valued up to ten million crowns," said Katarina. "And not only that; the truck belonged to the German wholesale company Celecia and was on its way to guess who?"

"To Hildeng's pharmaceutical warehouse," said Greger.

Katarina nodded.

"And besides the wrecked truck another truck is missing," she said. "The company drivers were found drugged and tied up behind a rest area. Both have been taken to the State Hospital in Oslo, and the police have promised to get in touch with us as soon as they know more."

"Do we know where Verne was during that time?" asked Greger.

"As far as we know he was and still is with his mother on Tjörn in Gunneby," answered Katarina.

"Has someone contacted Jon Hildeng and told him what's happened?"

"Yes, he's been told and the police in Oslo asked us to get in touch with him personally," said Katarina. "From what I understand, Jon was very upset and irritated when the Norwegian police asked if this could be an insider job."

"What indicated that the job could have come from the inside?" asked Greger.

"The trucks were unmarked; nothing on the outside reveals their cargo," said Katarina. "The truck that turned over was covered with a yellow tarp, and the one that's missing was driving covered. That's why it would be difficult for someone on the outside to know that just these two trucks were carrying narcotics in their cargo."

""It's time to bring in that rascal Verne Hildeng again," said Greger. "I don't believe in coincidences! He has to have been involved. We just have to get that shrewd bastard to make a slip of the tongue."

"Boy are you worked up!" said Katarina and laughed. "I'll

send Leif Griffén and Annika Thorsson to Tjörn. There's no point in calling in advance; that would forewarn Verne. Jon has probably called him already and told him about what's happened with the trucks in Oslo. Verne might be feeling safe in believing that he has a water tight alibi, but that could work to our advantage."

"I'm going to really enjoy showing photos where Verne is the main subject," said Greger."By the way, Charlotte had a question for you and Matthias. She wants you both to come over to our place for dinner this weekend, watch a beautiful sunset, and just relax. You can stay in the guest room! What do you say? Doesn't that sound like something you both need?"

"Something we both need? Yes, of course! The question is just whether or not it's possible. It'll depend on what happens with these trucks and whether or not we can get Verne to start cooperating with us," said Katarina. "And that's the part I don't have much faith in."

"Well, ask Matthias anyway. This might be just what he needs to be able to move on. How long has it been since the two of you have been alone?"

"We've been alone but haven't talked about Agneta's and the baby's death," answered Katarina. "I haven't dared to talk about it, and Matthias hasn't brought it up either."

"For our sake, ask if he'll come over this weekend. The worst thing that could happen is that he'll say no," said Greger, tilting his head to the side.

"Okay, I'll ask. But now we have to deal with Oslo and Verne," said Katarina. "I'll call Leif. We'll see what happens when they get back from Tjörn; hopefully they'll have Verne Hildeng with them," said Katarina.

Verne Gets a Visit from the Police

It was hard for Björn to conceal his smug expression as he accompanied Leif and Annika out onto the veranda and asked Verne to welcome his new guests. Kjell and Isabell stared at them in surprise. Verne glided along with a nonchalant attitude before looking up and recognizing them. The second he realized who it was he stiffened.

"We just want to talk about what happened in Oslo," said Leif and smiled at him, hoping Verne would relax.

Verne's mind was racing. He hadn't revealed the entire contents of the conversation he'd had with Jon in the morning. His explanation for being upset after the call was to say that something had happened with the trucks that were supposed to deliver medicine to the company's warehouse. The most important thing was that no one had been hurt. This was the moment he had prepared for. The police couldn't have made their entrance at a better time.

"What happened in Oslo?" asked Verne looking wide-eyed at them.

Annika wondered why he was pretending that he didn't

know? Was there some reason for this lousy performance?

"Haven't you spoken with Jon Hildeng?" asked Leif. "According to our information, he's called you. Or are you just making this up?"

"Excuse me? What are you implying by saying that?" snorted Verne. "Would you be good enough to speak plain Swedish?"

"I think you understand what I mean, and if you don't maybe you'd rather come with us to the police station and have someone explain it to you," said Leif with a voice that sounded like a low growl.

"No, that's not at all necessary. What I've been told is that two trucks carrying medicine have been hijacked and that they were on their way to our warehouse in Oslo," said Verne.

"Hijacked?" said Kjell joining the conversation. He had been standing off to the side, listening. He was surprised when he heard the word "hijacked" all of a sudden. Verne hadn't said anything about that before. Why had he hidden it?

"Are you Kjell Hildeng?" asked Annika and took a step forward.

He nodded.

"Are you also one of the pharmacy chain owners?" asked Leif. Kjell nodded again.

"Not a majority owner, but I'm very well acquainted with how the company is run. Our father, uh, Arne Holding, has been my mentor for the company the last five years. How did this happen? The hijacking I mean," asked Kjell.

"That's exactly what we want to know," said Leif. "That's why we'd like to exchange a few words with your brother."

"But he's only been in Oslo for four days," said Kjell. "Verne can hardly know how the company is run. It's better that you talk with me."

For each passing minute during the conversation between

the police and Kjell, Verne's confidence grew. He thought that his plan had so far truly been a stroke of genius.

"That's great," said Leif. "Can you come along with us to the station or can we sit down here somewhere and speak privately?" asked Leif.

"You can sit in the living room," said Andrea and showed the way. She felt confused. It wasn't because she had any idea about the ways Arne and Jon had split up the work load within the company. During the past twenty years, she'd been busy working as a lawyer and had neither had the time nor interest in getting involved with the company's business. When Arne had said about five years ago that he planned to let Kjell take over his share of the company, she had shrugged her shoulders and wished them luck. That Verne hadn't been present during that conversation was - she had assumed - his own choice. She thought that he simply wasn't interested in the company.

"I'd also like to participate in the dialogue," said Verne. "These days I have a little more influence in the company. Besides, I'd like to learn more; if that's okay with you Kjelle?" Kjell looked at his brother with raised eyebrows.

"Of course you should join us, if nothing else, as Jon's representative."

Björn longed to be transformed into a small fly on the flowery wallpaper in the living room. He watched them as they walked off and sighed.

"Why am I hearing you sigh and seeing longing in your eyes?" asked Andrea. "Have you started to idolize the police? Or a particular police officer?"

Björn chuckled, put his arm around Andrea's shoulders and walked back out to the veranda.

"We shouldn't let Isabell sit out there all alone," said Björn. "That's not polite."

286

Leif Griffén watched Verne while Annika asked Kjell questions about the company's security procedures. He thought that Verne looked far too pleased. Not upset, not bothered, but way the hell too pleased!

"How is it that you chose distribution and not the economy department?" asked Leif after Kjell had talked about Verne's four days together with Robert in Oslo.

"I had to start somewhere, so why not there?" answered Verne as his swept his tongue over his dry lips.

"Weren't the trucks on their way to that department when they were hijacked?" asked Leif.

"Yes, but there are only a few who know what time they should arrive and one of those persons is Robert, who has worked for us for fifteen years," said Kjell. We have complete confidence in him. Anyone who works with our medicines classed as narcotics has gone through a security check."

"But according to what Kjell just told us, you weren't satisfied with the security and pointed out changes for Robert. What was it that you thought was dissatisfactory?" asked Annika.

"It's a little difficult to go into details, but I'm convinced that if the changes I had pointed out had been carried through, this would never have happened," said Verne and stretched out.

Kjell looked at his brother and Leif could see traces of irritation in his eyes.

"Why do you think the hijacking was an insider job?" asked Kjell.

"We haven't made any conclusions that it was an insider job. We're continuing to investigate without preconceived notions and are keeping all doors open," said Leif.

"I should hope so," snorted Verne. "By the way, if this could be an insider job, why couldn't it just as well be someone from the German wholesale company?"

"Like I said, we're interrogating everyone who is involved and hope to find out who's responsible, whether it's one person or several," said Leif. It didn't seem as though they would get any more information for the time being. Leif nodded to Annika, and she got up to thank them, handing over her business card at the same time.

"We'll be in touch when we know more about the case," she said.

Kjell and Verne remained sitting alone in the living room after Leif and Annika had left. Kjell had become very angry with his brother during the conversation with the police. Sometimes Verne had an attitude that could irritate the hell out of anyone, he thought. Such as the way he sat ridiculing their questions in such a nonchalant way.

"I think I'm going to try and get in touch with Mette," said Kjell. "If she is willing to let me buy her shares, I'll get in touch with you. Isabell and I have planned to stay a few weeks at the house in Hovås before we start looking for something of our own," he concluded and walked out onto the veranda. He had the feeling he'd explode if he stayed one more second in that room with Verne. He and Isabell hadn't actually planned to stay at the house in Hovås. That just flew into his head the same moment the words came out of his mouth. Kjell walked quickly over to Isabell, who was sitting in the hammock together with Björn.

"We'll be right back," said Kjell.

An hour later they stood beside their car and hugged Andrea. Björn was waving good-bye to them, and Verne stood beside him.

"Phone me if there is anything you need," called Andrea after them as the car drove out of the driveway.

"I'm going to leave now, too," said Verne giving Björn a big grin. He hugged Andrea and walked away.

"Well, now it's just you and me," said Björn with a sigh of relief as he watched the rear of Verne's car disappear around the corner.

"Now you are sighing again," said Andrea. "Is Leif Griffén the object of your sighing?"

"Absolutely not," said Björn, pretending to have hurt feelings. "What kind of a person do you think I am? That I make a pass at any man just because he is big, handsome and muscular?"

Björn laughed out loud at Andrea's agonized expression and gently patted her on the shoulder.

"Let's just say to heck with all problems, pain-in-the-ass kids, whining parents and have a nice, comfortable evening at home. I can drive to Stenungsund and rent some movies," said Andrea. "While I'm gone you can make dinner. Whatever you make is always a delicious surprise when it's your own recipes."

Björn turned right around, walked into the kitchen and came back out with Astrid's apron on. He had wrapped it twice around his thin body and danced a pirouette in front of Andrea.

"Well, what are you waiting for? Drive off and rent the movies!" said Björn and blew kisses to her while walking backward into the kitchen.

Andrea laughed and felt playful and happy for the first time that day. And it was all thanks to her dear brother.

At the House in Hovås

The stale smell of used, dirty stockings greeted Isabell and Kjell when they opened the door to the house in Hovås.

"We'll open the windows on the upper floor and the balcony doors, so it will only take a few hours for this to ventilate," said Kjell.

While Isabell walked around the house opening windows, Kjell took the chance to call Mette.

"Hi, Mette! I should have called before, but you know how it is," said Kjell.

"Oh, hi Kjell! I'm so glad that you called," said Mette, feeling genuinely happy. She had thought of calling Andrea or Kjell several times since she'd come home to Strömstad and been confronted with the scene there but had never gotten around to it. "I'm sure you've heard the news," said Mette. "I just want you to know that I'm not at all angry with Andrea. There's another person whom my anger and disappointment are directed toward and I'm sure you can guess who that person is."

"Yes, I can," said Kjell. "It's amazing how quickly one's

life can change. I understand that your situation must be uncomfortable and wondered if you want to change your environment a few days? We want you to come and have dinner with us this weekend and spend the night? Would you like to and do you have the time?"

"Would I like to? Nothing could be better! I'm looking for a new home right now and could use a change of scene along with a good dinner."

"Are you going to move?" wondered Kjell. He didn't dare ask if she had filed for a divorce from Jon. That was too private a question.

"Actually, both Olav and I are getting new places," said Mette and laughed a little. "I'll tell you more when we get together. What time would you like me to come on Saturday?"

"Come at six p.m.," said Kjell.

"Okay! I'm looking forward to it!" said Mette. "Say hi to Isabell!"

"What a beautiful home you have, and it's so big," said Isabell when she met Kjell in the salon. "Have you lived here your whole life?"

"Yes, if you don't include the years in the USA. We're very unusual as a several generation family, living in the same house. But since the house is divided up into several apartments with doors in between, it never feels as though we are crowded. Everyone has their own private section," said Kjell. The house was built at the end of the 1800's and then rebuilt a few times after that." He looked longingly at his future wife. Isabell stood with her back to one of the panorama windows. The sunlight came in through the window and swept over her like a thin, delicate veil. Around her face and tousled blonde hair lay a silvery shimmer. Something shot through his body and tears pushed their way out through his eyes.

It was a painful and at the same time wonderful feeling to finally have her standing in front of him in his home. Kjell took a few steps, wrapped her in his arms and kissed her; a kiss that she returned.

"Finally alone!" she said and nibbled his ear.

He felt her warm breath and a wave of desire brushed over him like a warm summer wind.

"We're not expecting visitors anytime soon I hope?" said Isabell.

Kjell didn't answer. He just lifted her up in his arms and carried her to his part of the house.

Back in Strömstad Verne snuck back into the house. He didn't want to have to talk to Jon. First he had to handle an important conversation that was waiting for him. To be on the safe side, he locked the door just in case Jon got the idea to surprise him.

"We're not satisfied with the result," said the base voice.

"Well it's hardly my fault if one of your members couldn't manage to drive a truck," said Verne and snorted out loud.

"How is it going with your purchase of the shares?" asked the deep voice. "We need to be a majority owner."

"What are you talking about? We've never had any agreement saying that you would control the company," said Verne and felt his hands get sweaty.

"And what other options do you think you have?" asked the voice.

"This is the way it is: I am not a majority owner. My brother is together with my fa … Jon's wife. Even if I managed to buy her shares, I still won't be the largest owner," said Verne. He was starting to wonder how much they actually knew about him and his family.

"You'll just have to convince your brother that the best

thing he could do is to sell his shares to you," said the voice. "By the way, how does it feel to have a new father in your old age?"

Verne held his breath and tried to figure out how they could possibly know so many of the details in his life. Was he being followed?

"You didn't answer my question," said the voice.

"Yes, well it feels different but good," answered Verne and wanted to finish this conversation.

"That sounds nice! You should get your new father to help you convince his wife to sell you her shares. On the other hand, that may not be necessary. Mette is probably angry enough at Jon to want to sell her shares to anyone. And she'll want to sell to someone who can make life sour for him," said the voice and laughed.

The laugh Verne heard was hardly a pleasant one, and it made his skin crawl.

Chief Super Intendent Stefan Kronfeld

"Mondays are not what I would call the best day of the week," thought Greger as he opened the door to his room at the Serious Crime Division. This particular morning he hadn't even had time to sit down in his chair before his cell phone started ringing.

"Hope you've had a good weekend! Come to my office," said Stefan and hung up.

Greger muttered and walked slowly ahead in the corridor with swinging steps. He knocked on Stefan's door and opened it. Stefan was standing by the window looking out at the construction work for the new court building that was gradually developing.

"That's going to be a nice building, that one," said Stefan pointing. "Finally the costs of allocating a car for every prisoner behind bars can be used for better purposes. It has cost so much money to have special cars driven with guards back and forth several times a day, every day for weeks during trials. You should see those bills, Greger! You'd start crying," said Stefan and turned around.

"Well, what have we got so far?" Someone knocked on the door. Stefan looked up and made a face. "Come in if it's important," he said with a loud voice.

Charlotte came in with a paper in her hand.

"Hi, Stefan! I walked past Greger's room and heard that he was in here. Just as well, so you can also hear what I've found out." She walked over and put the paper down in front of Greger. "The bloody shirt button and gold earring have been analyzed. The shirt button belonged to the man who was shot on Norra Hamngatan, and the earring belonged to the one who was shot on Blendas gata on Hisingen," said Charlotte.

"The bag that these things were found in, did the lab find any fingerprints on it?" asked Greger scratching his head.

"No, that was clean," she answered.

"Why did we find belongings for two unknown victims on a farm that belongs to Heaven's Devils," wondered Greger, and his right eyelid started to twitch. Charlotte recognized that signal. He was either nervous or he'd done something wrong.

"Yes, that question would be a good one to have an answer for," said Stefan and leaned back in his chair.

Someone else knocked on the door.

"Come in and leave the door open! We might as well have a meeting in my room," said Stefan. "Hi Matthias, I hope you have some good news and some answers!"

"We've dug out a large arsenal of weapons on Xantino's farm outside of Biskopsgården. There was enough there to start a small war," said Matthias. "Right now our technicians are dusting for prints on the weapons. Some prints were found on the mini-excavator, one of them part of a palm. Now we're waiting for answers, as usual," he said.

Charlotte gave Matthias a copy of the paper she had just shown Stefan. He read it and nodded.

"What we in Special Investigations have concluded is that Amir and Hazim are good friends, not enemies like we thought earlier. That is if we are to believe what our telephone surveillance," said Matthias. "They chat about where they're going to eat, what girls they want and other things that aren't of interest. Not a word about business."

"Are you saying that Amir and Hazim are partners all of a sudden?" asked Greger. "If that's true, we have to re-plan our strategy!"

"What strategy? I didn't even know that you had one!" said Stefan and flashed a grin at Greger.

"Hey, thanks a lot! Since Massoud, who is a member of Xantinos, was at Packhuskajen when we found Black Pete, this whole time we've assumed that the gangs are rivals. In spite of our lousy budget, we'll have to try to track Verne twenty-four hours a day," said Greger. "I have a feeling it will be that little jerk who will give us the solution in the end. Do we know where he is right now?"

"Our last report says that he's returned to the house in Strömstad," said Matthias. His telephone is also tapped, but that hasn't yielded anything yet. What did Verne have to say about the trucks? Did we bring him in for interrogation?"

"No, his brother Kjell took over the conversation. His point was that Verne had only four days of experience in the company while he had over five years," said Greger. "I was really hoping Verne would have come along to the station, but I'll have to show him my photos the next time."

"How sure are you that there will be a next time?" asked Stefan. "From what I understand, we don't have an ounce of evidence on him. How did you think that we could bring him in for interrogation?"

"Verne is addicted to gambling and is going to make a mistake, I'm sure of it! All gaming addicts end up there sooner or later. There's a limit to how much money can be lost without completely emptying the cashbox and there comes a time when it has to be filled again. The question is with whose money?"

"Okay, keep Verne under surveillance twenty-four hours a day. I'll talk about the overtime with the economy department," said Stefan.

"Hi, everybody! Have we got some solutions within reach?" asked Katarina and stepped into the room.

"Come on in … I'm sure there's room for you too!" said Stefan. "You don't happen to have my wife along with you do you? I just mean that it would be nice to see her. It's been a while."

"Oh, you think so?" said Sara and came in right behind Katarina. "It was nice to hear that you miss me. I miss you sometimes too," she said and walked over to give him a pat on the shoulder.

"Excellent, and since it's lunch time I suggest that we all go out together and eat. My treat," said Stefan. It won't be McDonald's, just so you know," he said and turned toward Greger.

"That's too bad," said Greger and smiled broadly.

Verne Meets with Kjell

Verne paced back and forth outside of NK's main entrance. He was five minutes early, but Kjell was usually on time. He was optimistic and convinced that Kjell had succeeded in getting Mette to sell her shares. Verne had already decided to give Kjell double whatever he had paid. He could borrow money from his mother. If he told her what he wanted to use the money for, she would most likely not have any objections, especially because of the situation she had created for him. If he could then succeed in getting Jon to divide his shares fifty/fifty with his new found son then he would suddenly become the majority owner without Jon ever knowing about it. After that he would deal with those goddamn idiots who were under the impression that they were going to take over the action in his company. They were really stupid if they thought they could trick him into that, thought Verne and felt at peace with the situation.

"Hi, Verne! How are you?"

Kjell stood in front of him. Verne hugged his brother and patted him on the back. At the same time, he breathed a sigh of relief. Great that it seems to have worked, he thought.

"Shall we have a cup of coffee?" asked Kjell and pointed to a table with four empty chairs.

Verne nodded and walked ahead of Kjell into the entrance.

"Did she go along with it?" asked Verne as he put down a tray with two café lattes.

"Can't you sit down before we start discussing?" wondered Kjell.

"You must realize that I'm curious. It's about my future. Yours is already secure," said Verne and pretended to be hurt.

"Mette agreed to sell her shares to me," said Kjell.

"Great work, bro!" exclaimed Verne and patted Kjell on the shoulder. "When will we take them over?"

"As soon as the lawyer has written up all the papers. Fortunately, Jon had drawn up a prenuptial contract with Mette, which, in this case, is to her advantage and not his," said Kjell.

"My God, this is wonderful! We should celebrate!" said Verne and bent over toward Kjell. "And I'm sure you've guessed that I'm going to pay you double what you gave Mette."

"Of course I've understood that, but I have no intention of selling the shares. Not to you nor anyone," said Kjell and looked at Verne. Verne stared with wide-open eyes at Kjell. His mouth was half open, and his eyes flickered.

"But, what do you mean? We agreed …" said Verne and wiped off a drop of saliva that had run out from the corner of his mouth. "We had an agreement," he said with a harsh tone of voice and straightened up in his chair.

"We were in agreement that I should ask Mette if I could buy her shares, and that's what I've done," said Kjell. "But I never promised that you could buy the shares from me!"

"What in Hell? How can you be so goddamn unfair to me,

Kjell? First I lose my Dad, who isn't my Dad, just because Mom has been unfaithful. And due to that I lost my due part of the company, and now you won't even let me *buy* a share of the company! You're not acting like a brother!" hissed Verne out of the side of his mouth.

"That's exactly what I'm doing; behaving like a brother. I know that you have a problem with your gambling, and I'm not going to stand by and let you gamble away our family's business," said Kjell. He folded his arms across his chest and looked Verne right in the eyes.

Verne sank down in front of his brother, dropped his head, and started to cry out loud.

"You don't care about me one bit! If you did you'd let me buy those shares," he said and sniffled loudly. Kjell put his hand on Verne's shoulder.

"Come on Verne … don't cry. I know that you don't want to gamble, but you're sick and need help to break this addiction," said Kjell and moved closer to Verne.

Verne shook off Kjell's hand, straightened up and stared at him.

"I don't have an addiction!" said Verne and leaned back in his chair. "But if you don't want to sell the shares to me, I can't force you." He got up out of his chair and leaned toward Kjell.

"Believe me, you're going to regret your decision," said Verne and walked away from the table and out through the entrance doors.

Kjell remained sitting and watched his brother leave with raised eyebrows and a feeling of emptiness in his heart.

Mahtab and Massoud

Every night Mahtab locked the door to her room. Several times a night she woke up feeling sweaty and with her heart beating rapidly. She had locked the tapes that she got from Emelie at Hard Rock Café into her locker at work. At first she had thought to hide them at home, but ever since her brother revealed that he was proud to be a member of Amir's gang, she'd changed her mind. Mahtab had avoided her parents' questions about Massoud such as where he was during the evenings. Sometimes when she looked at the Parakeets in their cage in the living room, she realized she felt just as locked up as they were. Emelie had sent her several text messages, but she had neither wanted or dared to answer them. What should she do? She couldn't meet Emelie again and risk that Massoud would see her and discover their secret meetings. She didn't dare go to the police with the tapes; Emelie could get murdered. Her colleagues had pointed out that she looked tired and worn out, that she should see a doctor and get looked at. Was she anemic? Mahtab had brushed off their well-meant remarks by saying that she was just tired, that she had been sleeping poorly, but beyond that she was fine. It didn't feel good to lie … it never did. The only thing that kept her going and in a fairly good mood was her work. Mahtab had even lied to her own sister. And all of this was just to protect her from the same mess she was in. While she was getting dressed to go work the afternoon shift she heard someone knock on the door. Since she was holding a blow dryer in her hand she could hardly pretend that she wasn't home. The dryer was an older model and made a lot of noise. She shut it off and walked over to the door.

"Who is it?"

"It's me, Massoud. I want to talk to you! Open the door!"

She hesitated a few seconds but finally turned the key. After opening the door, she turned around and continued to blow dry her hair.

"Hi, Sis! Why are you locking your door these days?" asked Massoud and sat down on her bed.

"Because I want to. What do you want?"

"You know, Amir's girlfriend that you and I met at the café, Emelie … you remember her, right?" he asked.

Mahtab thought her heart would stop dead when she heard his question. In spite of being so afraid, she made an effort to keep her voice steady.

"Sure, I remember her. Nice girl. What about her?"

"She's gone!"

Mahtab shut the blow dryer off again and turned toward Massoud with her mouth wide open.

"What do you mean 'gone'?" she whispered.

"Just what I said," said Massoud. "Amir wanted me to ask you if you had seen her."

"When?"

"Yesterday, the day before yesterday, or sometime during the week," said Massoud.

302

"No, I haven't seen her for several weeks," said Mahtab and relaxed, since she was telling the truth for once. "Doesn't she have parents or sisters or brothers who know where she is?"

"Yes, a mother who doesn't care … she's an alcoholic," said Massoud and yawned. "If Emelie gets in touch with you in any way or if you see her in town, call me! Get it?"

"Is Amir mad because she took off?" asked Mahtab and ignored Massoud's demands.

"None of your business! Just do as I say," he said, left the room and closed the door.

Mahtab sat down on her bed, exhausted from the tense moment with her brother. Suddenly the thought of going to work wasn't as appealing. She wondered where Emelie had gone. Was there some friendly soul out there who had taken her in? Had she looked for help at the women's shelter? That last thought gave Mahtab some hope. That could be it! Emelie had mustered the courage to leave the jerk, thought Mahtab and breathed a sigh of relief.

A Random Police Check

After an unusually entertaining lunch in the company of Stefan Kronfeld, Greger sat in his room and heard someone approaching in the corridor with weight in their steps. It sounded as though someone was leaping forward! Leif Griffén suddenly stood in Greger's doorway.

"You're going to love this," he said and laughed out loud. Greger looked at Leif with big round eyes. He stood in the doorway waving a paper in his hand and choked up with laughter.

The sound of Leif's loud laughter brought out half of the department, including Stefan, who usually didn't fall for various outbursts. Leif looked around and waved to his colleagues to come closer.

"Now you're going to hear a really good story," he said and tried to hold back the laughter bubbling up inside of him. "Today the traffic police up in Kortedala had routine controls. They waved in a big, black Mercedes with toned windows. It rolled in, and the cop walked up and asked to see the driver's license as well as asking him to blow into a

304

breathalyzer. While one colleague checked the license, the other one asked the driver to blow. That didn't turn out very well. Anyway, the cop finally notices that his colleague has signaled."

"For God's sake Leif, don't take so goddamn long!" said Stefan and sighed loudly. Katarina grinned widely at Leif, and so did everyone else who by this time had circled around Leif and were waiting for the punchline.

"The driver's license was a forgery! The cop who stood by the Mercedes still hadn't paid much attention to who was sitting in the back seat, but when he heard that the license was a forgery, he took a look. Guess who was back there, like sitting ducks?" shouted Leif and started laughing again. Everyone shook their heads.

"Hazim and Amir," yelled Leif and doubled over with laughter. "Can you believe it? The idiots got caught in a routine check! And of course, the car was seized and, of course, it was filled with drugs! They had a gun in the glove compartment and one under the car seat!"

Stefan gave Leif a thud on the back that made him almost topple over.

"Hallelujah!" said Stefan and gave him another thud. "Now we finally have something we can use! I assume that Marianne Konttii has been informed and that she'll soon arrange a petition for their arrest?" he asked.

"You sure as hell can!" said Leif and smiled a big toothy smile toward his childhood friend. "She's already fixed it. What surprises me is that you haven't heard anything yet from their lawyers. You'd think they would've gotten here before me," he said.

Finally, thought Greger, time for take-off. He was so happy he got up gave Leif a cheerful pinch on the cheek.

"This is the best news I've had in ages. I'll get in touch

with Matthias right away. This is almost too good to be true," cheered Greger. "Now Matthias can interrogate Amir and Hazim. Things are going to loosen up after this; I'm sure of it. What about the guy who was driving?"

"He pleaded guilty to forgery on the spot and is already locked up. He didn't have a record with us. Seemed completely green, shook, cried and promised on his mother's grave that he didn't know what was in the car. He says he was just hired to be a chauffeur. I actually believe him," said Leif.

"Who was the car registered to?" asked Katarina.

"A woman in Hovås, Hilma Gustafson on Golfstigen 119," said Leif, reading from the report.

Greger looked at Leif and then turned to Katarina.

"Doesn't Andrea Hildeng live at the same address?" asked Gerger. "Where do we have our papers?" Annika hurried to get the notebook with all of the witnesses' names and addresses. She gave it to Greger.

"Of course it is!" said Greger and pointed. "Look here! Arne and Andrea Hildeng live on Golfstigen 117. They are neighbors with the lady who owns the Mercedes, the car they were in when they got caught in the traffic control. Has anyone talked with Hilma Gustafson?"

"We phoned, and it turns out that Hilma Gustafson is in Monaco on vacation," said Leif, "But she'll be home within a week according to her secretary."

"Ok, now we have her name registered," said Greger. "We'll see what that can give us. Strange that an older woman who is Andrea Hildeng's neighbor owns the Mercedes that Amir and Hazim are riding around in. It hasn't been registered as stolen has it?"

Leif shook his head.

"Very strange, I must say," mumbled Greger.

Matthias paced back and forth in Greger's room. He couldn't sit still. One minute he stood by the window and the next he was writing feverishly on a pad that lay on the desk. Greger sat quietly and waited.

"I think I know how I'm going to interrogate them now," said Matthias and sat across from Greger. "They're not going to be able to dodge anything this time. Who are their lawyers?"

"The one's they usually use, Pulman and Kovoski. Slippery as hell," said Greger. "Very expensive and we have to foot the bill as usual. By the way, Pelle called today from the National Criminal Police. I said that you would get in touch with them if you needed their help."

"I talked with their department head yesterday. I thanked him and all of that, but right now we have these guys right where we want them. How long will it take for the lab to give us an answer as to whose fingerprints are on the weapons that were found in the car?" asked Matthias.

"Katarina called, and it seems as though we'll get an answer tomorrow. The lab knows that this is a hot issue; they put aside everything else for our sake! Okay, it's time for our meeting in the assignment room," said Greger and looked at the clock.

"Can we tie them to the narcotics?" asked Matthias, turning to Charlotte.

She sat beside Katarina, thumbing through piles of documents and mumbled to herself.

"You want to know if our test results can prove that the narcotics have their origin from the hijacking of the trucks?" asked Charlotte.

Matthias nodded.

"Maybe, but I can't promise that," she said. "Right now

we're vacuuming the car and are going to take the whole car apart. If we have a little luck, we might find fingerprints on the packaging for the drugs."

"I wonder where they were when they re-packaged the narcotics? It's not exactly easy to hide a truck," said Katarina. "Which industrial areas have been checked? And which are still left? Has anyone found a truck?"

"That was a lot of questions all at once. Here are some of the answers," said Matthias and handed over some documents with a smile.

She felt warm and happy for the smile. A relaxed feeling spread through her, something like the way she felt when they had been at home with Greger and Charlotte. That night almost felt like their first, thought Katarina.

"We have no suspected areas left to search. Not in the Gothenburg area anyway," said Katarina as she was looking through the papers. "Maybe they got rid of the truck by dumping it or burning it up?"

"Everything is possible, but nothing unusual has been reported," said Matthias. "Now I want everyone to concentrate on the interrogation. Every single question to be put to these gentlemen needs to be x-rayed first. This might be the only chance we have to put these guys away forever! We can't screw it up! The list of questions will be sent out in plenty of time, just to be on the safe side. If you see so much as a period or a comma in the wrong place, I want to know about it!" said Matthias.

"A whole week has gone to hell! A whole goddamn week without one answer!" said Matthias, waving his hands and sighing. "The only thing we've gotten out of them is 'no comment'! Including their lawyers who just sit smiling through the interrogations. I'm going crazy soon!"

"I know how you feel. We can at least find comfort for now in that the weapons that were found in the car were used for the murders of the two men. One of them was used on Blendas gata and the other on Norra Hamngatan. But there were no fingerprints and, of course, both Amir and Hazim deny that the weapons are theirs. What could we expect?" said Katarina and made a face.

"What's happening with Verne's surveillance?" asked Greger.

"He met his brother, but that was a while ago. It looked like they were fighting about something and Verne left NK appearing upset. After that, he's been at the Casino in Gothenburg every single day. One of our men has also followed Verne inside the Casino but didn't see anything suspicious. He followed Verne into the men's room once where Verne talked to someone on the phone, but he couldn't hear any of the conversation. But since Verne's telephone is bugged he didn't worry about it," said Matthias.

"In other words there's not a lot happening with Verne right now," said Greger and raised his ringing cell phone to his ear. "Where are you? Have you sent the crime scene technicians and the coroner? We'll be there in a half an hour."

"Where are we going?" asked Katarina.

"We're going to Tjörn, or more specifically close to Gunneby. An elderly couple has found the body of a young woman," said Greger.

"Do we know who she is?" asked Matthias. And his jaws were tightly clenched.

Greger shook his head and got ready to go, and Katarina hurried down the hall after them.

When they arrived at the site that was already blocked off, Sara Kronfeld was there along with Charlotte.

"What have you found?" asked Greger.

"A young woman, pregnant," said Sara Kronfeld taking off her face mask.

Katarina didn't dare to look up at Matthias to see his reaction to this information. Without being aware of it, she braced her shoulders in preparation for what Sara was going to tell them.

"Can you see how she died?"

"Her body has been lying here for several days, maybe over a week, well-hidden. The elderly couple was taking an evening walk and had the luck, or rather the misfortune if we see it from their point of view, to find her. Some animal has probably sniffed around the body

and moved the branches away.

"Is it possible to get to the crime scene by car?" asked Katarina.

"We haven't found any car tracks; the terrain is inaccessible. But because the ground is hard and dry, we can't see if she has walked there, been murdered at the site or if she has been killed elsewhere," said Sara.

"Was there a handbag, cell phone or anything else that could help us with her identity?" asked Greger.

"Charlotte and her team are working their way toward the body, but so far they haven't even found a cigarette butt," said Sara and wiped the sweat off her brow with her arm. "When they are done, the victim will be sent to me for the autopsy. I'm probably going to call in a Forensic Entomologist, who's an expert on insects so we can better determine the time of death. After that, we'll see what we can find out. Whoever has the strongest stomach from your department can be present at the autopsy. It's not going to look pretty!"

Katarina looked at Greger and nodded. If she wanted to be present, it was okay with him. He had seen enough. Matthias had positioned himself at the blocked off area and watched

310

the crimes scene technicians at work. Katarina walked over to him and put her hand on his arm.

"How are you?"

"At first I felt a lot of rage, but then it passed," said Matthias. "Now I'm just thinking about the victim's family. But it's strange that we don't have any young, pregnant women reported missing."

"Maybe she's not Swedish," said Katarina.

"You could be right about that. Maybe it's just some poor soul that has been forced into prostitution, gotten pregnant and then been dumped," said Matthias turning to Katarina. "Can I come over to your place this evening?"

She stood still, looked into his blue eyes and nodded.

A Missing Girl Is Found

A day later Katarina stood together with Sara in front of the body of the young woman. Sara had called in a Forensic Entomologist who was walking around the body collecting insects. Sara had been right; this was not a pretty scene, thought Katarina, who was happy that she had only had a cigarette and a cup of coffee for breakfast. Even though she had sprayed her face mask with mint aroma, the stench of rotting flesh couldn't be avoided, and it was disgusting. Katarina could feel her stomach writhing from cramps several times, but she braced herself; this experience was a part of her job. Her salary was hardly worth what she had to endure, but there are certainly those who have it worse, thought Katarina. She let her thoughts wander back to last night with Matthias. They had made love, hard and intensely. Sometimes she had even had to protect herself from his powerful thrusts. Sweat had poured off him, and he hadn't opened his eyes once during their lovemaking. Afterward, he had gotten out of bed without a word, gone into the bathroom and stepped into the shower. She'd remained quietly in bed, listening to the sounds in and outside the room. Outside some inebriated young people were shouting and cars honked, but indoors it was the sound of Matthias in the shower that reached her ears. Still wet from the shower, Matthias had gotten back into bed with her and taken her hand to hold it and kiss it. Five minutes later he lay snoring by her side. She had sneaked out of bed, put on her bathrobe, lit a cigarette and sat out on the balcony. The air had felt fresh as if it had rained. Smells from the neighbor's window boxes filled with purple petunias were overwhelming and wonderful.

"How soon can we find out when this girl died?" asked Sara.

Katarina woke out of her dreams and stared at one of the test tubes that the Forensic Entomologist held in her hand.

"I think you could have an answer at the beginning of next week," said the woman taking her test tubes and walking toward the exit. She waved and left them alone with the body. Sara's assistant hurried over and took care of the victim. Sara pressed lightly on Katarina with her hands and signaled that she wanted to have a smoke. Katarina nodded.

"Days like this are few in number, fortunately," said Sara as she pulled the smoke down into her lungs, leaned up again the wall of the building and looked at Katarina.

"Funny that she hasn't been reported missing since the Forensic Odontologist thought that her fillings were probably made in Scandinavia."

"Not everyone who becomes a parent should become one," said Sara and lit another cigarette. Some should grow cucumbers instead!"

Katarina couldn't help but smile at her remark, in spite of the fact that just a few meters away lay a young woman whose life had been taken far too early and violently at that. But to be able to laugh, see the light in life, and not lose focus on one's work were all essential, thought Katarina and she, too, lit another cigarette.

The Owner of the Mercedes

Several hours after the autopsy, Katarina still felt the stench from it in her nose. Before welcoming the elderly lady who sat waiting on a chair outside her room, she took out a small bottle of perfume and sprayed a few drops behind each ear. She then opened the door and asked the woman to come in. As she sat down, Katarina noticed the way she was dressed. The light blue skirt with a matching jacket didn't have a single wrinkle in spite of this woman having sat in a police car for a half an hour. She wore dark blue pumps and had a matching bag. The lock on her handbag said that it was a Gucci. So obviously there were no issues with money, she thought. Hilma Gustafson sat down on the allotted spot and adjusted her skirt. Katarina could see that her hands were shaking. Outwardly she seemed calm, but inwardly she was probably nervous, concluded Katarina.

"Would you like a cup of coffee?" she asked.

Hilma Gustafson shook her head.

"As I'm sure you understand we are interested in finding out why you are the owner of a luxury model Mercedes

314

which has been used by notorious gang members from Gothenburg," said Katarina.

"That's not illegal, is it?" asked Hilma Gustafson and changed her position on the chair.

"No, but since the car was filled with narcotics and weapons, it would be good if you could explain how you are involved," said Katarina.

"How I am involved?" objected Hilma. "I'm not involved in anything at all that has to do with them!"

"Then tell me why your name is on the car's registration," said Katarina calmly and quietly.

"Does my husband have to find out about this?" asked Hilma Gustafson and changed her position on the chair one more time.

"That depends on what you have to say, but if it's not something illegal then there is no reason we have to speak to your husband about it," answered Katarina.

Hilma Gustafson cleared her throat, changed her position yet another time and then turned quickly around. She looked at the closed door, looked back at Katarina and then leaned forward.

"My son has gambling debts," she said and looked down at the floor. I've tried to help him with money, but since it's my husband who handles our economy I couldn't take out any more money from the account without making him suspicious."

"In what way did you come in contact with the persons who are driving around in your car?" asked Katarina.

"I wasn't the one who took care of that part. My son came home with the registration papers and asked me to sign them, so I did," said Hilma.

Katarina could see that it was difficult for her to talk and that her eyes were wet with tears.

"Did you get anything in exchange from your son?"

"No, but he said that if I signed he would be free from his debt."

"How are things with your son now? Is he still gambling?"

"Not as far as I know. He promised to get help since he has a wife and children," said Hilma.

"We'll make a record of your account of what happened, and after that we can drive you home again if you like," said Katarina. Hilma nodded and smiled for the first time.

"One more thing ... how well do you know your neighbors, the Hildengs?"

"What do you mean by 'well'? I say hello to Andrea when we meet; sometimes we've had coffee together at each other's homes. Is that what you mean?" asked Hilma. The smile had disappeared from her lips.

"I mean more if you see each other on a daily basis? Maybe go to the theater together? Take vacations together," said Katarina. "Exchange confidences with each other?"

"No, *so* well we don't know each other," said Hilma. She sounded very decided on that point. Apparently wealthy neighbors don't socialize more with each other than neighbors who are poor, thought Katarina and freed herself from a preconceived notion at the same time.

Mahtab Has Questions But No Answers

Mahtab wandered along the path that led to the trolley stop. She passed the kiosk on her way and without really thinking about what she saw let her eyes wander over the newspaper headlines. She stiffened when one sentence that she read abruptly registered in her mind. Young pregnant woman murdered! Mahtab started shaking in her whole body. Could it be Emelie? She finally decided to walk into the shop and buy one of the newspapers. With the newspaper in her hand, she walked to the covered stop and waited for the trolley. About ten people stood waiting together. Mahtab sneaked a glance at some of them, but no one seemed to take notice of her. The streetcar arrived at the stop on time, Mahtab got on and sat down. She held the newspaper tightly in her hand. Should she read it now or wait until she was at work? Massoud hadn't bothered her again after he had asked her about Emelie. For several days, she had waited for him to ask her to help look for Emelie. But the few times that they had met at home, Massoud had only said hi to her, as if everything was as usual. That had worried her at the beginning, but then she had forgotten her concern about Emelie and taken it for granted that everything was okay with her.

Thirty minutes later Mahtab stood in front of her locker. She had rolled up the newspaper and put it in her handbag. She said hello to her colleagues, and they walked together up to the Emergency Ward. It was time for the report. During the time that the nurse was telling them which patients they had right now in their department, which ones were waiting to see the doctor, and which ones had already been examined, Mahtab couldn't stop thinking about the newspaper that lay in her bag. Now it was locked up right here in a small locker. "I'll read it during my coffee break. Then I can sit outside Emergency at the front of the building," thought Mahtab.

Two hours later, with a coffee cup in one hand and the newspaper in the other, Mahtab sneaked away from her colleagues. She opened the newspaper with shaking hands. Unawarely she was holding the newspaper tightly. She read every sentence twice. When she had read the whole article, she felt nauseous. In spite of standing in the sun, she shook as if she were freezing. Suddenly she thought about the tapes that lay in her locker. Had Emelie said something about them? In that case, wouldn't Massoud have asked her about the tapes a long time ago? Suddenly Mahtab felt like the loneliest person on the planet. Who could she talk to and share her feelings?

"How are you, Mahtab? You're as white as a ghost," a voice said all of a sudden.

Mahtab turned quickly around and looked into a pair of green eyes that belonged to one of her workmates.

"I just wanted to sit in the sun a minute," said Mahtab.

318

"So you've also read about that poor girl who was pregnant and got murdered," said her colleague and pointed to the newspaper that Mahtab was still holding onto tightly.

"Yes, it's so terrible," said Mahtab and walked back in toward the Emergency Ward. "It was probably reading that story that made me feel sick," she said and tried to smile at her friend. Mahtab said a silent prayer that she'd be able to get through her work day.

The first member of her family that Mahtab met when she got home after work was Massoud. She greeted him, leaned up again the wall of the hall and took her shoes off. Suddenly he took out a newspaper, the same one that she had read and thrown into the wastebasket at work.

"Have you seen this?" he asked.

Mahtab nodded.

"Do you realize who has been murdered?"

She nodded again.

"Good. Then you understand what happens if you try to leave Amir," said Massoud. He crumpled the newspaper, opened the cupboard under the sink and pushed the newspaper down into the rubbish bin.

Without turning around, Mahtab walked slowly to her own room, shut the door and turned the key. Once alone, she realized she was breathing irregularly and opened the window widely. Gulping in the fresh air, she got a chair and put it by the window. The birds were singing, and a mild wind swayed the top of the chestnut tree back and forth. Mahtab watched two women gesticulating and laughing together. Some children were playing ball on the lawn. Everything she saw turned cloudy suddenly and she felt tears running down her cheeks.

Chief Prosecutor Marianne Konttii Is Informed

It was time to present the conclusions, and Greger twisted and turned in his chair. Katarina sat beside him and seemed to be lost in the paper she was holding in her hand. Everyone sitting in the assignment room was waiting for Chief Super Intendent Stefan Kronfeld and Chief Prosecutor Marianne Konttii.

"Excuse us please for being a little late," said Stefan and stepped into the room. "For those of you who have never met our Chief Prosecutor, I'd like to present Marianne Konttii."

She nodded briefly and had an austere look, with lips that didn't have the slightest hint of a smile. Marianne Konttii was just under five feet tall, wore heels all the time, but always managed to look small and delicate. Her thick hair was steel gray and cut short. Behind her metal framed round glasses were narrowly set gray-blue eyes. Her face was oval and decorated with a turned up nose. She stood up in front of her chair, looked out over the gathering of known and unknown faces and cleared her throat.

"I've read the report that's been put together and we can now charge Amir and Hazim with illegal carrying of a weapon and for possession of narcotics as well. Hopefully we'll be able produce stronger evidence that the narcotics belong to them," said Marianne and sat back down in her chair.

"Unfortunately, we didn't find any finger prints on the drugs that were found in the Mercedes. But the probability that the narcotics do not belong to them is ridiculous. However, we expect to find evidence that will hold up," said Matthias.

"We've spoken to Hilma Gustafson's son, and he corroborates her story. He claims that he is finished with gambling. After he had handed over the registration papers to someone who looked like neither Amir or Hazim according to photos we've shown him, he had no further contact with any member of the gang," said Leif Griffén.

"And we also found out that during the period he was gambling, he met Verne Hildeng at Casino Cosmopol several times. He claimed that they had simply said hi, nothing more," said Annika Thorsson.

"The identity of the murdered pregnant young woman has been determined. Her name was Emelie Lovarsson and was only nineteen years old. Her skull was crushed, and one of her arms was broken," said Sara, looking at Katarina as she spoke. "There is no doubt that she was murdered where she was found. We found a large quantity of dried blood under her head. We've done a DNA profile on the fetus, so when you get hold of the father, we can prove it's his child."

"Unfortunately, we didn't find any possible weapons at the scene of the crime," said Charlotte. "However we've collected evidence by taking photographs and video filming, mostly of blood spatters on leaves, blades of grass and tree trunks, which indicates that the blows to Emelie's head were powerful and lethal.

"What do we know about this girl?" asked Stefan.

"No home and out of work. Her mother is an alcoholic, her father is dead, and she has no brothers or sisters. She seems to have had a tragic life and was actually in our records for a few cases of shop lifting," said Katarina. "She didn't have any close friends and lived with several different persons, according to what we've found out."

Katarina was looking at Matthias. He sat with his arms folded across his chest with a facial expression that didn't seem to reveal any of his feelings. She did notice that he was tensing his jaws. To an outsider, it wasn't noticeable, but she recognized the signs.

"It could be the father of the unborn child who's beat her to death," said Leif. "Maybe she didn't want to have an abortion!"

"Since Emelie hung around in Hammarkullen, we checked with the health centers nearby in case she had gone in for a check-up, but she wasn't registered anywhere," said Katarina.

"Have we taken DNA samples from Amir and Hazim?" asked Stefan.

"Yes, but neither of their samples match the DNA of Emelie's fetus," answered Sara. "We're doing a search in our records, but that takes time."

"Well, with these results we can charge for illegal carrying of a weapon, for possession of narcotics and hope that more will show up in the meantime," said Marianne Konttii.

"Hammarkullen!" shouted Leif suddenly. "What was Emelie doing in Gunneby on Tjörn? That's where Andrea and her family lives."

Greger almost jumped out of his chair.

"What in hell!? That brings us back to Verne Hildeng again," said Greger. "Why was Emelie killed on Tjörn near the Hildeng's summer house? We should have asked ourselves that question long ago. Was this a warning to Verne?"

"Let's get in touch with Andrea Hildeng and hear what that family has to say," said Leif.

"Bring Annika along and leave right away," said Greger rubbing his forehead. "How could we miss this? Of course Verne is somehow involved!"

"Nothing is certain until there is evidence on the table," snorted Marianne.

"Do what you can! I hope and believe that you'll be able to solve this one too!" said Stefan and patted Greger on the shoulder.

"Speaking of the Hildeng family," said Sara. "There is a question noted here concerning Arne Hildeng. 'Did we take an HIV test?' You were lucky this time! I had a particularly zealous student assistant who took a sample, in spite of the fact that we don't do that as a routine procedure. The answer was positive. Arne Hildeng had HIV."

"But why would he kill himself for that?" asked Katarina. "Today there are excellent antiretroviral drugs!"

"Perhaps for the simple reason that Arne Hildeng hadn't told Andrea that he was bi-sexual. We found that out from watching the DVD we got from his lawyer, Örjan Grund," said Greger. "Don't you remember?"

"Yes, I do," said Katarina. "Or rather I still didn't think that that could be a reason. On the other hand, I suppose Andrea would have become suspicious if Arne suddenly wanted to use a condom. But still, to go so far as to take one's life …"

"Sometimes the line between wanting to live and wanting to die can be very fine," said Sara.

At the Summer House

At the summer house in Gunneby, Andrea and Björn had just sat down to have dinner when the doorbell rang.

"Who can that be? Are you expecting anyone?" asked Björn as he lifted the cover off of a pot filled with boiled new potatoes.

"No, and since neither Kjell nor Isabell are home it can't be one of their friends," said Andrea. She got up and walked out to the hall.

Björn looked up with raised eyebrows at Leif Griffén and Annika Thorsson, who were standing beside Andrea in the doorway to the kitchen.

"Hello, what can we do for you?" asked Björn and got up.

"We have some questions about the girl who was found murdered not far from your house," said Annika.

"Yes, what a terrible thing to happen!" said Björn and waved his thin hands in the air. "It's hard to believe that something like that could happen so close by. How old was the girl?" "Only nineteen. We wonder if you can remember anything unusual happening in the area here in Gunneby about two weeks ago. Maybe a car that was parked in a strange place? I understand that it can be hard to remember," said Leif and said no thank you to a glass of elderberry flower juice that Andrea offered.

"I can hardly remember what I did a week ago," said Andrea. "Can we sit in the living room?"

Leif and Annika followed along behind Andrea, and they all sat down around the coffee table. Björn sat down in an armchair and Andrea took her place on one of the sofas.

"Was she a summer guest?" asked Andrea.

"Summer guest? What makes you think that?" asked Annika.

"Because no one from Tjörn has talked about her. If she had been a resident, almost everyone would have known about her," answered Andrea.

"No, she was neither a summer guest nor a resident. She was from Hammarkullen," said Leif.

"Then what was she doing here?" asked Björn.

"That's the question we'd like to find an answer for," said Annika. "Has Verne been here recently?"

"It was a while ago, but I know when," said Andrea. "He was here the evening and night that it rained so heavily; it was the only rain we've had for weeks. The land is very dry!"

Leif thought back to what day it could be. When he knew what day it was, he realized that it could comply with the time of Emelie's death.

"Was Verne out alone at any point during that evening or were you together the whole time?" asked Leif.

Andrea clapped her hands together and stared at Leif with wide open eyes.

"Surely you can believe that …"

"We don't believe anything," said Annika, interrupting the conversation. "We just want to rule out the possibility!"

"Verne was not out of our sight the entire time that he was here," said Björn with a determined tone. Not liking the way Verne behaved was one thing; but murder would be going too far, he thought.

"When did Verne leave?" asked Leif.

"The day after, at lunchtime I believe," said Andrea with her shoulders slumping down. "We saw him drive off."

"Thanks so much and sorry to disturb your meal," said Annika getting up to leave. "If you remember anything else we'd appreciate it if you get in touch."

After Annika and Leif had left, Andrea sat down in the hammock and let the tears roll down her cheeks.

"What's happening with our family anyway? I don't understand. About a month ago Arne and I were heading for your exhibition in Skärhamn. We were happy! At least I thought so," said Andrea sobbing. "Now Arne is dead, Elsebeth, too, and my son is a gambling addict. A young girl gets murdered near our home, and Verne is suspected of murdering her. Oh my God, how will all this end?" asked Andrea and hid her face in her hands.

"Take it easy, don't worry about Verne. We know that he's crazy about gambling, but we also know that he's not a murderer," said Björn and put his arms around Andrea. "If you want me to, I can ask Kjell to talk with his brother. Maybe we can get Verne into a program for gambling addicts. We'll all have to support him."

Andrea grabbed onto one of Björn's arms, nodded and sniffed out loud. The phone rang at that very instant. Björn wiggled out of Andrea's grip and walked out to the hall to answer. Every word he heard that came out of the telephone made his body sink lower and lower. He felt faint and grabbed the wall, pressing his forehead against the cold,

326

glass hall mirror.

"We're on our way," he said and hung up.

How could he tell this to Andrea without her having a complete breakdown? Björn took a deep breath, straightened up and walked out to the veranda.

How Many More Victims?

"I got a call from the officer on duty," said Katarina. "A seriously injured person has been admitted to Emergency at Sahlgrenska Hospital. The injured person's relatives have asked for Greger Thulin."

Greger stared at Katarina.

"Do you want to come with me?" asked Greger.

Katarina nodded.

For the third time within a short time span, Greger and Katarina wandered around Sahlgrenska's Emergency Ward. A familiar face in a white coat rushed past, but Greger didn't catch her in time. At the reception, a young man sat thumbing through a magazine. Katarina knocked on the glass window, held up her police I.D. and pointed with her finger.

"We're looking for Kjell Hildeng, who came into Emergency together with Isabell Hirsch. They came about an hour ago. What room are they in?"

The young man's fingers moved quickly over the computer's tangents and then he turned toward Katarina.

"That patient is in surgery. The relatives are sitting in the surgical waiting room," he said.

Greger opened the door to Room 2 and Katarina came in behind him. There stood Björn Caling with an empty expression on his face. Andrea was sitting to the right of the bed with swollen eyes. The sight of this distressed family was heartbreaking. Kjell was sitting to the left of the empty bed and turned toward Greger to reveal a face twisted with anger. He wiped away his tears with the backside of his left hand and held out his right hand to greet Greger.

"What has happened?" asked Greger.

"Isabell and I were out walking in town. She wanted to shop at H&M at Femman Department Store, so I accompanied her to the store. While Isabell was trying on different clothes, I wandered around in the men's department," said Kjell and swallowed. "After about twenty minutes I thought it was strange that Isabell hadn't come out. She likes to show me the outfits she's trying on. I walked back over to the fitting rooms, but she wasn't there. Then I walked around the shop looking for her. I thought maybe she had missed me somehow. So I went outside and looked around outside the store, but didn't see her anywhere. When I was on my way back into the shop, my cell phone rang," said Kjell with tears running down his face again. "A male voice told me that if I wanted to see Isabell again I shouldn't call the police. Go to the Water Lily Pond in an hour and she'll be there."

While Kjell was talking, Greger snuck a look at Katarina, who was sitting on the bed comforting Andrea. He wondered if there would ever be a right time to tell Andrea about Arne's positive HIV test. That information might just push her over the edge.

"Could you see the number of the person who called you?" asked Greger.

"Yes, it was from Isabell's cell phone. That's how I knew they meant business," said Kjell. "But it was the last thing he said that made me think again and call you for help."

Greger gathered his thoughts and returned his complete focus on Kjell Hildeng.

"Say hello to your brother, he said, and thank him from us! It was as though I completely lost my breath."

"What did he mean by that?" wondered Greger.

Kjell told Greger what had happened at NK and Verne's interest in buying Mette's shares of the company.

Greger said "Uh huh," and felt that it was time to bring in Verne. "Excuse me … I have to make a call," he said and dialed Matthias' number.

"What happened next?" asked Greger returning to Kjell.

"I ran up to the Art Museum and walked round and round the statue of Poseidon. I didn't dare to go to the Water Lily Pond until the hour had passed. I was convinced that I was being watched even though I couldn't see anyone who was behaving unusually. But I didn't dare take any chances," said Kjell and wrapped his arms around himself.

"You did the right thing," said Greger and put his hand on his shoulder. Kjell's trembling body was vibrating under his hand.

"Exactly one hour later I ran up behind the museum over to the Water Lily Pond. A group of people had already gathered by one of the benches close to the pond. I rushed over and there she was!"

Kjell's voice cracked, and he hung his head.

"We're going to handle this! Concentrate on taking care of Isabell. I'm going to go find out what's happening with her operation," said Greger. "News of that might give you some peace." Kjell nodded and sobbed at the same time.

Greger left the room and walked out into the corridor. He didn't see anyone. "Typical," he thought and continued over to that department's reception. A male nurse was sitting behind the high counter. Greger introduced himself and asked him to call the operation room to if possible learn how the operation was going. Some minutes later Greger found out what he had been hoping to hear. Isabell's injuries were superficial. How damaging the emotional injuries were was something that only Isabell knew. Tragically she had lost the child, which was, the doctor explained, probably a result of having been violently raped. Greger shook his head, thanked the nurse for assisting and started walking slowly back to the room. Suddenly, the double doors to the Emergency Section opened and someone with a familiar face walked quickly toward him.

"You're Greger Thulin, right?" said Mahtab. Her hand was shaking as she held out a bag in front of him.

"Yes, that's me. What's in the bag? By the way, have we met before?"

"I need your help," said Mahtab as her eyes filled with tears.

Greger turned around, grabbed Mahtab, and pulled her along in the direction of the hospital room. He opened the door a crack and called to Katarina. She left Andrea, walked up to Greger and looked in surprise at Mahtab.

"What's going on? Has something happened to Isabell?" asked Katarina and shut the door behind her.

Greger shook his head and nodded toward Mahtab.

"I worked the day that the ambulance came in with Agneta," said Mahtab whispering. "She was the sister of Matthias Brodd."

Katarina nodded and encouraged Mahtab to keep talking.

"My brother was involved with what happened," said Mahtab as tears started to run down her pale cheeks. She stood absolutely still and didn't dare look Katarina in the eyes. Katarina put her arm around Mahtab's shoulders and pulled her toward her.

"Sweetheart, we're going to help you in any way that we can," said Katarina. "Come with me. We need to find a secluded place where we can talk."

"Take this bag along too," said Greger and handed the bag to Katarina. "I don't know what's in it, but Mahtab seems to want to get rid of it."

Katarina took the bag from Greger and with her arm around Mahtab walked into the personnel room. A young nurse sat at the table and drank coffee. Katarina let go of Mahtab and walked over to the nurse to show her I.D. She explained that she needed the room, and the nurse left.

"We can sit here in peace and quiet," said Katarina. "Even have a cup of coffee if we want. Would you like some?"

Mahtab shook her head. She sat down on one of the sofas and pushed her folded hands down between her legs. Katarina could see that her body was shaking and that Mahtab was struggling to breathe normally. Katarina had no difficulties in recognizing a frightened person when she met one and Mahtab was petrified.

"What's in the bag?" asked Katarina opening the bag to take out a handful of the tapes that were in there. "What are these?"

"I got them from Emelie," said Mahtab and struggled against her tears, but they overpowered her. Her teeth were chattering, and she couldn't sit still.

"Do you mean the Emelie who was murdered and found on Tjörn?" asked Katarina and tensed up unawarely.

Mahtab nodded.

"Have you listened to the tapes?"

Mahtab nodded again.

"Do you know who murdered Emelie?" asked Katarina.

Suddenly the door to the personnel room opened, and Mahtab threw herself down on the floor. With a wide open mouth, Katarina stared at Matthias, who was standing in the doorway.

"What's happened?" asked Matthias and looked at Mahtab, who was lying on the floor in a fetal position.

"Do you have anyone else with you?" asked Katarina and nodded in the direction of Mahtab.

"No, I'm alone," he answered and shut the door.

"Mahtab, it's ok. You can get up," said Katarina, bending over and stroking her over her hair.

Slowly Mahtab got up and sat beside Katarina, but didn't dare to look either of them in the eye.

"We need to get immediately in touch with the Protective Security Division," said Katarina. "Can you call them?"

"Sure, I'll arrange it," said Matthias and left them just as quickly as he had arrived.

"How did you meet Emelie?" asked Katarina and gently patted Mahtab's clenched hands. At the same time, she sent a thankful thought to Matthias who had understood immediately and not asked a lot of questions.

"Through my brother, Massoud," said Mahtab.

When Katarina heard the brother's name, she realized that the bag of tapes could be the zipper that would open the whole case. There was no way she was going to let Mahtab out of her sight.

"Does Massoud know that you have these tapes?" asked Katarina.

"I don't know," said Mahtab, "but I don't think so."

"If he knew, what would happen then?"

Even though she could figure that out herself, Katarina wanted Mahtab to say it.

"The same that happened to Emelie," whispered Mahtab and rocked her body back and forth.

There was a knock on the door, it opened, and Matthias stuck his head in through the open door.

"I've spoken to the Protective Security Division and there was no problem at all. They will send someone right away," said Matthias.

Katarina turned to Mahtab and explained what the name meant.

"It is a department that works specifically with protecting persons who are threatened. They have secret apartments all over the world. That means you can feel safe with them," said Katarina.

Mahtab nodded, but Katarina could see that she was still frightened to death. She got up from the sofa and opened the door. Matthias stood behind the door, and Katarina asked him to come into the personnel room.

"How is she?"

"I've told Mahtab what's going to happen, but it doesn't seem as though she really understands," said Katarina. She glanced quickly at the rocking body that sat on the sofa. Mahtab's wide opened eyes had a wandering gaze, and she was making small whimpering noises.

"I hope that she will be able to get over her fears one day," said Matthias and looked at her with an expression of sadness.

"Mahtab is Massoud's sister, and that's the guy with the burns who we interrogated in connection with the burned body at Packhuskajen," said Katarina.

Matthias sky blue eyes became dark, and his body stiffened.

"Does she know anything about the attack on me?" he asked looking into Katarina's eyes.

"Mahtab has given me some tapes that she got from Emelie. The answers might be on those tapes," said Katarina and put her hand on Matthias' arm. "Have you spoken with Greger?"

"Yes, it was he who called and asked me to help you," said Matthias.

"Has Isabell come back from her operation when you were with them?," asked Katarina.

"Kjell Hildeng's girlfriend, is her name Isabell?" asked Matthias.

Katarina nodded.

"Is that who I met when I was on the plane back to Sweden from the U.S.?" wondered Matthias.

"I don't know, but now that you mention it I remember there was an Isabell with long, gorgeous legs that you were pretty fascinated with. I haven't seen her yet, but that name isn't very common. I think Kjell was working in the USA when his father Arne died. It could be her," said Katarina. "What a coincidence!"

"What happened to her? How did she end up in Emergency?"

It suddenly occurred to Katarina that Isabell lost her child because of being raped and that Matthias would probably be reminded of what happened to Agneta. How could she prevent him from finding out about that?

"We don't know everything about the situation, but it all points to Verne Hildeng being involved in some way," said Katarina. "Now we have to take care of Mahtab. Can you stay with her? I have to talk to Greger."

Matthias nodded and walked over to Mahtab together with Katarina. She explained the current situation for Mahtab.

"Can I go change my clothes? My shift was over when I looked for Greger, but I would like to have my clothes with me," said Mahtab. Her teeth were chattering as she spoke, in the same way they would if she were standing in below-freezing weather in a summer dress.

"We'll take care of that. If you give me the key to your locker I'll see to it that you get your clothes," said Matthias. "But we have to wait until you are picked up by my colleagues. They are going to see to it that you are safe again."

Isabell lay on the bed when Katarina came into the room; Kjell and Andrea stood on each side of her. Björn was together with Greger by the window.

"How is she?" asked Katarina.

"Besides losing her child, being beat up and raped, her body is okay," said Björn and looked at Katarina. "What she will think and feel when she wakes up from the anesthesia is anyone's guess."

"I need to exchange a few words with you," said Katarina to Greger.

They left the room and walked out into the corridor. Katarina told him about Mahtab and what she was about to arrange for her.

"That's good. The Protective Security Division is good at its job," said Greger. "What you mentioned about Matthias, I can't see how we can avoid it. If nothing else, it'll come out during Verne's interrogation. Are you afraid he'll break down again?"

"I don't know," answered Katarina. "But there's been an overdose of abused women who have been pregnant; first Agneta, then Emelie and now Isabell. How much can a person handle? Police or not, we're human first and foremost, human beings with *feelings*."

"We'll have to see what the tapes reveal. Best thing would be for you and me to listen to them together with Stefan Kronfeld. At that point we'll know if there is any evidence that can prove who was behind Agneta's death," said Greger.

Katarina Can't Believe What She Hears

One day later, Verne sat in the interrogation room at the Serious Crime Division. He paced back and forth , without a break. Annika Thorsson watched him through the mirrored window. "He's probably worried that someone's going to grab him by the hair before his tricky lawyer arrives," thought Annika and leaned back in her chair. And while Verne paced back and forth in the interrogation room, Jon Hildeng sat in Greger's room wringing his hands.

"Why have you brought my son in for interrogation?" said Jon, asking the same question for the fifth time.

Greger sat at his desk with a printout of the transcribed tapes they had received from Mahtab. During the hours that Katarina, Stefan and he had sat listening to the tapes, there were many times he had wished that Amir and Hazim would just drop dead. Stefan and Katarina's facial expressions also revealed anger. When Jon Hildeng repeated his question for the sixth time, Greger turned to him and stared.

"One reason has to do with murder," he said.

"Murder! What do you mean? Do you think Verne is

involved with a murder? Those are ridiculous accusations," snorted Jon. "What proof do you have for that statement?"

"It's the prosecutor who decides whether or not there will be an arrest, not me. She has the evidence and will go through it all very thoroughly. After that, Marianne Konttii will decide whether or not your son will be arrested. Right now he is going to be interrogated. We're waiting for his lawyer," said Greger and went back to his documents.

"I want to be present at the interrogation," said Jon and got up.

"Yes, there's a lot we want in this world that can never happen," said Greger. "You are welcome to come back after the interrogation, but for the time being there is nothing more to add. I'll accompany you to the exit."

Greger stood to wait with Jon Hildeng in front of the elevator doors when Matthias came out of one of the other elevators. They nodded to each other and Matthias walked into the department to exchange places with Annika in the interrogation room.

"I demand that you call and tell me what's going on with Verne," said Jon Hildeng standing stiffly in the elevator. He had demonstratively placed his foot by the elevator door to prevent it from closing.

"Unfortunately we can't promise anything, but, as usual, we'll do our best," said Greger and turned his back to Jon.

When Greger heard the sound of the elevator doors closing, he breathed a sigh of relief. Now it was time to deal with Verne.

The lawyer greeted Greger and Katarina and introduced himself as Kurt Green. He was someone new, thought Katarina. His gray suit seemed to be two sizes too big. The arms of his jacket covered the knuckles on his hands. His shirt bulged out under his tie and drops of sweat on the top of his bald head reflected the light from the lamp that was hanging over the table. With a monotonous tone of voice, Greger explained how the procedure for the interrogation would be conducted and then leaned back and waited for the next move. "He seems to be as green as his name," thought Greger and watched coyly as the lawyer fumbled with his papers and pens. Lawyer Green almost fell out of his chair trying to grab on to all of his paraphernalia, but finally managed to sit up in his chair again.

"Verne is under suspicion for involvement in the murder of Emelie Lovarsson, the bomb attack on Matthias Brodd's home, the attack on Isabell Hirsch – fiancée to Kjell Hildeng – and the robbery of two trucks loaded with medications from the German company Celecio," said Katarina.

"Who the hell is Emelie? I don't know any Emelie and that I was involved in a bomb attack on your colleague Matthias is nothing but a bunch of lies!" screamed Verne.

Kurt Green made two pointless attempts to calm his client but gave up.

"Your brother's fiancée Isabell was kidnapped, raped and beaten up. What part of that are you involved with?" asked Greger.

Verne bent his head down toward the table, sighing deeply and loudly.

"I wasn't involved with anyone getting hurt," he said snuffling.

Katarina got out some paper tissues and handed some to Verne.

"Why did it happen then?"

"They threatened me!" said Verne and blew his nose loudly.

"Who is 'they'?" asked Katarina.

"You know who they are," said Verne. "These goddamn

gangs are running all of goddamn Gothenburg without you being able to do shit about it!"

"That depends on you," said Greger.

"On me? It's not my fault that they do what they do!" said Verne.

"What do they do?" asked Katarina.

"Threaten, murder, and rip money off you, amongst other things," said Verne.

"I want to know who it is that you are talking about. What are their names? We know that you have met several of them," said Katarina.

"I don't have the name of anyone," said Verne.

Greger got out a notebook and laid out several photographs. One picture showed Verne meeting Massoud at Järntorget receiving what looked like a weapon.

"Who are you meeting here? And what is it he's giving you?" asked Katarina.

"I have no idea what his name is. He never said his name. I got a bag that contained a charger for a cell phone."

"What did you need that for?" wondered Greger.

"I needed a new one because the first one was broken," said Verne.

"And you didn't go to a shop like the rest of us to get one; instead you set up a meeting with a member of a gang who comes and gives you a new charger! Do you think we are idiots?" hissed Greger and remembered the conversations he had heard on the tapes. Those conversations had revealed a completely different story than the one Verne just blurted out.

"Isn't it true that you received a gun? A gun that you were to hide in a particular place; a gun that would later be used to attack the two German truck drivers? Well, what's your answer to that question?"

"I want to speak with my client," said Kurt Green, finally doing something for his high hourly fees.

"Do you approve of your lawyer's wishes?" asked Greger.

Verne nodded, and Greger and Katarina left the odd couple alone.

"I think you should tell them about the threats toward you and your family," said Kurt Green staring at Verne.

"Would that change anything? They think I've murdered that girl," hissed Verne and leaned forward.

"Yes, but you are innocent of that, aren't you?" asked Kurt Green and felt how drops of sweat broke out on his forehead. Verne didn't answer the question and just shook his head, sighing loudly and heavily.

"I want them to continue with the interrogation," said Verne. "I want to get this done with!"

Greger and Katarina came back to the interrogation room. The taping procedure was explained one more time. The time the questioning started again was clearly stated, as well as who was present.

"Isn't it so that your visit to the pharmaceutical company was just an excuse for you to find out about the security procedures for the handling of narcotics? That all you did during those four days was to map out personnel and give the gangs the possibility to attack? Isn't that how it is?" asked Greger.

"Could it be that everything that has happened to you and your family has to do with your gambling addiction?" wondered Katarina. "Is it your gambling that's the reason Isabell has been beaten up and raped and consequently lost her child?"

Verne was silent and stared down at the table. Kurt Green leaned forward and pulled on one of the legs of his trousers. At the same time, he cleared his throat loudly.

"I had to do what they wanted. Otherwise, they would kill

me or someone else in the family. But I refused and they took Isabell."

"Who are they? These aren't just shadows we're talking about. You know who they are! Say their names!" said Katarina.

"Amir and Hazim," whispered Verne.

"You can speak louder," said Greger.

He repeated the names and looked straight into the mirrored window.

"How did you get in touch with Amir and Hazim?" asked Katarina. She wondered what Matthias was thinking as he sat listening through the one-way mirror. Matthias had been informed that Amir and Hazim lay behind the bomb that killed Agneta and that they had both ordered Emelie's murder. Now he just found out that Isabell had lost her child because of the rape. Katarina wondered how he was going handle all of this information.

Verne told them that he had called the telephone number he had been given by his friend Jan Kopec who was killed by a car bomb. The people he called always provided the cash that he needed to finance his gambling. There was never any problem in the beginning, he maintained. He always paid back, but all of a sudden his debt was almost one hundred thousand crowns and that was when he met Mahtab, who had tricked him.

"In what way did Mahtab trick you?" asked Katarina.

"By pretending to be interested in me and getting me to come to the Palace. But she never showed up. Instead, I was given a cell phone by the bartender. A voice told me what I had to do," said Verne. "From then on I was in trouble."

Verne started sniffling again and pulled the box of paper tissues toward him.

By listening to the tapes, they had discovered the motives for the killings on Blendas gata and Norra Hamngatan. Two teenagers, fourteen years old, had been practicing shooting at cans and bottles on Gårdstensbergen. The forensic technicians had found bullets that matched the bullets found in the men's bodies. The boys were future gang members, and the entrance examination was to shoot a person, anyone, anywhere. Katarina shivered when she remembered how she had felt as she heard Amir and Hasim talk about the murders. It was as though they had been sitting at a café, talking about what would be the best tie to wear for a funeral. Both of the boys had been taken into custody by social services, so now one could only hope that they would receive proper care. Otherwise, they could be back in a few years only to rob, abuse, murder, and rape. Katarina shook her shoulders and went back to concentrating on Verne's interrogation.

"We are going to transcribe this interrogation and then read it for you," said Greger and got up. At the same moment his cell phone rang. Katarina was about to join Greger when even her phone started ringing. Greger was already on his way out through the door when Katarina answered. As Greger ran through the corridor, he heard her scream. It echoed in his head all the way to the Custody section.

The first person Greger met was the head of Custody. His face was white, his glasses foggy and Greger could hardly see his eyes.

"I've called an ambulance, but I don't think that's going to help," he said and sat down on a chair that was placed next to the wall.

"What in hell has happened? You weren't very clear on the phone," said Greger and leaned up against the wall with one hand.

"What happened was that Matthias Brodd walked into Custody and asked to speak with Amir, which he was allowed. A minute later we heard two shots. We rushed in, and both of them lay on the floor. There was blood everywhere," he replied.

"Where's the ambulance?" screamed Greger. "Where in hell is the ambulance?"

Greger ran toward the crowd of guards and pushed his way through. In the door opening, he could see the guards on their knees beside someone, using Custody's hand towels. The cell walls were covered with blood. Through the roar of voices, he suddenly heard Katarina's voice. He would have to prevent her from throwing herself over Matthias. Greger took a deep breath and met her running toward him. He took a firm grip of her arms and wouldn't let go.

"Let me go, Greger, please let me go!" she whimpered. Katarina collapsed in his arms. Over her head, Greger could see the EMT's come running with a stretcher and their medical bags. In some strange way, it felt as though he was an actor in a film. Any minute now the director would show up and ask everyone to take their places again; the scene would have to be shot over; the first one had failed. Stefan Kronfeld's tall, lanky body came sailing through the corridor. Right after him was Leif and Annika. Hands patted him on the face, voices bubbled and he couldn't understand why their faces were so close to his own. It felt as though he was flying completely free. And strangely, it felt wonderful!

Greger opened his eyes and looked into Charlotte's dark blue eyes.

"Oh, dear sweetheart," she said and lay her head down on the pillow next to his.

Greger looked around and discovered that he was lying on

a bed in a hospital room. How did he get here and why? He lifted his hand and stroked Charlotte's hair. Suddenly he noticed a tube that was attached to his arm. Slowly he turned his head and caught sight of a machine on his right side. That was connected to something that looked like a thimble that was on one of his fingers.

"What happened?" asked Greger with a wheezy voice.

"Where shall I start?" said Charlotte with tear filled eyes. "You had a heart attack and sank to the floor at Custody."

"Where's Matthias? How is Katarina?" he croaked.

"Katarina is getting help," said Charlotte.

"What about Matthias? Is he also getting help?" hissed Greger from the corner of his mouth.

"Take it easy, darling. You have to stay calm. Don't get worked up," said Charlotte and was relieved when the door to the room opened.

"How's my patient?" asked the doctor as he walked over to Greger. "How are you feeling?"

"I don't know, but rather good I think," answered Greger.

"That sounds excellent. When it's time for you to go home, you're going to get a list with some dietary advice and an appointment with one of our dieticians. If you follow that advice you won't have to end up here again," said the doctor patting Greger on the hand before he walked off.

"Hardly a long visit from the doctor," said Greger and coughed.

Charlotte gave him some water from a glass with the help of a straw. Greger leaned back on the pillow.

"Can you please tell me how things are with Matthias?"

"He didn't make it," said Charlotte with tears running down her cheeks. "They did everything they could, but they couldn't save him. Matthias shot Amir right through one of his eyes and then he shot himself."

346

Greger felt the taste of salt in his mouth and realized it was from his own tears.

"Where is Katarina?"

"Stefan and Sara took her to the psychiatry ward. The last I heard, Sara was sitting with her. She was going to stay with her until she heard from the doctor. I don't know any more than that," said Charlotte.

Greger tried to remember what had happened. Fragments of the interrogation with Verne, the phone call from Custody, and Katarina running toward him all of it glided back into his brain. Why had Matthias shot Amir? What was he thinking? Those were questions that would never be answered; he knew that now. Matthias' parents must be heartbroken, thought Greger. "Why did you do it?" he said quietly to himself.

"What happened with Verne and Hazim? Are they under arrest?"

Charlotte nodded.

"Has Jon Hildeng been informed? Has anyone spoken to Andrea and Kjell? Mahtab, is she taken care of? Is she safe?"

She nodded again.

"I'm going to rest a minute. It feels like I need to," said Greger and squeezed Charlotte's hand.

"That's a good idea. I'll be back tomorrow," said Charlotte and pressed her lips to his forehead. That the fetus Emelie was carrying had Massoud as its father, if it had lived, I'll tell him tomorrow, thought Charlotte as she pulled the door closed behind her. She walked out through the entrance to Sahlgrenska, came out on the street and took a deep breath. Her thoughts were with Katarina now. The next thing to take place was a horror … attending the funeral of someone they loved and had worked with. It would be a difficult period for all of them. But Charlotte was convinced Katarina could handle this too. "We'll all stand by your side, just so you know," she said out loud to herself.

Letters From Out of the Past

Björn stepped into the apartment. He walked directly to the living room and opened a window. The air felt suffocating. It had been difficult to leave Andrea and Kjell alone in the house at Tjörn with his mother and father, but Andrea had assured him that it was fine for him to go back home. She understood that he had a lot to do, considering his new exhibition in the autumn.

Björn took out his easel, lifted the sheet, felt no inspiration and let the sheet fall over the painting again. He stood by the window and looked out over the cars zooming back and forth on the street. He then walked over to his yellow bureau, pulled out the top drawer, took out an envelope and sat down in his armchair in the living room. There was a photo and a letter in the envelope. It was the last photo of him and Arne together. They both smiled into the camera. The shot had been taken outside the house in Hovås.

349

In the letter, Arne wrote that not too long ago, he had been together with someone who had HIV. He excused himself by saying that it had been on the spur of a moment. He hadn't previously been unfaithful to Andrea since they had met. The young man had flirted heavily with him. Arne had been sitting alone in a bar in Germany, gotten drunk and was sad because he and Andrea had fought before he left. He ended up asking the young man to follow him to his hotel. In the morning when Arne woke up in his room, the money in his wallet was gone and the young man too. The suspicion that this man might be infected with HIV didn't occur to him until later that day. That was why Arne had decided to get tested in a private clinic in a nearby town. The result of the test was positive. In the letter, he asked Björn not to reveal the truth to Andrea. In one way or the other, he wanted to handle it himself. Arne finished his letter with the words: *I know that you have always loved me like a brother, and that's why I know you'll never reveal my secret.*

A tear dropped down onto the letter. Björn dried his eyes with the hem of his T-shirt. He put the photo and the letter in the envelope and put them back in the bureau drawer. Björn went out to the kitchen, opened the refrigerator, took out a bottle and mixed himself a gin and tonic. Then he sat down in his favorite armchair and raised his glass in a toast to Arne.

Mette stood with the telephone in her hand. For a whole hour, she had been listening to everything Andrea had to tell. She was on her way to visit Olav to congratulate him in his new house when Andrea had called. Mette had begun their conversation by saying how happy she was. She hadn't been in touch with Andrea because she and Olav had both found new places to live. With some of the money from the shares she had sold, she'd bought an apartment on Vasagatan right in the center of Gothenburg and Olav had bought a house on Tjörn, at Klädesholmen. "I want to be near the sea," he had said. The house wasn't cheap but was worth every penny. The divorce papers were signed, and Mette had felt relieved. But the conversation with Andrea brought her down. The happiness she'd just felt disappeared like a puff of wind out through the window. She grabbed the bouquet of flowers that she had left on the hall table and went out the door.

"I wonder if Olav knows what's happened," thought Mette when she stepped off the train at Stenungsund's center. According to Olav's directions, she should take the bus to Klädesholmen Östra. The bus left right on schedule, and she leaned back in her seat. It was a cool and refreshing ride. As they drove past the entrance to Skärhamn she caught sight of a sign on the left; in white letters on a brown background was written "Nordic Watercolour Museum". She felt tears burn her eyelids as she remembered everything that had happened during the past weeks. Mette looked around and noticed that there weren't a lot of passengers on the bus. She got up and changed to the right side, leaned her head up against the glass and felt the refreshing coolness. The nature she saw swishing by outside the window was beautiful with horses grazing peacefully in wide open fields. Suddenly the bus drove up on a bridge, and their speed slowed down. When Mette looked out over the sea and the islets, she realized why Olav had chosen to live there. The word fantastic was miles removed from what one actually felt, she thought. At the middle of the bridge, she could see the white houses that lay tightly next to each other on the island. The sun glittered on the water, and people strolled back and forth. This is truly a west coast environment, she thought and got ready to step off the bus. She got out her directions and read how to continue; she was to take Strandgatan to the right. Slowly she walked up the street and the steep hill that was lined with houses. At the top, she caught sight of Bojens grocery store. "That's where I can buy anything I need," had Olav said on the phone. It wasn't hard to understand why Klädesholmen was one of the most visited spots on Tjörn, she thought.

"Hi Mette, welcome to my humble abode," said Olav, accepting the flowers.

She stepped into the renovated captain's house. The view from the balcony was breathtaking. The white captain's houses had been built in harmony with the hills and looked something like a roller coaster. The sea lay still, and the gulls cried as they sailed over the houses. Everything would have been wonderful if she didn't have to think about the task that lay ahead. They sat down on the balcony and Olav took out two wine glasses and poured. During the time that it took for Mette to recount Andrea's report, the contents of the wine bottle sank. Toward the end of the narrative, Olav got up and fetched a new bottle.

"Tragic about that policeman and his family," said Olav. He closed his eyes, lifted his face up and let the last rays of sun warm his face.

Suddenly he jumped and sat straight up in his chair.

"I have a letter that I want you to read," said Olav. He went into the house, came out a minute later and handed the letter to Mette.

She read the two pages with increasing surprise. When she was done, she put the letter on the table and looked at Olav.

"Is this the letter that Örjan Grund gave you after the funeral?"

Olav nodded.

"Did you know about this?" asked Mette and her shoulders sank.

"No! It was as much of a shock to me as I can see it was for you," said Olav. "Sure, I thought it was strange that my father wanted me to marry the gardener's daughter, but since I thought I was in love with Elsebeth and she with me, I never protested. Now, knowing this, I understand why my father encouraged my interest in Elsebeth more than was normal."

"Just think … your father got Elsebeth's little sister pregnant! She was only fourteen years old. Was it because he had a high rank in society and a lot of money that he got away with that? Strange that Elsebeth didn't protest when they sent her little sister away to a convent."

"We don't always get the answers to our questions," said Olav and sighed out loud as he took a large gulp of wine.

"When they found the body of a child in the garden … did you know about it then?" asked Mette.

"No, I was doing my military service and didn't live at home," said Olav. "Gosh, that's enough bad news. I want to think about something more positive. What do you say to a cup of coffee and then a little brandy with it?"

"Sure, thank you; I might need it. There is one thing that I am very happy about in the middle of all the chaos and that is that I gathered the courage, with your support, to ask for a divorce from Jon. Thanks to that I avoided his son Verne and everything that he was connected with, including the coming trial," said Mette and raised her glass to Olav.

"Yes, it feels pretty good when one succeeds in giving someone a push in the right direction," said Olav. With a smile on his lips he got up out of his chair, went out to the kitchen and made the coffee.

Mette remained sitting and kept thinking about the contents of the letter. She thought about Elsebeth and how she had managed to keep that family secret. Maybe her death hadn't been an accident? Maybe she killed herself by throwing herself down the stairs? There were still lots of questions, but as Olav said, one doesn't always get the answers. Mette started to mull over whether or not she should dare to bring it up with Olav. Suddenly she heard him humming a tune as he rattled with the dishes. She shook her head. No, it was probably not a good idea to dig into Elsebeth's death. "No one could ever say that Olav misses her and neither do I," she thought, leaning back into her chair and closing her eyes. The smell of freshly brewed coffee swept out to the balcony and tickled her sense of smell. It would be, in fact, delicious to have a good cup of coffee, she thought.

***

A heartfelt thanks from the author to:

Chief Inspector Lars Ohlin from the Serious Crime Division in Gothenburg, who always gives me great support, suggests humorous angles, and guides me in the right direction as I walk on my murderers' paths.

Forensic Pathologist Fredrik Bäckström from The National Board of Forensic Medicine in Linköping, whom I met at his excellent lecture, "From Crime to Sentence". Through his lecture I have gained greater insight into a forensic pathologist's tough job.

Forensic Entomologist Anders Lindström from the Swedish University of Agricultural Sciences in Uppsala, who has taught me what flies and other insects can reveal when a body has been found and the time of death is uncertain.

Ann-Marie Sjöberg, Lennart Falk, and Bengt Welin, who all contributed with their expertise.

As a writer, I use my creative freedom to fantasize within what I consider to be reasonable limits. That reality surpasses fiction is not an entirely unfamiliar statement. However, possible similarities in this book with any living person are pure coincidence. Any errors in the book are my responsibility and no one else's.

Ramona Fransson

Previously published in english.

Precious love 2012

Can be bought as POD-book and downloadable MP3.

Precious Love is the popular Swedish author Ramona Fransson's first in a series of detective novels with Chief Inspector Greger Thulin. There are ten in the series so far.

Gothenburg, Sweden

During a break-in at the luxurious home of Kenneth and Viola Svalborg, someone has neatly sliced valuable paintings from their frames. Also missing is the neighbor's beautiful 15 year old daughter, Elina Gullberg, who was babysitting for the Svalborg's two sons. Did she follow the thieves of her own accord? Was she involved with the break-in? Her parents, Daniel and Miriam Gullberg, are sick with worry. Chief Inspector Greger Thulin is called in and senses tension between the two families.

Kenneth Svalborg wants to divorce his wife, the mother of their two children. Viola suspects he has met another woman, which Kenneth flatly denies. A month after the break-in at Svalborgs, a young woman is found naked in the woods, beaten to death. Shortly thereafter, the body of a young man is found in the Mölndal River, shot to death. Greger Thulin and Crime Scene Investigator Charlotte Engman start to see a pattern. Is there some connection between the victims and the two families?

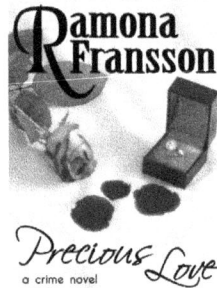

Murder in Skarhamn 2013

Can be bought as POD-book and downloadable MP3.

On the west coast of Sweden, in Skärhamn on Tjörn, Chief Inspector Greger Thulin thinks he lives at an idyllic spot. But even the most beautiful painting can have a faulty stroke of the brush. Hiding behind the walls of Bleket School, are bullying and drug addicted students. Homeroom teacher, Jonas Blomgren, lives on Rönnvägen. Amanda Durén and Belinda Wallin are pupils in his class. Amanda wears designer clothes, spreads money around and lives in a mansion, while Belinda's family is grateful if there's enough money to cover their basic needs. Belinda's mother, Margit Wallin, has a bad feeling about her daughter's teacher. Could he be following Belinda, and if so, why?

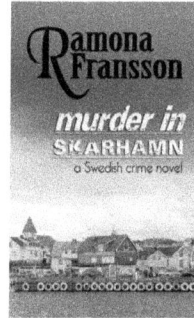

When the first murder victim shows up on Lyckebacken in Skärhamn, Greger Thulin is convinced that it won't take long for them to find the murderer, but starts to get discouraged when the investigation drags on. Inspector Katarina Linde and Forensic Detective Charlotte Engman are called in and try to put the pieces of the puzzle together from the clues they manage to find. It turns out the victim had an apartment on Eklandagatan in Gothenburg. What was he doing there? Soon Katarina starts to suspect that behind the victim's family façade, is a man who may be capable of even more than beating his wife. Greger Thulin is forced to ask the unavoidable question; has the peace and quiet of Skärhamn been put in a backpack, thrown on board a boat, and been transported out to sea?